A History of Methodism in East Norfolk

Ben Milner

A History of Methodism in East Norfolk

Published by Alder Carr Publishing, 9 The Fairway, Gorleston-on-Sea, Norfolk, NR31 6JS
aldercarr@googlemail.com

ISBN 978-0-9564495-0-4

British Library Cataloguing in Publication Data
A catalogue record for this book is available from the British Library

First published 2009

Printed and bound in the United Kingdom by Page Bros (Norwich) Ltd, Mile Cross Lane, Norwich, Norfolk, NR6 6SA

Contents

Acknowledgements

The publication of this book would not have been possible without the help and support of a great many people and my thanks go to those listed below. I would like to give special thanks to Mrs Glenda Tooke, Mrs Colleen Palmer and Mr Walter Moss for providing much information on Methodism in Martham, Acle and Great Yarmouth, respectively. I would also like to thank Mrs Sylvia Milner, Mr Glen Johnstone and Dr Jonathan Darch for the constructive comments that they have made and for their proof-reading of this book.

Joan Arbon
Mike Bennett
Christine Brady
Joy Brock
Alec Brown
Sylvia Brown
Roger Burghall
Wendy Burghall
Brian Callan
Hazel Cole
Doris Coleman
Doreen Collicott
Jean Cooke
Myrtle Cross
Jonathan Darch
Billy Delf
Frank Elliott
John Fenn
Margaret Gee
Joan Gill
Barbara George
Brenda Green
Margaret Harrison
Melanie Harvey
Debra Hunt
Margaret Kemp
Glen Johnstone
Alison Milner
Sylvia Milner
Walter Moss
Coleen Palmer
Don Peers
Ken Saul
Brenda Searle
Ian Stewart
Mark Stolworthy
Glenda Tooke
Roy Wooltorton

RWM Data Management
Norfolk Picture Archive
Norfolk Record Office
Brian Ollington Photographers
Old Chapel Guesthouse, Horsey
Ludham Archive
Kings Church, Great Yarmouth
Archant

Preface

It seems that every one hundred years someone writes a book on the history of Methodism in Great Yarmouth. First was Mr Abraham Watmough's *A history of Methodism in the town and neighbourhood of Great Yarmouth.* This was published in 1826 and described the early Wesleyan Methodist circuit in Great Yarmouth. Next, in 1903, was Arthur Patterson's *From Hayloft to Temple* which described the expansion of Primitive Methodism in Great Yarmouth and the surrounding villages. Now, in 2009, comes this book – *A History of Methodism in East Norfolk.*

Action for Children charity

The proceeds from the sale of this book will be given to the children's charity Action for Children. Action for Children is one of the UK's leading children's charities and has been supporting children and young people affected by poverty, disability, abuse or neglect for 140 years. Action for Children helps nearly 156,000 children, young people and their families across the UK.

Action for Children (previously known as National Children's Home – NCH) was founded in 1869 by a young Methodist minister, Thomas Stephenson. Shocked by the plight of homeless children on the streets of London he, with the help of two Methodist friends, converted a disused stable block into a children's home. They called it The Children's Home as they wanted to provide the same quality of care that other children received in a loving home – a vision that was radically different to the workhouses of the day. The work grew and developed, and it was initially Methodists, staff and volunteers who developed new ways of caring for children and young people.

Action for Children's ethos is deeply rooted in Methodist principles and the charity maintains close links with the Methodist Church. The charity's Council of Trustees is appointed by the Methodist Conference and many of its supporters and volunteers come from Methodist churches.

List of Figures

List of Tables

Chapter 1

Introduction

1.1 Methodism in East Norfolk

Methodism has been in East Norfolk for just over 250 years, having been first introduced to Great Yarmouth in 1754. Over this time, Methodist societies have been created, grown, merged, argued, closed and re-built. At its peak in the late nineteenth century, Methodism in East Norfolk had over 2,000 members, spread across 48 societies and belonging to five different circuits. Almost every village in East Norfolk had a Methodist chapel, and many had two. At one time, the two towns of Great Yarmouth and Gorleston had 11 Methodist churches that were all open simultaneously. In fact, in its 250 year history, Methodists in East Norfolk have opened over 100 churches and chapels. Twenty-one of these remain open today and they serve as a living monument to those early preachers and pioneers who introduced Methodism to East Norfolk. Of course, not all Methodist churches and chapels have survived. For many no trace remains of their past in terms of either the society or the building. Fortunately, many buildings have survived and these are now used for many different purposes such as housing, community venues, or by other religious groups.

The county of Norfolk has been a hotbed of nonconformist religious activity ever since the sixteen-hundreds, with Baptists, Congregationalists, Unitarians, Quakers and Methodists all establishing networks of societies. Of all of these nonconformists, the Methodists have been the most successful in East Norfolk. In fact, of the counties in the east of England, Norfolk is second only to Lincolnshire in terms of the number of Methodist societies that have been established. Methodism was first brought to Norfolk by James Wheatley in 1751, when he established a Tabernacle on Timberhill in Norwich from where he would preach. Soon afterwards, violent anti-Methodist riots ensued which lasted for almost a year and resulted in the Tabernacle being pulled down. Shortly after the destruction of the Tabernacle a new society was formed in Norwich. It was from this Norwich society that Methodism was first introduced to Great Yarmouth. In 1754, Thomas Olivers, who was stationed in the Norwich Methodist Circuit, travelled to Great Yarmouth and began preaching in the Market Place. He was met with similar violence as had occurred in Norwich and Mr Olivers was forced to flee back to Norwich. It wasn't until 1760 that Methodism was more firmly established in Great Yarmouth, this time by Captain Howell Harris. From these early steps, Methodism in East Norfolk began to establish itself, first in Great Yarmouth and then further afield into the surrounding towns and villages.

During these early days of Methodism in East Norfolk, visiting preachers would hold services wherever they could. These would be outdoors in fields or on a village green, or in the spare room of a house or other vacant building. As societies developed they would seek to find more permanent places for worship which usually meant either building or buying a chapel. Methodist chapels were not usually found in such prominent positions in a town or village as the Anglican church. In many cases funds were limited and a society wishing to build a chapel was forced to buy cheaper land that was on the outskirts of a village or town. In some cases the land may have been donated, meaning that it would often be in the corner of a field or of an irregular shape. Secondly, there was often hostility to these new Methodist societies by the local villagers, and in some cases by the local squire and parson too. It was therefore easier for societies to operate away from the centre of a village and thereby away from hostilities.

Building a new chapel was not cheap. Land had to be obtained, building materials had to be sourced and labour was needed to construct the chapel. For a few societies, a rich benefactor provided all, or a large proportion, of these costs, but this was rare. It was more usual for a society to engage in fundraising to pay for a new chapel. Often loans or mortgages were taken out and societies frequently took many years to pay off these debts. An effective method of fundraising was through foundation stones. Wealthy or influential local people, such as JPs, landowners or the local MP, would often be invited to lay a foundation stone during the early stages of building a chapel. In return for having their name on the stone, they would be expected to make a generous contribution to the fundraising.

1.2 A brief history of Methodism

The evolution of Methodism in East Norfolk over its 250 year history has followed closely the national changes in Methodism. To appreciate the history of Methodism in East Norfolk it is useful to examine the changes that have taken place in Methodism since its conception in the eighteenth century. It is not the aim of this book to present a detailed history of the Methodist Church, but instead to provide a brief history that is sufficient to put into a national context the developments that have taken place in East Norfolk.

Methodism was started by the brothers John and Charles Wesley in the eighteenth century, and its governing body, the Methodist Conference, was established soon after in about 1744. At this time Methodism was not separate from the Church of England as it is now, but instead operated as a number of local societies. After John Wesley's death in 1791, many of these Methodist societies were divided on whether Methodist preachers who were not ordained could give Holy Communion. In an attempt to resolve these disputes the Connexion published a "Plan of Pacification." For some Methodists the plan did not go far enough to distance the new Methodist Church from the Church of England. Two of these preachers were Alexander Kilham and William Thom. They refused to sign the Plan of Pacification and, together with another five Methodists, were excluded from the list of Methodist preachers. Kilham and Thom then formed an alternative connexion in 1797, which was known as the Methodist New Connexion, and members of this connexion were known as "Kilhamites." This meant that there were now two branches of Methodism – the traditional Wesleyan Methodists and the Methodist New Connexion. Both of these were highly active in establishing new societies and building chapels, in many cases in the same towns and villages as each other.

Divisions and breakaways

This was only the first such break-away from traditional Wesleyan Methodism and over the course of the next 50 or so years, several more divisions would occur. A second break-away from Wesleyan Methodism occurred in 1812 with the establishment of the Society of Primitive Methodists. By the early eighteen-hundreds, Wesleyan Methodists were seen by some as having become rather too comfortable and "middleclass", with the result that they were reluctant to disrupt social orders that existed within societies. Contrary to these perceived ideas, two Methodist preachers, Hugh Bourne and William Clowes, had begun to hold "Camp Meetings." Camp Meetings were an American idea which encouraged large crowds to attend meetings that were held outside, often in quite remote places. People would bring camping equipment and basic provisions, and over the course of a few days hold prayers and listen to "revival addresses." This was not in line with the conservative attitude of the Wesleyan Methodist Conference. They had heard that such meetings caused "violent emotionalism" which was "mixed with sexual licences." This led to Bourne and Clowes being expelled from the Methodist Conference, with the result that they formed the Society of Primitive Methodists. This now added a third branch of Methodism – Primitive Methodists – who were also actively establishing societies and building their own chapels.

Two further break-aways from the Wesleyan Methodist Conference took place a few years afterwards. The Bible Christian Society was formed in 1815 and the Protestant Methodists in 1827, although nationally these were much smaller than the other Methodist connexions. The final break-away from Wesleyan Methodism occurred in about 1849 when several ministers felt that too much power was held by too few people in the Wesleyan Connexion. These ministers tried to bring change to Methodism but were instead expelled from the Wesleyan Methodist Connexion. The ministers then established the Wesleyan Reform movement which, during the early 1850s, attracted many Methodists away from Wesleyan societies and into the new reform societies.

Unifications

After over 50 years of disputes and arguments, these breakaway Methodist movements began to unite. This started in 1857 with the Wesleyan Reformers and the Protestant Methodists joining to become the United Methodist Free Churches. In 1907 the United Methodist Free Churches joined with the Methodist New Connexion and the Bible Christians to become the United Methodist Church. Finally, at the Uniting Methodist Conference in 1932, the Primitive Methodists, United Methodists and Wesleyan Methodists united to become the Methodist Church as it is today. These divisions and unifications of the Methodist Church are summarised in figure 1.1.

The effect in East Norfolk

The three main branches of Methodism – Wesleyan, Primitive and United – all had large numbers of members and many chapels that were spread across the entire country. Depending on the particular part of the country, some branches of Methodism were often

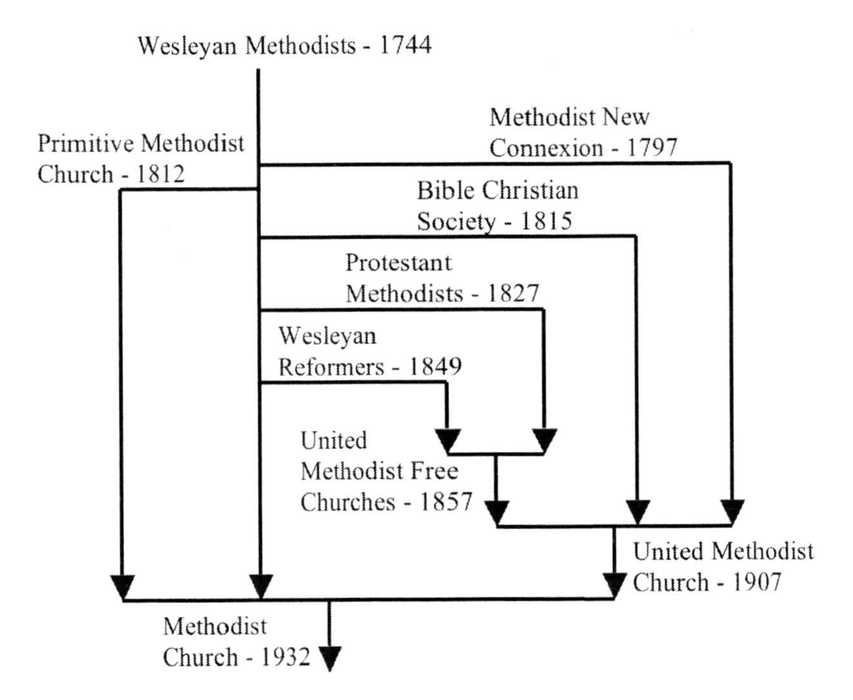

Figure 1.1: Illustration of the break-aways from the Wesleyan Methodists, starting with the Methodist New Connexion in 1797 through to the Wesleyan Reformers in 1849. This is followed by their eventual uniting, leading to full unification in 1932 to form the Methodist Church as it exists today.

more successful than others. For example, Primitive Methodism appealed particularly to rural and working-class areas. In East Norfolk, the Wesleyans, Primitives and United Methodists all had significant numbers of chapels. The Primitives were possibly the most successful, primarily because of the rural nature of East Norfolk, which was traditionally a stronghold for Primitive Methodism. In the larger towns of Great Yarmouth and Gorleston, Wesleyan Methodism was more successful, although the Primitives still maintained a strong presence. The United Methodists were the least successful in East Norfolk, although during the period of the Wesleyan Reform Movement, they did attract many of the Wesleyan Methodists.

Each of the three branches of Methodism built its own chapels, with many of these being close to one another in the same town or village. Towns such as Great Yarmouth and Gorleston had at least one church from each of the main branches of Methodism. This was also true in some smaller villages. For example, villages as small as Fleggburgh, Stokesby and Ludham had both Wesleyan and Primitive Methodist chapels. In some cases these were at opposite ends of the village, but in others, such as Acle, they were just a few hundred metres apart. This meant that in comparison to other nonconformist churches, the number of Methodist churches was many times greater.

The Methodist Uniting Conference of 1932 left a substantial over-provision of churches, not just around Great Yarmouth, but also nationally. Getting the different Methodist societies to unite in local areas was not an easy task as many members did not wish to join with other societies, particularly if this would result in their church being closed. The effects of the Second World War did provide some rationalisation with many churches being damaged or destroyed and members transferring to an existing church. The period from the end of the Second World War to the present day has also witnessed the closure of many Methodist churches, particularly the more rural societies and those near larger societies. Declining memberships and the increasing costs of maintaining ageing buildings are the primary reasons for these closures. However, some societies have grown in strength in this period and new churches have been built – in East Norfolk alone, five new churches have been built in this post-war period.

1.3 Layout of the book

The area of east Norfolk that is the subject of this book is based loosely on the area covered by the East Norfolk Methodist Circuit which was formed in 2007. This covers Great Yarmouth and Gorleston and the areas around Acle and Martham, going to Sutton in the north and across to Lingwood in the west. One structure for this book would be to take each society in turn and report on its history. However, such a structure is not able to describe the broader and interrelated history of the Methodist societies in East Norfolk, nor the influence of events in Methodism nationally. Instead, this book is divided into five broad historical periods, each concerned with wider-scale developments in Methodism.

The first period is from 1750 to 1833. This covers the introduction and early growth of Methodism around Great Yarmouth. This period was dominated by Wesleyan Methodists, although towards the end of this time Methodist New Connexion and, to a lesser extent, Primitive Methodism had begun to establish societies in East Norfolk. Chapter 2 of this book covers this period.

The second period considers the next one hundred years, from 1833 to 1932. This was a time of large-scale growth for all branches of Methodism and resulted in many churches and chapels being built nationally. The same was true for East Norfolk which saw many new societies formed and chapels built. Great Yarmouth and Gorleston witnessed the construction of several big churches with seating capacities of over 300 and one giant church which was reported to be able to seat 1,200 people. Wesleyan Methodism in this period is described in chapter 3. Primitive Methodism is covered in chapters 4, 5, 6 and 7, divided into the regions of Great Yarmouth (chapters 4 and 5), Martham (chapter 6) and Acle (chapter 7). Finally, United Methodism in this period is described in chapter 8.

The third period is much shorter and examines the effect of Methodist unification in the years from 1932 to 1938. Nationally, the Wesleyan, Primitive and United branches of Methodism unified in 1932. However, it wasn't until 1938 that unification had formally taken place in East Norfolk. Chapter 9 explains the effect of unification in East Norfolk and, related to this, chapter 10 discusses the opening of Great Yarmouth's new Central Hall in 1938.

The fourth period examines the effect that the Second World War had on Methodism in East Norfolk and covers the years from 1939 to 1960. The war disrupted Methodism in East Norfolk virtually from the start of its outbreak in 1939, but the effects of the war were felt for many years afterwards, certainly into the 1950s. This is described in Chapter 11.

Finally, the fifth period examines the more recent history of Methodism in East Norfolk, starting in 1960 and going on to 2009. This was a time when many chapels closed, but it was also a period when many have celebrated centenaries and even new churches have been built. Chapters 12, 13 and 15 cover this period and finish with an examination of the East Norfolk Methodist Circuit that was created in 2007. Chapter 14 is rather a misfit. It examines some of the organs that have existed in Methodist churches and chapels in East Norfolk, which have had such an important part in Methodist worship.

Throughout this book the words "church" and "chapel" are used to describe buildings for worship. No strict rules have been applied as to which word is used, although in general, larger buildings are referred to as churches and smaller buildings as chapels. Some terms that are used in this book refer to the organisation of the Methodist Church, such as Connexion, Circuit, District, etc. Brief explanations of such terms are provided in Appendix A at the end of this book.

Chapter 2

The beginnings of Methodism in Great Yarmouth and East Norfolk – 1750 to 1833

2.1 Introduction

This chapter describes the early history of Methodism in East Norfolk, starting from around 1750 and finishing in 1833, by which time Methodism had firmly established itself in the area. During this period, three different factions of Methodism began to establish themselves in East Norfolk. First to arrive were preachers from the traditional Wesleyan Methodist organisation who came from Norwich as early as 1754. As breakaway Methodist movements began to establish themselves nationally, they sent preachers to East Norfolk. In 1806 the first Methodist New Connexion preachers arrived in Great Yarmouth with the intention of setting up their own societies. Similarly, in about 1820 the first Primitive Methodist preachers arrived in Great Yarmouth. Each of these three separate organisations began to form their own societies and build their own chapels.

At the beginning of the period 1750 to 1833, the few Methodist societies that had begun were small and part of the Norwich Methodist Circuit. These early Methodists didn't have their own chapels, but instead held services in a variety of places such as in the open air, in a kitchen or spare room of a house, or for larger societies, in a rented building. It wasn't until the societies became more established that they were able to move into purpose-built chapels. Over time, with many ups and downs, these societies grew and were joined by more societies in neighbouring towns and villages. Eventually, the societies around Great Yarmouth were separated from the Norwich circuit to become part of a Great Yarmouth circuit. The Great Yarmouth (Wesleyan) Methodist Circuit was established in 1792, while the Great Yarmouth Primitive Methodist Circuit began in 1825.

The remainder of this chapter examines the early histories of the Wesleyan Methodists, the Methodist New Connexion and the Primitive Methodists in East Norfolk up to 1833.

Figure 2.1: Mr Thomas Olivers. Mr Olivers was the first person to introduce Methodism to Great Yarmouth. This was in 1754, but he was not successful and was chased out of the town by an angry mob.

2.2 Wesleyan Methodism

Wesleyan Methodism was brought to East Norfolk by preachers from the Norwich Methodist Circuit. These preachers attempted first to establish Methodism in Great Yarmouth. After a difficult start, and with the help of John Wesley, they were able to form a Great Yarmouth Methodist Circuit. The preachers from this circuit then began to expand preaching into the surrounding towns and villages. This section tells how Methodism began in these areas.

2.2.1 Early Wesleyan Methodism in Great Yarmouth

Wesleyan Methodism in Great Yarmouth has a long history which involves a great many preachers and laymen, whose dedication and faith enabled them to overcome many adversities to establish Methodism in the town.

Mr Thomas Olivers – 1754

Wesleyan Methodism was first brought to Great Yarmouth in 1754 by Mr Thomas Olivers – see figure 2.1 – who, at the time, was stationed in the Norwich Methodist Circuit. Thomas Olivers was born in 1725 in Tregynon in the Welsh county of Montgomeryshire. He became a travelling Methodist preacher in 1753, having been converted after hearing the preaching of both George Whitefield and John Wesley. This would have made his stationing in Norwich one of the first places that he visited and his preaching in Great Yarmouth was only one year into his ministry at the age of 29 years. Mr Olivers spent many years as a travelling preacher and it is said that he covered over 100,000 miles on a single horse that cost him £5. He also wrote several hymns, the most famous being "The God of Abraham praise, who reigns enthroned above", which is in the Methodist hymn book, *Hymns and Psalms*, number 452.

At the time of Thomas Olivers, Great Yarmouth was an un-Godly place and the townsfolk made no secret of the fact that they did not want to be introduced to Methodism.

Figure 2.2: Captain Howell Harris. Captain Harris successfully introduced Methodism to Great Yarmouth in 1760 with the help of soldiers from his regiment.

Mr Olivers was aware of this and for support took with him a companion from the Norwich circuit. They arrived in Great Yarmouth on a Sunday and, after attending the parish church, went to the Market Place where they sang a hymn and said prayers. As they were doing this, a crowd began to gather around them. When Mr Olivers began his sermon, the mood of the crowd changed and they began to attack the preacher.

The pair managed to escape from the mob and hid in a house in the Rows, where upon they sent for their horses so that they could escape back to Norwich. However, the mob followed Mr Olivers' horse and tracked him down to his hiding place in a row house. Eventually the pair were able to leave, but as they rode through the narrow rows they had sticks, stones, turnips and potatoes thrown at them. The women from the row houses also joined in and threw basins of waste water and filth at them as they passed. Great Yarmouth was not yet ready to receive Methodism and it would be another six years before anyone else was brave enough to try again.

Captain Howell Harris – 1760

In 1760, a group of soldiers, led by Captain Howell Harris, had been sent to Great Yarmouth to recruit soldiers in defence of a rebellion that had occurred in Scotland. Howell Harris – see figure 2.2 – was an officer in the Brecknock Militia, which was based in his home county of Brecknockshire and is now part of the Welsh county of Powys. Howell Harris was no ordinary army captain, but was in fact close friends with many of the leading Methodists of the time, including John and Charles Wesley, George Whitefield and the Countess of Huntington. He had devoted much of his life to preaching in both his home of south Wales and further afield, although he was never ordained and referred to himself as an "exhorter." He achieved a great many things for Methodism, including being a founder of Welsh Calvinistic Methodism and establishing a college for the training of ministers. To put into context his popularity, it is said that at his funeral 20,000 people attended and nine sermons were preached!

Upon Captain Harris's arrival in Great Yarmouth, he asked whether there were any

Methodists in the town, to which he was told of Mr Olivers and his attempt at introducing Methodism. Having considerable preaching experience, Captain Harris decided to try again and employed the Town Crier to announce that a Methodist preacher would be holding a service at the Market Place.

As had happened with Mr Olivers, a mob assembled on the Market Place armed with sticks and stones with the intent of disrupting the forthcoming service. However, Captain Harris was more cunning than his predecessor and also had the advantage of being able to use the soldiers from his regiment to help him. Just before the service was scheduled to begin, Captain Harris began exercising his men on the Market Place and enquired of the mob what was happening. He was informed that a Methodist preacher was supposed to have been coming and was told "It is well he has not made his appearance, as he otherwise would certainly have been put to death." To calm the crowd, Captain Harris offered to sing a hymn, pray and give some words of advice. During this, he was in his full regimental uniform and climbed up on a table and was surrounded by his soldiers who joined in heartily with the singing. This scene both astonished and terrified the assembled mob – perhaps more so as the soldiers were armed and ready to defend their captain if the need arose. The result was that no disruption to the service took place. This was a turning point for Methodism in Great Yarmouth and Captain Harris continued to preach in the town with no one daring to oppose him.

Rev John Wesley – 1761

John Wesley was supportive of the Great Yarmouth Methodist society and visited the town on several occasions to preach. In 1761 he described Great Yarmouth in his journal as "a large and populous town, and as eminent both for wickedness and ignorance, as even any seaport in England." It was at about this time that John Wesley formed the first Methodist society in the town. Over the next few years the people of the town became more accustomed to Methodism, and in a visit by John Wesley in 1763, he reported that he found the Great Yarmouth Methodists "quiet and comfortable, without any jar or contention." By 1765, Methodism had grown even stronger, with John Wesley writing of Great Yarmouth in his journal that "There now seems to be a general call to this town; surely some will hear the voice which raises the dead."

This early success was rather short-lived. A local preacher in the Great Yarmouth society, Mr Benjamin Worship, began to have Calvinist ideas which were in opposition to John Wesley, and he began to cause division in the society. The situation deteriorated and Mr Worship declared openly his opposition to the doctrines and leaders of the Methodist society. At the peak of the discontent the chapel used by the Methodists (previously built for the Anabaptists in one of the rows) was taken over by Mr Worship. By 1767, the society had given up and Methodism in Great Yarmouth had all but finished with just a few members remaining. John Wesley visited Great Yarmouth in that same year and tried to resume the Methodist society, but by this time the people of the town had become indifferent and uninterested. Over the next two years, through the efforts of two preachers in the circuit, the society began to grow again, with John Wesley writing in early 1769: "The congregation was the largest I ever saw at Yarmouth." However, the society was not strong and suffered many ups and downs. The society began to diminish and by 1779, almost twenty years after its establishment in the town by John Wesley, Methodism in Great Yarmouth ceased to exist.

Mr Samuel King and the Row 8 chapel – 1780

Methodism was restored in Great Yarmouth by Mr Samuel King, who was a brazier in the town and had previously been a member of the first Methodist society that had been established by John Wesley. When Methodist preaching in the town had formally stopped, Mr King began to invite his neighbours into his kitchen on Sunday evenings where he led them in scripture readings, hymn singing and prayer. This informal worship continued and the number attending began to grow – in no small part due to Mr King's wife who encouraged many new people to attend. In 1780, out of respect for Mr King's efforts, one of the Methodist preachers from the Norwich circuit, Mr James Wood, preached for the Great Yarmouth Methodists in the General Baptist Chapel, which had been hired for the occasion.

This was a success and represented a new start for Methodism in Great Yarmouth, with Mr Wood being invited to return to preach again in the town. The congregation moved through several locations for services as the numbers attending gradually built up. The first services were held in a house belonging to a widow. They then moved to a Mr Calthorpe's house near to Fuller's Hill, and then to an empty house which was adapted so as to create a single large room for services. The Norwich circuit was unable to supply enough preachers to Great Yarmouth, so Mr King took it upon himself to lead worship by reading from scripture, giving short sermons and leading prayer. Eventually a new Methodist society was formed in Great Yarmouth.

John Wesley visited this new society in 1781, and wrote in his Journal "there was a prospect of good, the two hindrances having taken themselves out of the way." By 1782 the society had grown to about 60 members, and Mr Wood left the Norwich circuit and was replaced by Robert Brackenbury, Esq. from Raithby Hall in Lincolnshire. Mr Brackenbury found his congregation to be rather small and so he decided to preach in the open air. As had happened many years before when this was tried, a mob formed with the intention of disrupting the service. Mr Brackenbury was taken to the town mayor whereupon the two men developed a mutual respect for each other. The mayor apologised for the rude behaviour of the townsfolk and arranged for an escort to take Mr Brackenbury back to his lodgings. John Wesley returned to Great Yarmouth about two months later and preached "to the largest congregation he had seen there for many years."

The increasing size of the membership led the society to think about obtaining a larger building for worship. To help the society achieve this ambition, a corn merchant in Great Yarmouth, Mr Lee, generously donated a piece of land on the north-west side of Ferry-boat Row for a new chapel, and also a quantity of bricks. Ferry-boat Row was numbered as Row 8 and ran from North Quay to Northgate Street, close to Fuller's Hill. In October of 1783 the chapel was finished and, excluding the land and bricks, cost £315 to build, which was raised through a combination of donations and a loan.

Road development work in the 1970s meant that Row 8, and many other rows in this area, were demolished. Today very little remains of Row 8, with only a few buildings on the extreme eastern part still standing that were part of the original row. Figure 2.3 shows the approximate position of the Row 8 chapel, which is now part of the Fuller's Hill car park and some new housing developments, close to the centre of Great Yarmouth.

The Row 8 chapel was opened on 22 October 1783 by John Wesley, who, at that time, was eighty years old. He wrote in his Journal of the event:

"Wednesday the 22nd I went to Yarmouth. Often has this poor society been well nigh

Figure 2.3: The approximate location of the Wesleyan Methodist chapel in Row 8. Row 8 was demolished in the 1970s for redevelopment and has been replaced by the Fuller's Hill car park and, more recently, by housing.

Table 2.1: Churches in the Norwich Methodist Circuit in 1783.

Norwich	Thurne	Yarmouth
Lowestoft	Cove	Beccles
Wheatacre	Haddiscoe	Thurlton
Heckingham	Hempnell	Loddon
Barford	Hardwick	Stratton
Fasburg	Dickleburgh	Winfarthing
North Lopham	South Lopham	Diss

shattered to pieces; first by Benjamin Worship, then a furious Calvinist, tearing away nearly half of them; next by John Simpson turning Antimoniam, and scattering most that were left. It has pleased God, contrary to all human probability, to raise a new society out of the dust; nay, and to give them courage to build a new preaching house, which is well finished, and contains about five hundred persons. I opened it this evening; and as many as could get in, seemed to be deeply affected. Who knows that God is about to repair the waste places, and to gather a people that shall be scattered no more?"

During the opening service at the new chapel, John Wesley preached from a wooden pulpit. This pulpit survives today and is known as the "Wesley Pulpit." It has had a long history in Great Yarmouth Methodism and can now be found at Lowestoft Road Methodist church in Gorleston – see figure 2.4.

At the time of the Row 8 chapel opening, Great Yarmouth was one of twenty-one churches that made up the Norwich Methodist Circuit – see table 2.1. The Norwich

Figure 2.4: The Wesley Pulpit. John Wesley preached from this pulpit in 1783 at the Row 8 chapel. It was then moved to the new Wesleyan church on King Street in 1792, where it remained until 1812. Next it was moved to the Wesleyan chapel in West Caister where it stayed until 1876. It was then stored until 1929 when it was bought, restored and presented to Dene Side Methodist church in 1932. Following Dene Side's closure in 1937 it was given to Lowestoft Road Methodist church in Gorleston, where it remains today. American Methodists offered to buy the pulpit for £1,800 in the 1970s to pay for re-roofing of the church, but fortunately the offer was rejected.

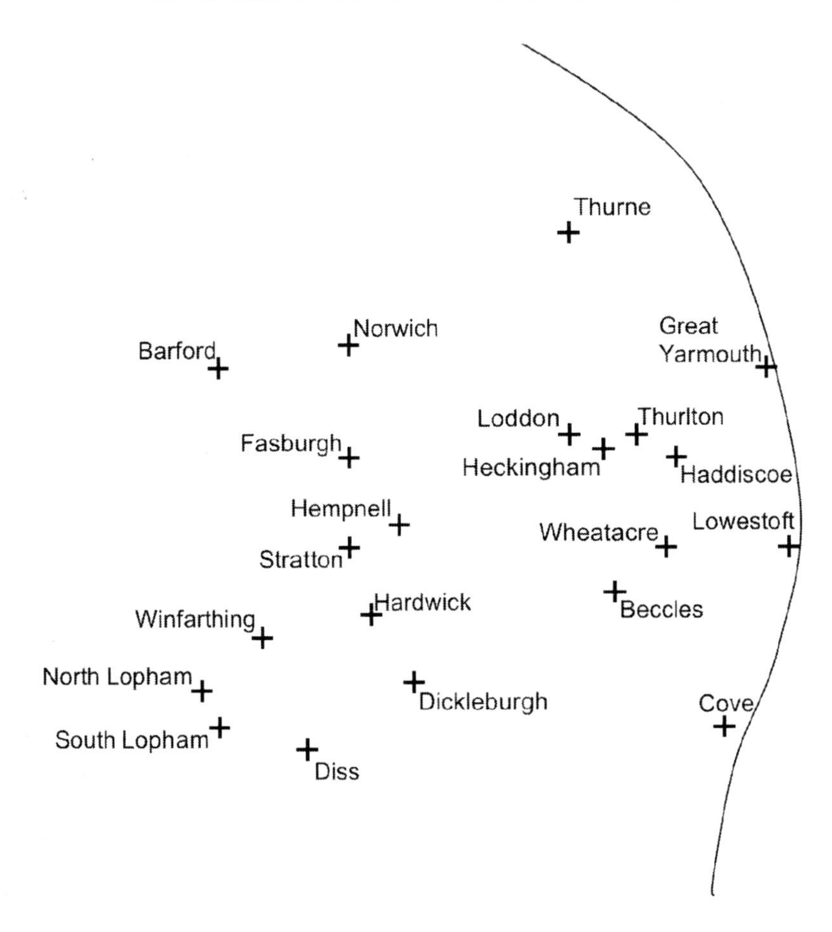

Figure 2.5: Map showing the extent of the Norwich (Wesleyan) Methodist Circuit in 1783 which comprised twenty-one chapels.

circuit covered a sizeable area, extending to Thurne in the north and Diss in the south, the extent of which is illustrated in figure 2.5. The Norwich circuit had only four ministers to cover this large area which meant that Great Yarmouth did not have a regular minister. Most services were conducted by local preachers who were based in the towns and villages that made up the circuit. Consequently, Mr Samuel King led many of the services in Great Yarmouth and this was of considerable assistance to the hard-pressed Norwich circuit. However, another preacher, a Mr Hindmarsh, had recently joined the circuit and also began to take some of the services in Great Yarmouth.

At first, Mr Hindmarsh's residence in Great Yarmouth was considered a great benefit. However, it was not long before Mr Hindmarsh's preaching became the source of much discontent in Great Yarmouth. As time went on, many of the worshippers in Great Yarmouth took preference to Mr Hindmarsh's preaching over that of Mr King's preaching. The extent of this grew and at some services, congregations, upon finding out that Mr King was to preach, got up and left in search of Mr Hindmarsh's preaching. After a few years, Mr Hindmarsh decided to leave Great Yarmouth, although the hostility towards Mr

King remained. The hostilities were kept up for three years until, in 1786, John Wesley wrote of Great Yarmouth "Once more the combatants here have laid down their arms and solemnly promise to live in peace." Even this was temporary as the prejudice against Mr King still remained and eventually Mr King left the society and formed a separate society for himself and his own band of followers. This was short-lived and in 1790 Mr King and his followers returned to the Methodist church as ordinary members. In the same year, in his last report on Great Yarmouth, John Wesley wrote in his Journal:

"I went to Yarmouth, and at length found a society in peace, and much united together. In the evening the congregation was too large to get into the preaching-house; yet they were far less noisy than usual. After supper a little company went to prayer, and the power of God fell upon us; especially when a young woman broke out in prayer, to the surprise and comfort of us all."

This was John Wesley's last visit to Great Yarmouth; his first visit had been thirty years earlier and in this time he had witnessed, several times, the rise and fall of Methodism in Great Yarmouth.

A new chapel – 1792

Seven years after the Row 8 chapel had been opened, membership at the Great Yarmouth Methodist society had grown considerably and the building was becoming too small for the congregation. Money was rather scarce in the Great Yarmouth society at this time so a set of trustees was formed, comprising ten men from the society, with the task of obtaining a larger chapel. The trustees acquired a large building on the south-west corner of Regent Road and King Street, which was chosen for its "central position in a respectable part of the town." This was converted into a place of worship that could seat almost 1,000 people, which made it twice as large as the Row 8 chapel. Figure 2.6 shows the location of the chapel today, where the position is now occupied by a gentlemen's clothes shop. The cost of the building and its conversion to a chapel was £1,300, of which £272 was raised from subscriptions and the remainder borrowed.

The new chapel was opened in the autumn of 1792 by Rev Charles Boon who delivered an appropriate sermon from the Old Testament book of Haggai, chapter 2, verse 1:

"The latter glory of this house shall be greater than the former, saith the Lord of hosts: and in this place will I give peace, saith the Lord of hosts."

Following the transfer of worship to the new chapel, the chapel at Row 8 became redundant and was eventually converted into three cottages. Figure 2.7 shows the three cottages that were the former chapel. Some time after their conversion to cottages a plaque was set into the wall of one of the cottages to commemorate its former use as Great Yarmouth's first Wesleyan chapel. The cottages survived until the 1970s when the area was redeveloped and the area around Row 8 was converted into the Fuller's Hill car park. A newspaper article from the *Eastern Daily Press* on 13th December 1960 mentions the proposed redevelopment around Fuller's Hill and states that the Great Yarmouth Town Planning Committee recommended that the plaque be replaced into the nearest building to the original site of the chapel. Sadly, investigation around the Fuller's Hill area has revealed no such plaque to be on display.

The large debt incurred when the new King Street–Regent Road chapel was built was a source of considerable anguish for the Great Yarmouth Methodist society. As a result, the society often found itself in need of money to enable the debt on the chapel to be

Figure 2.6: The location of the King Street–Regent Road Wesleyan Methodist chapel. The chapel opened in 1792, closed in 1838 and was demolished some time afterwards. Greenwoods shop now stands close to the site of the former chapel.

serviced. This wish was about to come true for the society in a very strange way.

An army Drum-Major by the name of Richard Thompson had served in many places overseas and had been subject to much hardship, leading him to question where his life was going. He was quite a wealthy man as, in addition to his own army pay, his wife ran the only shop in the garrison, which brought the couple considerable extra income. This way of life began to trouble Mr Thompson and he began to worry about the salvation of his own soul. He recognised that the only way to save his soul would be to resign from the army and take up a better life – which he did in 1786 aged 47.

Mr Thompson first retired to Scotland but, after concerns over the Scottish methods of religious teaching, moved to Norwich and joined their Methodist society. This was at the same time as the new Great Yarmouth chapel had been opened. One night, Mr Thompson had a dream where he thought that he was in Great Yarmouth and saw the inside and outside of the new chapel. Having had such a curious dream, Mr Thompson felt compelled to travel to Great Yarmouth and see for himself whether such a building existed or not. To his surprise he found that the new Great Yarmouth chapel was identical to the one he saw in his dream. He enquired of the trustees the financial position of the society and on hearing their plight lent them £650. He stayed in Great Yarmouth for twelve years, until his death in 1804, and became a member of the Methodist society, sitting in the same seat that he believed he occupied in his dream.

Figure 2.7: Three cottages that were formerly the Row 8 Methodist chapel. The plaque on the middle cottage reads: "This building, consisting of cottages numbered 16, 17 and 18, was the first Methodist chapel erected in Great Yarmouth, and was opened for public worship by the Rev John Wesley, MA on October 22 1783." (This picture has been included by kind permission of Archant)

Great Yarmouth becomes a circuit – 1792

Following the opening of the King Street–Regent Road chapel, the membership of the society was quite large, with about 150 members. It was decided that this was enough members for Great Yarmouth to become a circuit in its own right and separate from the Norwich circuit. The Great Yarmouth society, along with Lowestoft, Framlingham and several other smaller societies, formed the new Great Yarmouth Methodist Circuit.

In 1795, new ministers were appointed to the Great Yarmouth circuit with the superintendent being a Mr Anderson. During this time, the ministers agreed that they should try and increase the size of the circuit by preaching in some of the surrounding villages. One of the first places they tried was at Filby and a service was held in the open air on the green. Mr Anderson was a hard-working man and a good preacher, and in the three years of his superintendency in the circuit, from 1795 to 1798, membership increased considerably from 398 to 574. The circuit, however, was not able to maintain this growth, and by 1799 had declined somewhat. Membership had reduced by 20 members and the newly formed societies at Filby and Caister had been lost. A new society at Gorleston was also struggling and in decline. In the same year, the Framlingham section of the circuit split off, leaving a geographically more dense Great Yarmouth circuit.

The fortunes of the circuit improved over the next few years and by 1804 a new superintendent was appointed by the name of Mr Robert Miller. Mr Miller was viewed as someone who was rather frivolous with the circuit's money and he had alterations carried out at both the chapel and the chapel house. To pay for this building work, Mr Miller demanded more money from the members and increased the quarterly subscriptions. Mr Miller only stayed in the circuit for a year and was replaced in 1805 by a Mr Yates. In the period between Mr Miller's departure and the arrival of Mr Yates, the society steward, a Mr Sewell, proposed to reign in the circuit's spending, primarily by reducing the allowance paid to the minister. Upon his arrival Mr Yates was not pleased with this reduction and relations between him and Mr Sewell got off to a bad start, and deteriorated further as time went on.

At one of the circuit quarterly meetings, Mr Yates called into question Mr Sewell's conduct with the finances of the circuit. Mr Sewell had been responsible for the circuit accounts for the last twenty years and during this time had become quite secretive with them. Upon investigation the accounts were found to be in a mess, so Mr Yates appointed two new society stewards to assist Mr Sewell with the book-keeping. Mr Sewell did not agree with these appointments and took the action as a personal insult.

While this internal squabbling was happening a group of Kilhamites (who are also known as the Methodist New Connexion) were in Great Yarmouth trying to promote their version of Methodism. At this time, the Methodist New Connexion was considered to be an enemy of the more traditional Wesleyan Methodism. Mr Sewell's dispute with Mr Yates and the circuit led him, and his son, to support this rival Methodist faction. This was to such an extent that Mr Sewell provided funds to establish several Methodist New Connexion chapels in the area, while still being a senior member of the Great Yarmouth Wesleyan Methodist Circuit. More details of Mr Sewell and his support of the Methodist New Connexion are given later in this chapter in section 2.3.

In 1810 the Great Yarmouth circuit extended south quite some distance past Lowestoft, but in a northwards direction it was more limited in size. The circuit leaders decided to try and advance the circuit northwards and began preaching at places such as Winterton, Hemsby, Martham, Ormesby and Filby.

By 1812, the Great Yarmouth circuit was divided once again, with Lowestoft being separated off, as Framlingham had been some years earlier. The Great Yarmouth circuit now comprised nine societies with a total of 428 members – table 2.2 lists these societies along with their memberships in 1812. The Great Yarmouth chapel was also altered and enlarged, with more pews added and the gallery enlarged. The alterations left insufficient space for the Wesley Pulpit and it was subsequently moved to the Wesleyan chapel at West Caister. The cost of the modifications was £700, although even after this had been carried out, more room was still required as people were often turned away because of a lack of space. To accommodate the extra people, a former Methodist New Connexion chapel, the Providence Chapel, was hired and in 1814 a third preacher, Rev Richard Eland, was brought to Great Yarmouth. However, this second chapel was very close, too close in fact, to the principal Wesleyan Methodist chapel on the corner of King Street and Regent Road and it struggled to develop. About a year after its opening the third minister was relocated leaving two ministers again in Great Yarmouth, namely Rev Isaac Bradnach and Rev James Bromley. The Providence Chapel was subsequently purchased by the Countess of Huntington Connexion who worshipped there until they erected their own iron chapel on Southtown Road, at the top of Albany Road, in Great Yarmouth.

Table 2.2: Great Yarmouth Wesleyan Methodist circuit churches and memberships in 1812.

Church	Membership
Great Yarmouth	297
Caister	24
Filby	20
Stokesby	33
Hemsby	7
Winterton	7
Martham	11
Ludham	17
Bradwell	12
Total	428

Some preaching developments also occurred south of Great Yarmouth during this period. In 1814 a small society was established at Hopton (also called Lound on some plans) in the former Methodist New Connexion chapel. At about this time the society that had been established at Bradwell was given up, with some of the members transferring to the Great Yarmouth chapel.

The end of the Napoleonic Wars in 1815 led to a decline in membership of the Great Yarmouth circuit. Great Yarmouth had been a sizeable military base and the Yarmouth Roads were a well-used rendezvous point for the navy. Not only were military personnel removed from the area, but also the many people who had provided support for these large numbers of servicemen no longer had work and were forced to move away. Over the next three years the circuit membership was reduced by 155 members. Great Yarmouth's link with the navy did, however, continue when the superintendent minister began preaching on board ships. The first of these on-ship services was held in 1821 on a boat named *Thetford* which was bound for Naples from Hull.

2.2.2 Gorleston

The first attempts at introducing Methodism to Gorleston began in the early 1790s by local preachers who had travelled from Great Yarmouth. However, congregations were small and disruptions by aggressive mobs were frequent. The early Methodists in Gorleston faced similar hostilities to those in Great Yarmouth, risking both abuse and physical harm. In 1792, the Rev Boon from Great Yarmouth began preaching in Gorleston. Rev Boon was said to be "a man of superior talents as a preacher, who drew large congregations" and he had more success in establishing Methodism in Gorleston.

A Gorleston river pilot by the name of Mr Thomas Dawson attended these early services and began to appreciate greatly the words of these preachers from Great Yarmouth. Mr Dawson was in a lucrative business as a river pilot, but when one of the ship owners for whom he worked came to hear of his Methodist tendencies, he threatened to give his employment to someone else if he continued "in that scandalous way." Mr Dawson did continue with Methodism, although he lost his contract and faced similar threats from some of his other employers. He eventually became torn between giving up religion and retaining his lucrative employment, or remaining faithful and giving up the money. One night, when Mr Dawson was asleep, he had a dream which showed him heaven and hell and from that moment on he decided to continue with his faith. In 1793 he hired and fitted out a schoolroom, at his own expense, from which services could be held.

Methodism had still not been wholly accepted in Gorleston and in an attempt to stop angry crowds from disrupting services, Mr Dawson would stand outside the schoolroom and keep the mob quiet. On one occasion, Mr Dawson chased a particularly troublesome youth with the intention of keeping him quiet. However, when Mr Dawson caught up with him, the youth drew out a pistol and pointed it at Mr Dawson's chest. Fortunately, the gun was not fired and Mr Dawson was able to return to his chapel.

The Gorleston society grew with Mr Dawson as leader and by 1794 had grown to 13 members. Two years later membership had risen to 20 and the following year, in 1797, Mr Dawson built a Wesleyan Methodist chapel on Duke's Head Lane, which was just off the High Street in Gorleston town centre. This was again built at Mr Dawson's own expense and cost £300, by which time membership had increased to 23. The following year, membership had reached 28 and one of the local preachers from Great Yarmouth now acted as their leader. However, by 1800 membership had declined to 14 members, and in 1802 membership was down to just ten. The decline continued and as a result preachers were not always allocated to Gorleston, which caused more disruption. The situation got worse and in 1803 Gorleston was removed from the Great Yarmouth circuit plan. By 1804 the chapel was closed and converted into cottages. This caused considerable financial loss to Mr Dawson, who had funded the construction of the chapel single-handedly with no trustees to support him. The Wesleyan Methodist society in Gorleston was broken up in 1805 and it would be seven years before Wesleyan Methodism returned to the town.

Wesleyan Methodism returned to Gorleston in 1812 when Mr Dawson bought the former Methodist New Connexion chapel which was also located on Gorleston High Street – see section 2.3 for details on this chapel. A new Gorleston Wesleyan Methodist society was opened by the Rev Barnard Slater, who was the Superintendent Minister of the Great Yarmouth circuit. Rev Slater left the circuit in 1814, but by this time the Gorleston society had a membership of 32. Further growth continued with Rev Philip Jameson being Superintendent Minister in 1819 and by 1829 membership had reached 43. In October 1835 Mr Dawson died, having lived in one of the cottages that had been converted from the chapel he had built on Duke's Head Lane in Gorleston in 1797.

2.2.3 Caister

In Caister, Wesleyan Methodist services began not long after they had begun in Great Yarmouth. These were held by a Mr Kerridge and took place in the home of Mr Isaac English. This saved worshippers from Caister the long walk to Great Yarmouth. By June of 1785 the first society of Wesleyan Methodists was formed in Caister and had a membership of 13 with Mr James Edmonds as their leader. The following year, on 25 November, John Wesley visited Caister and preached from Mr English's cottage where he said of the worshippers "once more the combatants here have laid down their arms, and solemnly promise to continue in peace and love."

Shortly afterwards, in 1788, permission was given for a Baptist preacher to preach at Mr English's home. This caused much dissent within the Wesleyan Methodists of Caister with the result that the society came to an end. By 1805 some recovery of

Wesleyan Methodism in Caister had taken place and in 1807 a membership of 14 was reported with services being held in the house of a Mr Clement Burton who lived in West Caister. Mr Burton had originally taken a sceptical view of Methodism and had attended John Wesley's service in 1786 with a pocket full of stones with the aim of causing disruption. However, he was so impressed by John Wesley that he was converted to Wesleyan Methodism.

In 1809, the society had grown sufficiently to warrant building their own chapel, although there were still only 20 members. The circuit superintendent, Mr Bownell, encouraged them to do this although they were worried that they were too few and too poor. He advised them to make weekly subscriptions for a year and then see how much money they had accumulated. After a year they had saved £36. From this money they purchased land from Mr Burton that was adjacent to his house for £10. The Lord of the Manor permitted them to dig brick earth from waste land in the village and by 1811 the first Wesleyan Methodist chapel in Caister was built at West Caister. The site of this chapel is close to the western side of the footbridge that crosses the Caister bypass – figure 3.9 in chapter 3 shows the location of this chapel. The chapel was demolished many years ago but the nearby road takes the name Chapel Corner which serves as a reminder of the former chapel.

2.2.4 Filby and Stokesby

Filby was one of the first villages where the Great Yarmouth Methodist Circuit tried to establish a society. The first service was held in the open air on the village green in 1795. This was not a success and the preacher, Mr Robert Page, was beaten with sticks, brickbats and rotten eggs, and it is reported that his eyes and face were so swollen that he was hardly recognisable. One of the Filby residents at the time, a Mr John Martin, who was not in favour of the Methodists, did not like the way that Mr Page had been treated and began to wonder whether it was actually the villagers who were wrong. This played on Mr Martin's conscience and to put matters right he hired a room where preachers could hold services. Within a few months a small class of ten people was established. This society, however, did not last for many years and by 1799 had disappeared.

A few years later in 1804, a Mr Simon Long moved to Filby. He had previously been a gardener at Felbrigg Hall in North Norfolk, but fell out with his employers over his Methodist views. Mr Long joined the Great Yarmouth Methodist society and walked there twice a week from Filby, which was a considerable distance to travel on foot. On one instance, along with some other villagers from Filby, he attended a service at Caister and was recognised there by the preacher. Following a conversation, the preacher offered to travel to Filby to take services in the village. Mr Long was willing to have the services held in his house but he needed to obtain a licence to do so. To obtain a preaching licence, Mr Long required his landlord's consent, but he knew that he was not a religious man, although he was a man of good will. Mr Long enquired of his landlord as to whether he could have his house licensed, to which the landlord replied "O that I will, at once, I have sometimes thought of that myself: It is a convenient house too for the purpose, standing so close by the road-side." Realising his landlord's confusion, Mr Long replied "But, Sir, that is not what I mean; I mean a licence for preaching the gospel in it." This was a different view to the landlord's thinking of establishing a drinking house, but he did consent to Mr Long's request and a preaching licence was duly obtained. Preaching was thus resumed at Filby and the services at Mr Long's house became the start of this new society.

In about 1810 a wealthy villager, Mr James Norton, began attending services in Great Yarmouth and then at Filby. He was a great supporter of the Filby society and encouraged them to build their own chapel. Land, measuring 47 feet by 26 feet, was purchased in 1811 and a chapel was opened on the site later in the same year.

At nearby Stokesby, prayer meetings and preaching were started in the rented cottages of Mr John Davison and Mr John Goulder. Shortly afterwards the ownership of these cottages was transferred to Mr Norton, but this was before his conversion to Methodism. Naturally, Mr Davison and Mr Goulder were concerned as to whether their new landlord would permit them to carry on holding services from their cottages. However, it was in this period that Mr Norton found Methodism and so he continued to support their services. This was to such an extent that he, having supported the building of the chapel at Filby, supported the building of a similar chapel at Stokesby and by 1811 a chapel was built. Mr Norton and his wife then became members of the Stokesby society.

2.2.5 Winterton, Hemsby, Thurne and Ormesby

In about 1810 the Great Yarmouth Methodist Circuit extended south quite some distance, past Lowestoft, but northwards was more constrained. The circuit leaders decided to try and advance the circuit northwards and began preaching at places such as Winterton, Hemsby, Martham and Ormesby. By 1814, preaching at Hemsby had ceased and preaching was moved to Ormesby where a small chapel was built on land owned by Mrs Norton, who, with her husband, had previously established chapels in Filby and Stokesby.

Further growth occurred at Thurne, which by 1814 had 11 members. In the same year a chapel was built at Martham, but it was reported that patience was needed "until the peculiarities of Calvinism can be made to disappear." In Winterton, a house owned by Mrs Ann Kemp was licensed for preaching in 1811 and soon afterwards in 1814 a chapel was built for £50. However, there was found to be a problem with the deeds for this new building which resulted in the society loosing the chapel. This signalled the end of preaching at Winterton.

The chapel at Ormesby was subjected to a lot of disruption by groups of people objecting to Methodism in the village. Several villagers were issued with summonses to stop them disturbing preaching, but many of these people were quite wealthy and preferred to pay the summons and keep causing disruption! One particular person was a well-known agitator and had once taken a horse into the parish church at Caister! He would come into the Ormesby chapel, half drunk, and as soon as the preacher began speaking, he would speak at the same time. This would go on for some time, and eventually the preacher would have to dismiss the congregation. Eventually, he was summonsed to the Magistrates Court in Norwich in 1815 and was fined £40 for his actions. However, the cost of bringing this matter to court cost the Ormesby Methodists £60. Even with all this disruption, the Ormesby society prospered and they opened a new chapel on 10 January in 1822.

2.2.6 Ludham

The first Wesleyan Methodist society in Ludham began in 1812, which was during the time that the Great Yarmouth circuit decided to expand northwards. In 1812 the society had

12 members and by 1816 the Ludham Methodist society appeared on the Great Yarmouth Methodist Circuit plan. For its first nine years, until 1821, the society met in a stable that belonged to the Kings Arms Inn in the village. During this time the prosperity of the society fell but by 1821 it was increasing again to such an extent that the members decided to build their own chapel.

On 24th April 1821 the Superintendent Minister of the Great Yarmouth Methodist Circuit, Rev William Bacon, on behalf of the Ludham society, purchased a plot of land in the village from a Mrs Sarah Rust. The land cost £5 and was alongside a road called Baldwyns Lane which is now known as Malthouse Lane. The chapel was built quickly and opened on 8 November 1821, measuring 24 feet by 28 feet. The chapel is reported to have had galleries along both sides and along the front, and to have had a high pulpit. The chapel is also said to have had a choir, but "with no-one who could read music very well!" At its opening, the Ludham society had the following nine trustees:

- James Norton from Stokesby, a farmer
- Edward Rice from Ludham, a marshman
- John Beverley from Martham, a shoemaker
- Martin Sandall from Ludham, a farmer
- John Thurgate from Ludham, a shoemaker
- William Carrier from Rollesby, a farmer
- Robert Beverley from Martham, a farmer
- George Simpson from Great Yarmouth, a shoemaker
- James Sparison from Great Yarmouth, a tailor.

2.2.7 Wickhampton, Freethorpe and Moulton

The earliest reports of Methodism in the Wickhampton, Freethorpe and Moulton area date as far back as 1803, when a Mr Farman of Freethorpe hired a house at Moulton for services and preaching. This early society progressed and six years later in 1809, Mr Farman bought a house in Freethorpe and turned it into a chapel. The chapel was opened on Christmas Day in 1810 with a service conducted by Rev Gilfin who was the Superintendent Minister in the Norwich Methodist Circuit. The chapel was well attended and soon became too small for the growing band of worshippers. One of the congregation was a Wickhampton farmer by the name of Mr John Crown. Mr Crown donated a piece of land from his farm on the corner of Church Road and Mill Road, measuring 47 feet by 30 feet, for the erection of a larger chapel. He also made a gift of £30 to help with its building costs. In January 1814 the new chapel was opened and the congregation of the original Freethorpe chapel transferred to the new Wickhampton chapel. The opening services were reported to have been so well attended that they were held in the open air. These services raised £11.9.2, which, together with subscriptions, amounted to £109.9.2 towards the chapel. In the early years of the Wickhampton chapel, the society was part of the Norwich Methodist Circuit. It wasn't until 1831 that the chapel was transferred into the

Figure 2.8: The former Wesleyan chapel at Wickhampton, pictured in 2008. The chapel was sold in 1988 and is now a private house.

Great Yarmouth Methodist Circuit – chapter 3 continues the story of the Wickhampton chapel. Figure 2.8 shows the chapel as it was in 2007, having been closed for about 20 years.

The trustees of the new chapel later mortgaged the building for £400 which they planned to use for investment. The farmer who donated the land, Mr Crown, died in 1819 and left the chapel £100 in his will. His executors subsequently donated a further £100 which halved the debt on the chapel to £200. Over the next few years the chapel was improved by the addition of a gallery in 1823 at a cost of £30. In 1826 additional land was purchased from Mr Bernard Crown for £15 to provide space for a stable and the chapel was also enlarged at a cost of £70.

2.3 Methodist New Connexion

As has been described in the previous section, the Wesleyan Methodists in Great Yarmouth during the early 1800s had some serious problems with which to contend. One of the senior members of the circuit, Mr Sewell, had been a trustee, class leader and society steward for over 20 years. During this time he had kept the society and circuit accounts, but had not kept a sufficiently close watch on them with the result that they had become in a state of confusion. In August 1805, the newly appointed circuit superintendent minister for Great Yarmouth, Rev Yates, appointed two new stewards in an attempt to clear up the mess made by Mr Sewell. Mr Sewell took umbrage at this and, together with his son who was in agreement with his father, started to cause considerable unpleasantness in the

Great Yarmouth chapel and circuit.

This began when Mr Sewell invited members of the Methodist New Connexion (who were also known as Kilhamites after their founder Rev Alexander Kilham) to come and preach in Great Yarmouth. The Methodist New Connexion was set up in 1797 as a break-away from the Wesleyan Methodist movement and at the time they were trying to poach Wesleyan Methodists into their society. Unsurprisingly, the Methodist New Connexion accepted Mr Sewell's invitation and began to establish preaching in Great Yarmouth. These services were supported by Mr Sewell, who was a man of considerable wealth and influence in the town.

Mr Sewell had further plans to disrupt the Wesleyan Methodists, which involved bringing the Methodist New Connexion preachers into the new church that the Wesleyans had built on the corner of King Street and Regent Road in 1792. Mr Sewell's plan was to propose this during the 1806 Wesleyan Methodist conference when the superintendent minister would be absent. Mr Sewell revealed his plans to another of the Wesleyan trustees who was shocked at Mr Sewell's scheme and informed the other trustees. During the meeting that followed, the trustees stood firm and together defeated Mr Sewell's plans. This left Mr Sewell unable to bring the Methodist New Connexion preachers into the Wesleyan chapel on King Street. Instead, Mr Sewell procured a large building in the town which was converted into a church for the Methodist New Connexion, in effect setting up a rival to the Wesleyan Methodist church. During all this scheming, Mr Sewell remained a leader with the Wesleyan Methodist church and even attended leaders' meetings. It is also said that on Sundays, Mr Sewell would take his wife to the Wesleyan chapel and then take himself off to the Methodist New Connexion service!

By 1807, a Methodist New Connexion chapel had been built in Great Yarmouth and soon after chapels were built in Gorleston and in Lound (the society at Lound is also referred to as Hopton on some plans). Mr Sewell financed much of this new building work and became a trustee of all three chapels. The location of the Methodist New Connexion chapel in Great Yarmouth is not known precisely, but is thought to have been somewhere in the King Street area, close to the Wesleyan chapel that was on the corner of King Street and Regent Road. The chapel in Gorleston was on the High Street, near to where the Gorleston Shopping Precinct is now. The location of the chapel in Lound (Hopton) was close to the Lound Water Works and is thought to be the chapel shown on the map from 1891 illustrated in figure 8.2.

These three Methodist New Connexion societies were not successful and after only a few years had closed their chapels. In 1814, the Methodist New Connexion chapel in Great Yarmouth was hired by the Wesleyan Methodists to accommodate their growing congregation. The chapel on the High Street in Gorleston was also subsequently taken over by Wesleyan Methodists in 1812 and later rebuilt in 1844. The chapel at Lound was used by Independents for a while, before being hired by Wesleyan Methodists. A Wesleyan Methodist society was later formed in Lound although services discontinued in about 1851.

On 1 January 1823 Mr Sewell died and in a letter he was given a glowing tribute for all he had done for Wesleyan Methodism in Great Yarmouth. In particular, he was praised for giving his heart and house to receive John Wesley. This is not the end of the Methodist New Connexion's link with Great Yarmouth, as they did have a more successful return in 1833. This is discussed in chapter 8, which examines several of the various break-away movements from Wesleyan Methodism that would later become known as the United

Methodist Church in 1907.

2.4 Primitive Methodism

The third group of Methodists to establish themselves in Great Yarmouth and the wider East Norfolk area were the Primitive Methodists. The Primitive Methodist movement began in 1810 and reached Great Yarmouth about ten years later. Much of the early history of Primitive Methodism in Great Yarmouth is taken from accounts made by elderly Primitive Methodists that have been recorded in Arthur Patterson's book *From Hayloft to Temple* that was written in 1903. The people providing these accounts were in their eighties at that time of writing in 1903, so they would have been just able to recollect the early days of Primitive Methodism in Great Yarmouth.

The Primitive Methodist movement was established in 1810 and began to gather strength in the Midlands during the 1810s and then began to move eastwards towards Norfolk. In the early 1820s, towns such as Fakenham, Kings Lynn and Norwich became centres for the Primitive Methodists in Norfolk. Preachers from Norwich started coming further east and first arrived in Great Yarmouth in about 1819, although some sources claim this to be in 1820 or 1821. The first Primitive Methodist preacher to hold services in Great Yarmouth is said to be Mr Turnpenny and he preached on the Denes in Great Yarmouth, close to the Jetty, as early as 1821. Other accounts state that he also held classes about a year later in 1822 from a house in one of the rows. Open air services were also held in the same year at Hog Hill by Mr Turnpenny and Rev Brame. Hog Hill was outside the Fishermen's Hospital at the northern end of Great Yarmouth Market Place and the location is shown in figure 2.9 in a drawing from the book *From Hayloft to Temple*. If the weather was too wet for outdoor services, preaching was moved to a gig-shed in Row 8 that was owned by a Wesleyan couple by the name of Fryer. It is interesting to recall that the Wesleyan Methodists had also worshipped in Row 8, although by the time of the arrival of the Primitive Methodists in the 1820s, they had moved to their new chapel on the corner of King Street and Regent Road.

Soon after these services had become established, the two preachers formed a Primitive Methodist society in Great Yarmouth. This was known as the "Yarmouth branch of the Norwich Circuit." In its first preaching plan, for the period 26 October 1823 to 18 January 1824, the society had two travelling preachers, S Chapman and J Bryant, three local preachers and two exhorters. Eleven preaching places were listed on the Sunday plan and six for the week-night plan, and these are listed in table 2.3. In these early days, the area covered by the Great Yarmouth plan was large, from Westleton in the south to Martham in the north – a distance of about 40 miles.

2.4.1 The Hayloft

The new Primitive Methodist society in Great Yarmouth soon required permanent covered premises and in 1824 had rented the upper floor of a stable which was situated on what is now Temple Road in Great Yarmouth, near to the town wall. The upper floor was a hayloft, although it was subsequently fitted out for public worship and became known as the "Hayloft." The building was about 20 feet long and lit by three small leaded windows. These had been installed by the Primitive Methodists as previously there had been no windows in the openings which made it rather draughty. The worship area could seat

Figure 2.9: A sketch of Hog Hill, next to the Fishermen's Hospital on Great Yarmouth Market Place, where some of the first open-air Primitive Methodist services were held. Note the parish church in the background with its spire. The picture comes from the book *From Hayloft to Temple.*

Table 2.3: Sunday-night and week-night preaching places in the Yarmouth branch of the Norwich Primitive Methodist Circuit in 1823.

Sunday-night plan	Week-night plan
Great Yarmouth	Ludham
Wangford	Martham
Beccles	Halesworth
Mutford Bridge	Westleton
Lowestoft	Blythburgh
Thurne	Southwold
Rollesby	
Burgh	
Geldeston	
Norton	
Wrentham	

Figure 2.10: A sketch of the Hayloft which was the first permanent location for the Great Yarmouth Primitive Methodists and was located on Priory Plain in the town. The picture is based on a description of the Hayloft and comes from the book *From Hayloft to Temple.*

about 50 people on stiffly built seats. Surrounding the Hayloft were stables, almshouses and a large saw pit. Even during the Primitive Methodist occupation of the Hayloft, horses and carts were stored in the stable below. Figure 2.10 shows a sketch of the Hayloft which appears in the book *From Hayloft to Temple* and was drawn using descriptions provided by several elderly Primitive Methodists.

Services at the Hayloft were not without disruption from gangs intent on annoying the worshipers. A common trick was for groups of lads to take into the Hayloft a pocketful of sparrows and then release them during services and watch the distraction that they caused. In another incident, a dead cat was thrown at the person leading prayer. The poor condition of the floor of the Hayloft was also the source of mischief. The floor had many holes and gangs would congregate in the lower floor of the building and thrust stable-brooms up through holes in the ageing floorboards.

A circuit plan beginning 17 April 1825 indicated that Great Yarmouth had been made a Primitive Methodist circuit in its own right, by using the heading "Yarmouth Circuit. A plan of the Preachers of the Primitive Methodists, called Ranters." In the same year one of the most ungodly men in the town, Robert Key, was converted to Primitive Methodism. Robert Key subsequently went on with this good work and became known as the "Norfolk Evangelist."

2.4.2 The First Tabernacle

A new superintendent minister was appointed to the Great Yarmouth Primitive Methodist Circuit in 1827 by the name of Rev Samuel Atterby. He realised that the Hayloft was not suitable for worship and set about collecting subscriptions to fund a more appropriate building. The congregation had grown very quickly following the establishment of the Hayloft and by 1829 membership had increased to 280. This represented an increase of 137 members in one year and the society decided to purchase the Hayloft and convert it into a proper chapel. This new chapel measured 57 feet by 28 feet and was 16 feet high and galleried on three sides. It was known as the First Tabernacle and cost £700. The back of the chapel was built on the old town wall and descriptions of it do not portray it as an elegant building. In fact, it is described as a "small, meagre and stuffy place." Even so, the Rev T Swindell wrote in the *Primitive Methodist Magazine* of November 1850 that the Tabernacle could hold 650 people!

2.4.3 Early Primitive Methodism in Gorleston

Occasional Primitive Methodist preaching took place in Gorleston in the early nineteenth century, but it wasn't until 1833 that Primitive Methodism was established in Gorleston with a membership of 15. Meetings were held in an old chapel on Burnt Lane which was galleried on all four sides with a deep pit in the centre without any seating. This gave the chapel the name "the sandpit." The galleries were high and the ceiling low, giving a dim feel to the inside. The chapel was said to be a trying place to hold services and keep the congregation interested. In fact, it is reported that "on many a Sunday more than half the congregation sometimes collapsed, and some would temporarily enliven proceedings with a hearty snore." Next to the chapel was a pigsty "the tenants of which would sometimes sing when the congregation did not!"

2.4.4 The villages around Great Yarmouth

The period around 1830 was a time of much new missioning work by the Primitive Methodists in the villages to the south, west and north of Great Yarmouth. Many new societies were formed, and taking the year 1833 as a cut-off date, missioning had begun in Hemsby, Martham, Thurne, Catfield, Upton, Rollesby, Reedham, Belton, Fleggburgh, Limpenhoe, Winterton, Freethorpe, Berney Arms, Halvergate, South Walsham, Acle, Stokesby, Runham, Potter Heigham, Caister and Repps. Chapels had not yet been constructed in these villages, so services tended to be held in rooms in members' houses.

At Belton, for example, which was first put on the plan in 1832, there was no chapel and instead preaching is reported to have taken place in a labourer's cottage in a room shared with a large mangle! A similar account is taken from Horsey, where early worshippers met in the kitchen of Mrs Sarah Watts, who lived in a farm opposite the Nelsons Head Inn.

After 1833, all branches of Methodism continued to expand. The next six chapters chart the history of the Wesleyan, Primitive and United Methodists in the next 100 years up to 1932.

Chapter 3

Wesleyan Methodism – 1833 to 1932

3.1 Introduction

The period from 1833 to 1932 was a time of growth and consolidation for Wesleyan Methodism, both nationally and locally in East Norfolk. Nationally, in 1833 there were about 200,000 members of the Wesleyan Methodist Church, and by 1932 this had increased to over 500,000. In East Norfolk, over the same period, similar levels of growth were witnessed. The number of members in the Great Yarmouth Wesleyan circuit grew from about 270 in 1833 to almost 600 in 1932.

These numbers, however, hide some of the problems that Wesleyan Methodism suffered during the period 1833 to 1932. Already, several disputes had taken place within the Wesleyan Methodist movement that led to alternative Methodist connexions being established, the most significant being the Methodist New Connexion (1797) and the Primitive Methodist connexion (1810). One of the biggest disputes within Methodism was over the increasing power and centralisation of the Wesleyan Connexion. This argument began after John Wesley's death in 1791 and continued for many years, gradually becoming more objectionable for more and more members as time went on. Grievances came to a head during the 1849 Wesleyan Methodist Conference when several ministers who were strongly in favour of reform were expelled. Shortly afterwards the Wesleyan Reform Society was established and this took with it large numbers of Wesleyan Methodists. Nationally, the effect of this was serious, with, by 1854, the Reformers having almost 50,000 members; mainly taken from Wesleyan Methodist societies. In East Norfolk the Reform movement caused serious disruption to the local Wesleyan Methodist societies. Several Wesleyan societies saw more than half of their membership leave and in some cases Wesleyan chapels actually closed, as happened at Gorleston, or merged, as happened at Caister. By the end of the 1850s the losses to the Reform movement had subsided and Wesleyan Methodism began to grow again.

Wesleyan Methodism was successful in the towns of East Norfolk, but its societies in the more rural areas often struggled against competition from the Primitive Methodists. The villages that had a Wesleyan Methodist society generally also had a Primitive Methodist

Table 3.1: Wesleyan Methodist societies in East Norfolk and their memberships, taken from Great Yarmouth circuit plans in 1892, 1903, 1913, 1922 and 1932.

Society	1892	1903	1913	1922	1932
Dene Side	255	287	265	244	285
Lowestoft Road	66	64	81	101	134
Caister West	29	26	13	2	–
Caister East	27	30	18	35	42
Ormesby	21	20	19	17	17
Stokesby	20	19	11	16	25
Ludham	21	9	15	9	14
Fleggburgh	26	26	11	12	11
Wickhampton	20	21	9	11	20
Acle	6	5	9	8	9
Mission Room	27	27	38	16	34
Total	518	534	489	471	591

society. This inevitably caused some tensions, with the two Methodist societies vying for members. There seems to be no reason for the success of one society in a village and the demise of the other. For example, at Stokesby the Wesleyans were more successful than the Primitives and eventually took over the Primitive chapel. In nearby Acle, the opposite was true with the Primitives outliving the Wesleyan Methodists.

Comparing the list of societies in the Great Yarmouth Wesleyan Methodist Circuit in 1812 (see table 2.2 in chapter 2) with those in 1892 (from table 3.1) shows much change to have taken place. Many societies that existed in the early 1800s did not survive, but several new chapels had opened by the end of the 1800s. Of the nine societies listed in 1812, only four survived – Great Yarmouth, Caister, Stokesby and Ludham. The smaller societies of Filby, Hemsby, Winterton, Martham and Bradwell did not survive. The precise cause of these closures is unknown, but it is likely that the strength of the Primitive Methodist movement in these more rural areas was a contributing factor. In fact, all five of these villages eventually had Primitive Methodist societies.

Broadly speaking, Wesleyan societies were more likely to be found in the towns and larger villages of East Norfolk – those probably large enough to support both Wesleyan and Primitive Methodist societies. The eleven societies listed in table 3.1 occupied nine towns and villages – Great Yarmouth, Gorleston, Caister, Ormesby, Stokesby, Ludham, Fleggburgh, Wickhampton and Acle. All of these, with the exception of Wickhampton, also had Primitive Methodist societies. However, most of these places were generally more populous than the villages surrounding them. In addition to these eleven societies, early plans from the Wesleyan circuit show that services took place at "Great Yarmouth Workhouse" and "Military Department." Services at these venues did not last for long, but they do serve to illustrate how the circuit brought Methodism to those in need.

The remainder of this chapter discusses the development of Wesleyan Methodist societies in East Norfolk in the period from 1833 to 1932.

3.2 Great Yarmouth

In the early part of the 1800s, Great Yarmouth Wesleyan Methodists continued to worship at the chapel on the corner of King Street and Regent Road, where they had moved in 1792. In the period to 1932, two significant developments were to take place. The first was to move from the King Street–Regent Road chapel to a new church on Dene Side in Great Yarmouth. The second was to establish a new society, the Tower Street Mission, in the southern part of Great Yarmouth.

3.2.1 Dene Side

During the early 1830s the King Street–Regent Road chapel was allowed to deteriorate. The decay was to such an extent that by 1836 the trustees reported on the "very dilapidated state of the building" and the need to "spend considerable amounts of money" to have it restored. The building must have been in very bad condition as the trustees advised that it would be better not to spend such a large sum on restoration. Instead, they suggested that a new and more spacious church should be built in Great Yarmouth. In their search for premises, the trustees found a builder's store that was for sale. This was on the corner of Regent Road and Dene Side and had the advantage of being on an open road and just inside the town wall. The trustees considered this as being "most suitable and convenient" as the site for the new church. The site was bought by the trustees, together with some adjacent shops, for £684. More land was also purchased south along Dene Side for £22. The owner of the land generously donated the £22 towards the cost of building the new chapel.

Building work on this new "Dene Side" church began in 1837 and a foundation stone was laid by Mayor William Barth Esq on 14 August 1837. During the stone laying ceremony an address was given by Rev Thomas Rowland of Norwich. Building work progressed quickly and an opening service for the Dene Side church took place on 14 June 1838, where sermons were preached by Rev Robert Newton of Leeds. The total cost of the new church was £4,200. The now disused Methodist church on the corner of King Street and Regent Road was sold in 1838 for £830. The upper picture in figure 3.1 shows a picture of the Dene Side church in 1902. The lower picture in figure 3.1 shows the Dene Side site as it was in 2006, having been replaced by the Great Yarmouth branch of BHS. Dene Side closed in 1937 and was sold for commercial development – see chapter 10 for more details.

The entrance to the 1792 Wesleyan chapel on the corner of King Street and Regent Road had a north-facing entrance. This often caused problems for the church as sand and snow tended to drift across the doorway and would then need to be cleared away. The Methodists wanted to avoid this problem in their new building and so designed the church to have a south-facing main entrance. At the time that Dene Side was opened, the land to the south of the church, known as the chapel yard, was unoccupied as it was a requirement to allow the residents of Dene Side an uninterrupted view of the sea. This made a south-facing entrance possible. It was only later that the entrance was moved to the north side of the church to lead in from Regent Road.

Inside Dene Side were side galleries and also a north gallery which was accessed by its own stairway. This was a very narrow and winding staircase and worshippers referred going up to the gallery as "going up the spout!" There was also a large pulpit which could

Figure 3.1: Dene Side Methodist Church. The upper picture shows the Dene Side church in 1902 and the schoolrooms and lecture hall. The church was closed in 1937 and demolished soon after. The lower picture was taken from the same position in 2006 and shows that the Great Yarmouth branch of BHS now occupies the site.

hold up to four preachers at any one time, although there was no organ in the church when it first opened.

Disaster almost struck Dene Side shortly after it had opened. In August 1838 a large congregation was packed inside the church for the farewell service of one of the ministers who was leaving. At this time lighting inside the church was provided by gas lights. During the sermon, air in the gas pipes feeding the lights caused the flames to flare up and someone shouted out that the church was on fire. In response, the congregation caused a stampede as they rushed to get out of the building and it was fortunate that no one was injured. Following the incident, the gas lights around the pulpit were replaced by candles, which seems a rather backward, although possibly safer, step.

Over the years, Dene Side grew to be one of the leading Methodist churches in Great Yarmouth and was described as the "Cathedral church of East Anglian Methodism." In 1848 the church was modernised and an organ was installed. The north gallery was taken down, along with the "spout." The decision on whether or not to install an organ was an extremely close call and was decided by just one vote at a meeting of the Dene Side trustees. To celebrate the installation of the organ a recital was given by Mr Joseph Reddie of St Margaret's church in King's Lynn. Some of the music played was Mr Reddie's own composition and it was reported that at times, when his hands were fully engaged, some notes had to be played with his nose – a skill that, sadly, is infrequently displayed by organists today!

In 1886 the church was renovated, new pews added, the vestry re-built and the pulpit and entrances altered. This cost £2,000 and gave a seating capacity at Dene Side of 1,000 people. At this time the Great Yarmouth Wesleyan circuit supported three ministers. In 1900, the Dene Side society bought a magic lantern and held a range of slide lectures, with titles such as "Scenes from the Life of Christ", "Joseph and his Brethren", "Natural Phenomena" and "Buy your own cherries" – this was a Victorian tale about saving a drunkard from the devils of drink!

The new Lecture Hall

Dene Side expanded again in 1904 with the opening of a rather grand lecture hall and Sunday school room, which together cost £3,500. By this time the restrictions on building along Dene Side had been relaxed. This allowed the Methodists to build on the chapel yard to the south of the church. Figure 3.2 shows the new schoolroom on Dene Side and figure 3.3 shows one of the classrooms inside. The lecture hall was highly ornate with beige coloured terracotta tiles outside and glazed tiles inside. Inside was a large hall, around which were ten smaller classrooms. These could be opened out to make one very large room which was suitable for lectures, meetings and bazaars.

The Gourlay Wesleyan Day School

In 1867, the Mayor of Great Yarmouth, Mr David Gourlay JP, had recovered from a serious illness and as an act of gratitude he gave £1,000 to support Methodism in Great Yarmouth. The Methodists decided that the best use of this money was to build a Wesleyan day school to support the young people of the town. A plot of land was bought on Dene Side for £260 that was a few hundred metres south of the church. The school was built on the site and named the Gourlay Wesleyan Day School. The school prospered for many years and was a great help to Methodism in Great Yarmouth. Eventually the

Figure 3.2: The Dene Side Sunday school. To the left of the Sunday school buildings can be seen the west side of the Dene Side church.

Figure 3.3: One of the schoolrooms inside the Dene Side Sunday school and lecture hall.

Gourlay School was converted into the Sunday school rooms for the new Central Hall in 1938 – this is explained in more detail in chapter 10. Figure 3.4 shows the former Gourlay School building in 2008.

3.2.2 Tower Street Mission – 1883

In 1883 an evangelistic minister by the name of Rev Thomas Cook preached at Dene Side. Rev Cook caused quite a stir and, as a result of his preaching, many young people became converted to Methodism. The young people formed themselves into a mission band, with one of the local preachers, a Mr Berry, serving as their leader. About 80 young people were in the mission band and they would go out into the streets of Great Yarmouth and sing, thus continuing the evangelism introduced by Rev Cook.

At around this time an old dance hall was being advertised for sale. This had on occasions been used for church services and was formerly the dance hall of the Victoria Pleasure Gardens, on the corner of Tower Street and Malakoff Road in the southern part of Great Yarmouth. The Victoria Pleasure Gardens had opened in 1855 and was a spacious outdoor area for relaxation, containing a fountain, stage, dance hall, gardens and the Victoria Gardens public house. The gardens closed in about 1872 and the land was sold, subsequently being replaced by two new roads – Tower Street and Boreham Road. Figure 3.5 shows three maps of the area for the years 1867, 1906 and 2009, where the dance hall, Tower Street Mission and present-day layout can be seen.

With this large influx of young people at Dene Side, the trustees wished to make use of their enthusiasm and so bought the old dance hall with the purpose of establishing a mission in the southern part of Great Yarmouth. Once opened, the building was called the

Figure 3.4: The former Gourlay Wesleyan Day School. The building has now been converted into self-contained bedsits and is owned by Orbit Housing.

Tower Street Mission and regular services and a Sunday school were held there. Figure 3.6 shows a picture of the Tower Street Mission, along with some of its members including Mr Berry, in the 1920s.

3.3 Gorleston

Wesleyan Methodism in Gorleston continued at the chapel in the High Street for many years until the Wesleyan Reform movement caused irreparable divisions in the society, leading ultimately to its closure. The remaining Wesleyan Methodists then had to travel to Great Yarmouth for services until, in 1866, the Methodist Church on Lowestoft Road in Gorleston was built. Thus, the Gorleston Wesleyan Methodist society occupied two churches in the period 1833 to 1932, first on the High Street and then on Lowestoft Road.

3.3.1 High Street

Wesleyan Methodism in Gorleston did not have an easy start at the end of the eighteenth century. These early Methodists suffered much abuse as they attempted to establish a

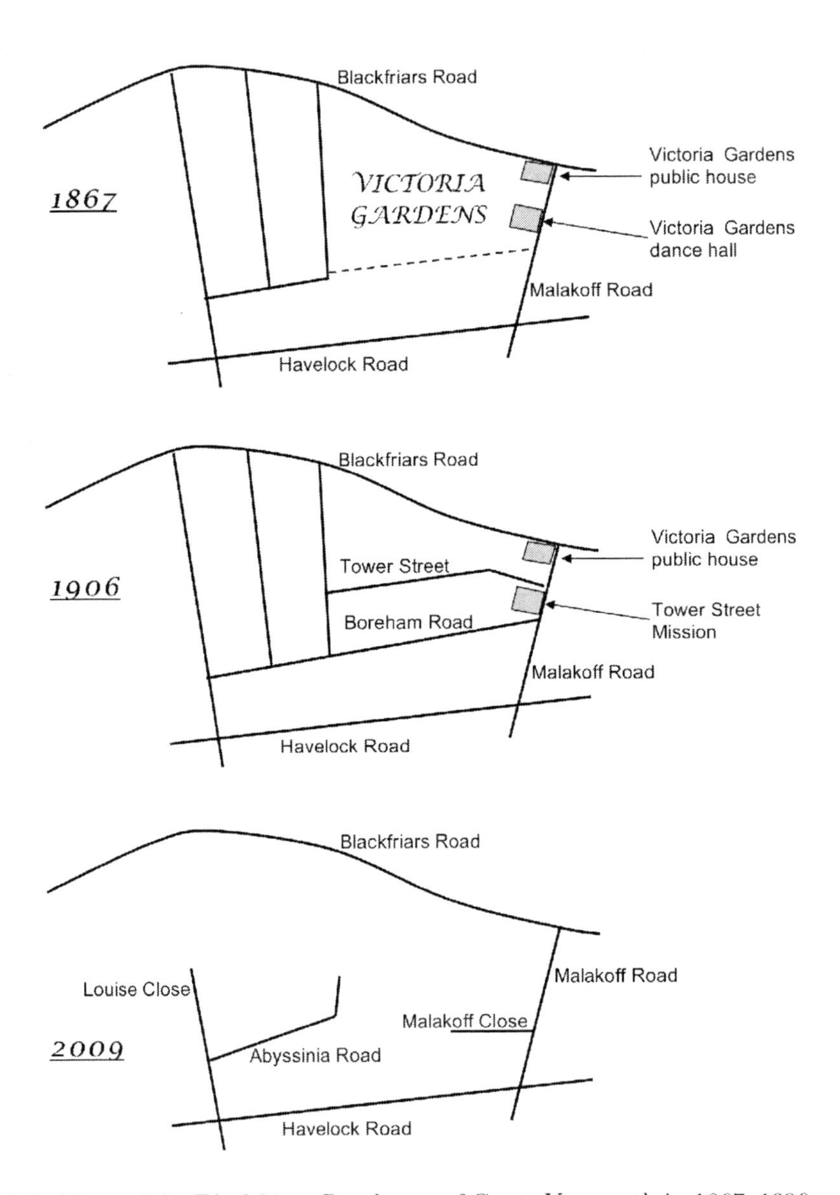

Figure 3.5: Maps of the Blackfriars Road area of Great Yarmouth in 1867, 1906 and 2009. In 1867 the area was occupied by the Victoria Gardens with its own public house and dance hall. After the Victoria Gardens had closed, new roads were put through the area and the former dance hall was bought by Wesleyan Methodists and became the Tower Street Mission. The area was further developed in the 1970s and is now occupied by flats.

Figure 3.6: The Tower Street Mission in the 1920s. This was on the corner of Tower Street and Malakoff Road in the south of Great Yarmouth. It was opened in 1883 but was closed during the Second World War having been damaged by enemy bombing.

society in Gorleston. By the early nineteenth century, however, their fortunes had picked up and the High Street Methodist church in Gorleston began to prosper. Congregations had grown to such an extent that by 1844 the High Street church was no longer big enough. In response to this growth, the trustees decided that the best course of action would be to demolish the building and build a larger church on the same site. Foundation stones for the new church were laid on 20 August 1844 by Rev William Fowler, who was a supernumery minister living in Great Yarmouth. At this time the membership of the Gorleston society was a very healthy 79 members, which was the highest number since Wesleyan Methodism had been introduced to Gorleston. However, shortly afterwards membership began to decline and by 1850 it had reduced to 48 members – a sizeable drop in just six years.

The influence of the Wesleyan Reform movement in the early 1850s caused a big division in the membership of the society. Many members left to join the Wesleyan Reformers which caused a further fall in members to just 23 by 1851. Membership numbers continued to fall, eventually to such a level that it became impossible to keep the church open. In what was a very difficult time for the remaining Wesleyan Methodists, later in 1851 the church was sold to two of the Wesleyan Reformers – Mr James Lawn and Mr Michael Field. The pair had previously been members of the Wesleyan society and had left during the agitation caused by the Reformers. Once Mr Lawn and Mr Field had taken ownership of the church they opened it as a Wesleyan Reform chapel. This later became a United Methodist Free Church chapel, when the Wesleyan Reform movement merged with the Protestant Methodists in 1857 – see chapter 8.

The sale of the church in 1851 left the remaining Gorleston Wesleyan Methodists with no meeting place in Gorleston. They did, however, continue worshipping by hiring a nearby room for their services. Even after losing their church, the fortunes of the Wesleyan Methodists in Gorleston remained in decline and membership was still falling. In 1852 membership had reduced to 17 – a reduction of over 60 members in just eight years. By 1854 membership had reduced to 12 and in 1855 the rented room used for services was given up. The few remaining Wesleyan Methodists in Gorleston now had to travel to the Dene Side Methodist church in Great Yarmouth to attend services. To add to the Gorleston Wesleyan Methodists' problems, it transpired that proper procedures in accordance with the Wesleyan Methodist Chapel Building Committee had not been followed when the High Street church was re-built in 1844. The sale of the building to the Wesleyan Reformers had not cleared the mortgage on the church and this now had to met by the few remaining Wesleyan trustees who were each faced with a debt of £18.

3.3.2 Lowestoft Road

The need to travel to Great Yarmouth for services was not ideal for the Gorleston Wesleyan Methodists. At a local preachers' meeting, held at Dene Side Methodist church in 1865, a decision was made to build a new Wesleyan Methodist church in Gorleston. A plot of land for the new church was bought on the corner of Lowestoft Road and Suffield Road. At the time, this was considered quite a strange location for a new church, as this was some distance from the centre of Gorleston and considered very much out of town. The foundation stone for the new church was laid in April 1866 by Mr Francis Lycett of London. Mr Lycett was a wealthy Wesleyan Methodist who had recently given £6,000 for the construction of churches in his own district. During the foundation stone laying ceremony, Mr Lycett addressed the congregation with the following words:

"The laying of a foundation stone of a new chapel is unquestionably one of the most important works that can at any time engage the attention of a Christian Church. I am glad to find, by the prospectus your indefatigable minister has presented me with, that you propose in this scheme to reduce the debt upon the Yarmouth Chapel by £500. You also propose the erection of this chapel which I am glad to find is to be upon a larger scale than was originally intended. Although my impression was, as we came out of the village, that we were nearly going outside the bounds to erect a chapel, finding that you have a large population in the rear, and will very soon be surrounded by an increasing population, I think you have done well and wisely in coming into a new neighbourhood. I am glad to find that by this movement you identify yourselves with other Christian Churches in making provision for the increase in population by providing them with sittings in chapels, vieing also with the Metropolis and other large towns in spreading Scriptural Holiness throughout the land by Methodist agency. Our motto is still the same as it ever was. We are the friends of all and the enemies of none. I am thankful to say that at no period of our history have there been such extraordinary exertions made, as are being made in the erection of new chapel, in the building of schools, in the increase of the ministry, so that in a few years, we shall I believe, become a very large and a very important body. And surely Methodism is as much needed now, as it was when Mr Wesley, more than a century ago, was going up and down the length and breadth of the land. When we behold the Sabbath desecration, the profligacy, the immortality, the spiritual destitution by which we are surrounded, Methodism, I say, is as much needed now as it ever was. We have

the same simple living truths preached in all our pulpits, and repentance toward God, and faith in our Lord Jesus Christ, and I believe that we have greater opportunities for the perpetuity and for the furtherance of the preaching of these Gospel truths than any other church. Then too, we have the same social advantages as were enjoyed in Mr Wesley's day. Our class meetings are the same, our lovefeasts are the same and we have the same hymns sung in every chapel in the land from John O'Groats to Lands End. Well, ladies and gentlemen, I trust when this sanctuary has been properly prayed for by the Chairman of the District, that no accident will happen to any of the workmen while erecting it, when the sanctuary is opened that the Great Head of the Church will smile upon the undertaking, that sinners may be converted to God, that many will be turned from darkness to light, from the power of sin and Satan to serving the living God. If such results as these crown your efforts, you will feel that you have not laboured in vain, or spent your strength for nought, and in that great decisive day, when God the nations shall survey, may it before the worlds appear, that crowds were born for glory here."

The Lowestoft Road church cost £500 to build and was designed to seat 300 people. The architect was Mr J Bottle and the church was built by Mr G Godbolt of Brockdish. The church was opened in the autumn of 1866 by Rev Luke Wiseman and Rev David Solomon.

The congregation of the new church grew rapidly and it soon became too large for the building. In 1896, additional land was purchased to the south of the existing building in readiness to build a new and larger church. On 18 March of that year the trustees met at Dene Side Methodist church and asked the Quarterly Meeting for consent to build a new church. The Quarterly Meeting agreed unanimously. Plans were soon drawn up and memorial stones laid on Whit-Monday, 30 May 1898. The church was designed by the Great Yarmouth borough architect, Mr W B Cockrill, and was built by Southtown builder Mr G Beckett at a cost of £2,300. The church opened on 21 May 1899 (Whit-Sunday) with a service taken by Rev John Gould. Rev Gould was the minister at Lowestoft Road when plans for the new church were started and he was also considered as being "practically the 'Bishop of the Wesleyan Methodists' of East Anglia." Of the £2,300 cost of the new church, £1,800 had been raised already. This included grants from the Connexion Fund and Extension Fund of £335 and £250 respectively, and cash donations of £707. By the time of the opening ceremony the building was not completely finished, with the tracery of the windows still needing to be filled with glass. Figure 3.7 shows two pictures of the original 1866 church and the new 1899 church on Lowestoft Road.

On the following day, an opening service was taken by Rev W T Barber who was the headmaster of the Leys School in Cambridge, and he preached a sermon on the "Vision of Isaiah". This was followed by a large tea meeting, held in the old church, with about 300 people in attendance. In the evening the Superintendent Minister, Rev Condor Nattrass, thanked members for the money raised so far, but re-iterated that £500 still had to be found. This prompted several people to make generous donations, including the Mayor of Great Yarmouth and a Mrs Quant.

The return of a Wesleyan Methodist society in Gorleston prompted the Great Yarmouth circuit to make a request for a second minister to be stationed in the town. In response to this call, the Stationing Committee sent a missionary who had just returned from being abroad for 20 years. However, he found Gorleston much too cold and left within a year!

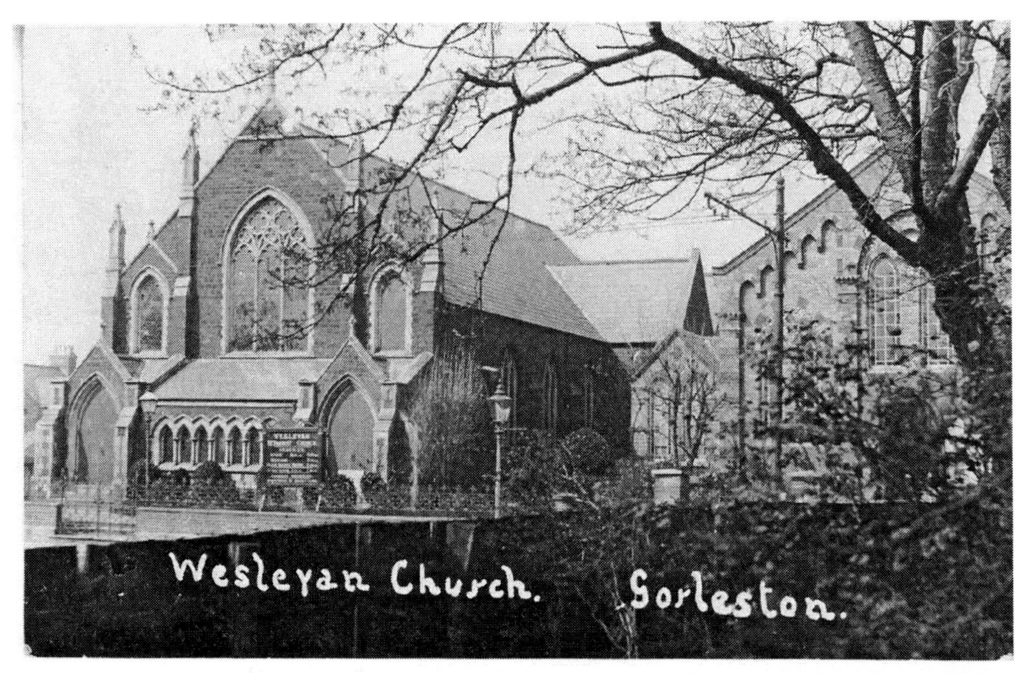

Figure 3.7: Lowestoft Road Wesleyan Methodist church. The upper picture shows the new church on the left, only a few years after its opening in 1899, and to its right the original church which subsequently became the schoolroom. The lower picture was taken from the same position in 2009 and shows very little to have changed. The wrought iron fence at the front of the church has been removed and the noticeboard has since gone.

Figure 3.8: Caister Methodist chapel in 2008. This was built in 1886 as the Caister Wesleyan Methodist chapel, following the merger of the East Caister and West Caister Wesleyan societies.

3.4 West Caister and East Caister

West Caister had a prosperous Wesleyan Methodist society in the first half of the nineteenth century – by 1844 the membership was a healthy 43. However, West Caister was another Wesleyan society that was very badly affected by the Wesleyan Reform movement. In the period 1851–1852 almost all of the society left to join the Reform movement, leaving only seven members. As a consequence, the Wesleyan Reform movement in Caister grew rapidly and by 1855 the society was renting a chapel on Caister High Street from a Mr Spendlove. By 1869 the Wesleyan Reform movement had dwindled, and by mutual agreement the Wesleyan Reformers and the Wesleyan Methodists joined. The society held services in the rented chapel on the High Street and became known as the East Caister Wesleyan Methodist society. This left Caister with two Wesleyan Methodist societies, East Caister and West Caister. This was in addition to the Primitive Methodists who also had a chapel on the High Street. Following Mr Spendlove's death in 1876, rent for the chapel was doubled from £5 to £10. This was considered too expensive by the East Caister Methodists and they stopped renting the chapel. Instead, the Wesleyan Methodists from the East Caister and West Caister societies decided to merge and build a new chapel on Beach Road in Caister. The Beach Road chapel was completed in 1886 and a schoolroom added soon after in 1888 at a cost of £700 for both buildings. By 1893 the merged Wesleyan Methodists at Beach Road had a membership of 55. Figure 3.8 shows a picture of the chapel in 2008.

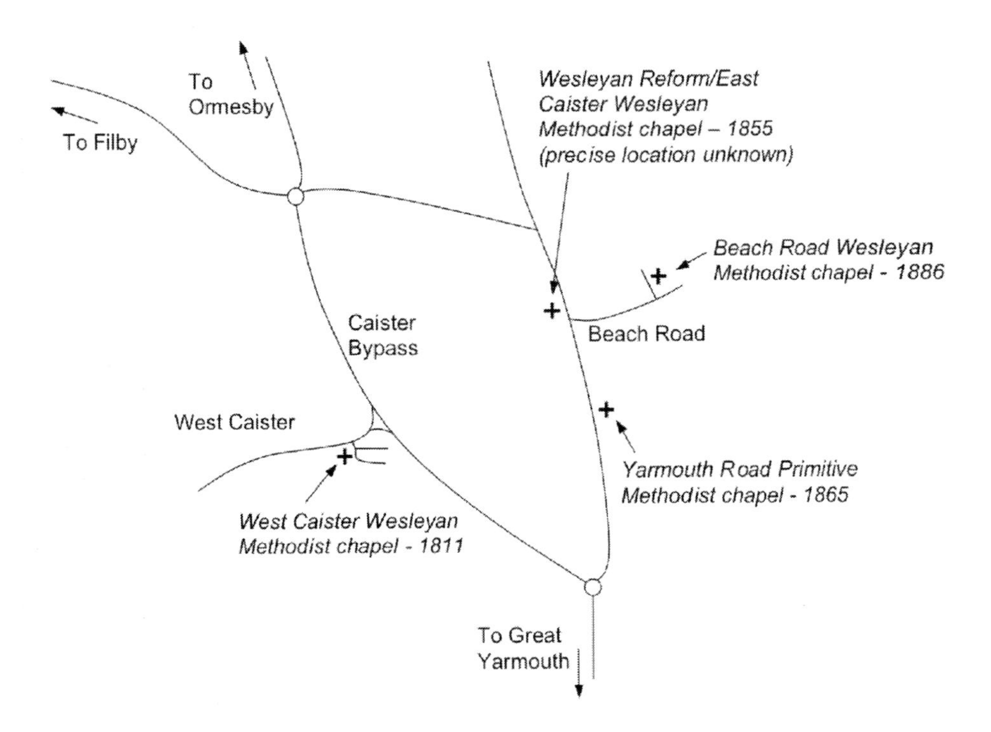

Figure 3.9: Map of the Methodist chapels in Caister – showing West Caister Wesleyan, Wesleyan Reform/East Caister Wesleyan, Beach Road Wesleyan and Yarmouth Road Primitive Methodist.

During this time the West Caister chapel was in need of repair and in 1876 it was thoroughly repaired and re-seated at a cost of £69, making it "a very comfortable place of worship." It was at this time that the Wesley pulpit was removed and put into storage – see figure 2.4 on page 13. The West Caister chapel finally closed in 1914 and was sold in 1924 for £10. No trace remains of the chapel, although the road in West Caister where the chapel was situated takes the name "Chapel Corner."

To illustrate the locations of the four Methodist chapels that Caister had, figure 3.9 shows a map of the village with the chapels shown, together with opening dates.

3.5 Ludham

In the early days of Methodism in Ludham, worshippers met in a stable that belonged to the local public house. By the early 1820s a Wesleyan chapel had been built in the village and the society prospered to such an extent that by 1841 it had a membership of 45. After this date, records show that membership fell – down to 35 members in 1844 and to just 14 members by 1853. This most recent fall in numbers was most likely a result of members joining the Wesleyan Reform movement.

Membership began to rise again after the demise of the Wesleyan Reform movement and had increased to 17 in 1857 and 24 by 1862. Membership continued to grow rapidly and by 1866 the original chapel had become too small for the society and a decision was made to build a new chapel. In the same year Mr Aaron Neave, who was a local farmer, gave the society a plot of land on which they could build the new chapel and schoolroom. A stone laying ceremony for the new chapel took place at 2pm on Good Friday in 1866. The ceremony began at the old chapel, where a hymn was sung, and then moved to the site of the new chapel. Between five and six hundred people came to the ceremony, which was led by the Rev George Barnley who was the Superintendent Minister of the Great Yarmouth Wesleyan Methodist Circuit. Rev Barnley read from the Old Testament, 1 Chronicles, Chapter 29, verses 1 to 15, and from the New Testament, Ephesians, Chapter 2. This was followed by another hymn "Thou who has in Zion laid, the true foundation stone" and then the foundation stone was laid by William Twitchell, Esq. of Willington near Bedford. Four corner stones were laid by Misses Neave, Skinner, Hacon and Huke, who were young ladies from the society. Finally the National Anthem was sung and the group moved on to Mr Neave's farm for a tea that had been prepared by the ladies of the society. During the day £50 was raised for the new chapel which had been estimated to cost £350 to build.

The chapel was built by Mr Chaplin, who was a local builder from Ludham, and opened on 17 April 1867 in a service conducted by the Rev George Barnley. Figure 3.10 shows two pictures of the chapel – in about 1900 and the other in 2008. The cost of the chapel far exceeded its original estimate and eventually cost £565 to build. The old chapel was sold to Mr Chaplin, the builder, but with a clause preventing him, or any of his heirs and successors, from erecting a public house or beer shop on the land.

3.6 Fleggburgh

According to the Great Yarmouth Wesleyan Methodist Circuit plan of 1812 (see table 2.2 on page 19), a society at Fleggburgh had not yet been established at that time. Precise details on when the first Wesleyan society began at Fleggburgh do not appear to be recorded, although a best guess would be in the 1820s or early 1830s. Records do, however, indicate that a Wesleyan Methodist, by the name of James Penman, was granted a certificate to use a house owned by Robert Durrant for worship. This seems to be the earliest record of Wesleyan Methodist worship in Fleggburgh. This young society grew and by 1841 had built its own chapel in the village. The chapel still stands, as shown in figure 3.11, although it is now privately owned having been sold in the late 2000s. By the end of the nineteenth century membership of the Fleggburgh society reached 26, which was slightly more than neighbouring societies in Stokesby, Ormesby and Ludham. By the start of the First World War membership dropped to 11 and remained around this number until Methodist Unification in 1932.

3.7 Wickhampton

When the Wesleyan chapel at Wickhampton opened in 1814 it was part of the Norwich Wesleyan Methodist Circuit. However, in 1831 the Norwich and Great Yarmouth Wesleyan circuits decided that the chapel would be more easily worked by being transferred to the Great Yarmouth Wesleyan Methodist Circuit – the circuit already had chapels close to Wickhampton. The Wickhampton society was in a very healthy state with 63 members

Figure 3.10: The upper picture shows the Wesleyan chapel at Ludham in around 1900. The lower picture shows the same scene in 2008 with the chapel still in use and holding regular Sunday morning services. (The upper picture has been included by kind permission of the Ludham Archive).

Figure 3.11: Former Wesleyan chapel in Fleggburgh in 2008. The chapel was opened in 1841 and remained in use until the mid 2000s, when the congregation moved into Fleggburgh village hall. The building was subsequently sold.

recorded in 1837, and many of these coming from the surrounding villages. This was about the peak of the Wickhampton society, and in the following years membership fell. In 1849 membership was 52 and by 1855 had reduced to just 20 members. The Wickhampton society lost members on two counts – to the Wesleyan Reform movement and due to the influx of Primitive Methodism in the area. Wickhampton was deep inside a concentrated area of Primitive Methodist societies that included Acle, Freethorpe, Halvergate, Limpenhoe and Beighton. These were all only a few miles away and generally appealed to the more rural communities, such as Wickhampton. Membership of the society did pick up again in later years and had risen to 36 in 1860, presumably as the Wesleyan Reform movement declined and people returned to the Wesleyan society.

A serious problem for the Wickhampton chapel began in 1878 with the death of its last surviving trustee, a Mr Bately. Since the formation of the chapel in 1814, a £200 debt on the chapel had not been reduced and had actually accrued £50 of interest. Upon Mr Bately's death, the executors of his will requested that this debt be repaid to them. This led to over a year of legal wrangling and numerous letters to and fro between the executor's solicitor and Rev John Jones, who was the Superintendent Minister of the Great Yarmouth Wesleyan Methodist Circuit. Rev Jones stated that it was not in his power to resolve the matter, while the executors were adamant that they should receive payment of the debt. Eventually the executors proposed that the matter could be resolved if the Methodists paid £150 by 1 January 1880. A new group of trustees was put in place for the Wickhampton society and they were advised by the Methodist General Chapel

Committee to borrow the £150 required to pay Mr Bately's executors.

The wranglings over the previous few years had left the chapel in a poor state of repair and in need of thorough renovation. In 1884, Rev Daniel Pearson, who was the new Superintendent Minister of the Great Yarmouth Wesleyan Methodist Circuit, decided to renovate the chapel and remove its gallery. This was completed at a cost of £117, and further repairs were also carried out in 1895. The society was in decline at this time, having a membership of 20 members and reaching a low point in 1913 with just 9 members. The society did grow again, and by 1932 had a membership of 20.

3.8 Stokesby, Acle and Ormesby

The three villages of Stokesby, Acle and Ormesby all had both Wesleyan and Primitive Methodist societies. In Stokesby, the Wesleyan society was the more successful, while in Acle the opposite was true. In Ormesby, both societies existed together with healthy membership numbers.

The first Wesleyan chapel at Stokesby was built in 1811 and this society prospered – only one year later a membership of 33 was recorded. The Primitive Methodists arrived in Stokesby some years later, but after an encouraging start their membership went into terminal decline. Primitive membership was 25 in 1883, but had fallen to just seven by 1922, even though a new Primitive Methodist chapel had been built in the village in 1907. In contrast, Wesleyan membership in Stokesby was 20 in 1892 and had increased to 25 by 1932.

In the early 1920s, the Wesleyan chapel was in poor condition and in need of major repair work, which was expected to cost in the region of £325. Repairing the chapel was one option for the Wesleyan Methodists, but a second option arose in the form of the Primitive Methodist chapel in Stokesby. This had been built in 1907 and was in a practically new condition. The chapel was not used very often and had been closed for worship since the middle of 1925. Following discussions between the Wesleyan and Primitive Methodist societies in Stokesby an agreement was made to sell the Primitive chapel to the Wesleyans. The Wesleyan Methodists paid £250 for the chapel and for the repair work, which was considerably less than was needed to repair their own chapel. The new Wesleyan chapel in Stokesby was opened in 1926 by Mrs H Needham and a sermon was preached by Rev WH Heap who was Chairman of the East Anglia District. This was followed by a public tea. Figure 3.12 shows the chapel in 2007, having been converted to a house since its closure in 2002.

In Ormesby, the division of power between the village's Wesleyan and Primitive Methodist societies seems to have been more balanced. Wesleyan Methodism was established in the village first, with a chapel opened in 1822. The Primitive Methodists didn't arrive until 1836 with a chapel not opened until later still. Both societies prospered, with 17 members at the Wesleyan chapel and 31 at the Primitive chapel in 1932. Figure 3.13 shows a picture of the Wesleyan chapel in about 1910. Below it is a picture taken in 2008, with the building now being a Baptist church.

Acle was in a similar position to Stokesby and Ormesby, having both Wesleyan and Primitive societies. However, the Wesleyan society at Acle seems to have struggled in comparison to its Primitive neighbour. The two chapels were literally around the corner from one another. The Primitive chapel was on Reedham Road and the Wesleyan chapel

Figure 3.12: The former Wesleyan chapel at Stokesby, which was bought from the Primitive Methodists in 1926, having been built in 1907. The chapel was closed in 2002 and is now a private house.

on Middlesex Street – a distance of about 100 metres. Figure 3.14 shows the Wesleyan chapel which was tucked away down a narrow lane.

The Acle Primitive society seemed to go from strength to strength, with 21 members in 1883, growing to 45 members by 1932. In comparison, the Wesleyan society struggled to grow, having just six members in 1892 and nine in 1932. Presumably it was the strength of the Primitive society, combined with their better position in Acle, that led to the Wesleyan society's closure in the late 1930s.

Figure 3.13: The upper picture shows the Wesleyan chapel at Ormesby in around 1910. The lower picture shows the same scene in 2008. Following its closure in about 1979, the chapel is now a Baptist church. The building looks very similar, except for the addition of a more modern porch at the front.

Figure 3.14: The former Wesleyan chapel at Acle which closed just before the Second World War. It is now used for storage.

Chapter 4

Primitive Methodism in Great Yarmouth – 1833 to 1932

4.1 Introduction

This chapter describes the history of Primitive Methodism in Great Yarmouth in the one hundred year period from 1833 to 1932. The end of chapter 2 described how Great Yarmouth became a branch of the Norwich Primitive Methodist Circuit in 1823 and two years later became a Primitive Methodist circuit in its own right. By 1832 the Great Yarmouth Primitive Methodist Circuit had built the First Tabernacle on Priory Plain and had also established several smaller societies in the surrounding towns and villages. At this time very few of these societies had purpose-built chapels and instead worshipped in a room of a member's house or in a rented building. Many societies even had no undercover worship area and instead met on a village green or in a field. Life was difficult for the early Primitive Methodists, especially as many villagers disapproved strongly of these societies and often went to considerable lengths to disrupt services.

As time went on these societies became more accepted and new societies were established in other areas, widening the area of the Great Yarmouth Primitive Methodist Circuit. In less than 30 years, to 1852, the Great Yarmouth Primitive Methodist Circuit had grown from having just a few small preaching places to having 41 societies. These 41 societies are listed in the first column of table 4.1. As the table shows, the circuit covered a large area across east Norfolk and north Suffolk, stretching from Lowestoft in the south to Catfield in the north and west as far as Mundham. Given that the main methods of transport available to people at this time were either horseback or walking, having such a large circuit put considerable strain on the preachers. In March of 1870 a request was made by the Lowestoft branch of the circuit "That we earnestly request to be made a circuit with one married and one single preacher, and request our Yarmouth friends to help us." This request was accepted and by May of 1870 the societies in the south of the circuit were split off to form the Lowestoft Primitive Methodist Circuit. This itself was divided in 1911 to create the Loddon Primitive Methodist Circuit. The second column in table 4.1 shows the 34 societies remaining in the Great Yarmouth Primitive Methodist Circuit in 1870.

Table 4.1: Societies in the Great Yarmouth Primitive Methodist Preaching Plan for 1852, 1871, 1875 and 1886.

1852	1871	1875	1886
Yarmouth	Yarmouth	Yarmouth	Temple
Gorleston	Gorleston	Gorleston	Gorleston
Caister	Caister	Caister	Caister
Scratby	Scratby	Scratby	Scratby
Filby	Filby	Filby	Filby
Belton	Belton	Belton	Belton
Runham	Runham	Runham	Runham
Great Ormesby	Great Ormesby	Great Ormesby	Great Ormesby
Bradwell	Bradwell	Bradwell	Bradwell
Fleggburgh	Fleggburgh	Fleggburgh	Workhouse
Acle	Acle	Acle	Queen's Road
Stokesby	Stokesby	Stokesby	
Horning	Horning	Horning	
South Walsham	South Walsham	South Walsham	
Beighton	Beighton	Beighton	
Ludham	Ludham	Ludham	
Hemsby	Hemsby	Hemsby	
Martham	Martham	Martham	
Thurne	Thurne	Thurne	
Catfield	Catfield	Catfield	
Upton	Upton	Upton	
Rollesby	Rollesby	Rollesby	
Reedham	Reedham	Reedham	
Limpenhoe	Limpenhoe	Limpenhoe	
Winterton	Winterton	Winterton	
Freethorpe	Freethorpe	Freethorpe	
Halvergate	Halvergate	Halvergate	
Repps	Repps	Repps	
Hickling	Hickling	Hickling	
Horsey	Horsey	Horsey	
Berney Arms	Berney Arms	Berney Arms	
Heigham	Heigham	Heigham	
Lowestoft	Queen's Road	Queen's Road	
Haddiscoe	Rollesby No 2		
Mundham			
Toft			
Moulton			
Burgh St Peter			
Norton Street			
Corton			
Hales			

Table 4.2: State of the Great Yarmouth I, Great Yarmouth II, Acle, Loddon, Lowestoft and Martham Primitive Methodist circuits in 1924.

	GY I	GY II	Acle	Loddon	Lowestoft	Martham
Number of chapels	9	4	9	8	8	13
Cost of chapels	£13,190	£3,412	£4,748	£4,303	£6,989	£6,035
Present debt	£1,880	£90	£70	£367	£1,370	£221
Church members	440	140	290	150	314	390
Class leaders	30	6	11	15	20	20
Local preachers	32	5	44	17	32	68
Sunday school scholars	941	225	575	330	663	480
Sunday school teachers	70	28	96	45	63	65

In 1883 two more circuits were created out of the Great Yarmouth Primitive Methodist Circuit when the Martham Primitive Methodist Circuit and the Acle Primitive Methodist Circuit were established. At a meeting of the Great Yarmouth Primitive Methodist Circuit on 5 March 1883, a Mr Waters from Panxworth proposed that Acle become a branch of the Great Yarmouth circuit. This proposal was amended by a Mr Bell of Great Yarmouth that Acle be made into a circuit in its own right. This amendment was agreed. Seeing that Acle was now to become a circuit, a Mr Whittleton from Hickling moved that Martham also become a circuit. This was also agreed at the meeting. The new Acle Primitive Methodist Circuit was made up of 12 societies: Acle, Upton, Reedham, Limpenhoe, Freethorpe, Halvergate, Beighton, Stokesby, South Walsham and Panxworth. The new Martham Primitive Methodist Circuit was made up of 13 societies: Martham, Hemsby, Thurne, Catfield, Rollesby, Winterton, Repps, Hickling, Horsey, Somerton, (Potter) Heigham, Fleggburgh and Horning. The history of the societies making up the Acle and the Martham Primitive Methodist circuits, in the period from 1833 to 1932, is the subject of chapters 6 and 7.

This chapter is concerned with the history of the societies that remained in the Great Yarmouth Primitive Methodist Circuit after 1883, which are listed in the final column of table 4.1. The table shows 11 societies in 1886, although the circuit continued to grow after this period, establishing societies at Cobholm, Nile Road in Gorleston and Browston. The growth was to such an extent that a Great Yarmouth Number II Circuit was formed in 1909. At its peak, this had four societies: Queen's Road, Belton, Bradwell and Browston. This left nine societies in the Great Yarmouth Number I Circuit: The Temple, Scratby, Caister, Beccles Road, Runham, Great Ormesby, Filby, Nile Road and Cobholm.

The division of the Great Yarmouth Primitive Methodist Circuit to form these other circuits is shown in figure 4.1. The state of these circuits in 1924 is illustrated in table 4.2, which lists the number of chapels, their cost to build, their debt, the number of members and several other figures. These figures show the circuits to be in a healthy state with good levels of membership and relatively small debts in comparison to the cost of their chapels.

The remainder of this chapter describes the history of the societies in the Great Yarmouth area. Much of the material for this chapter has been found in *From Hayloft to Temple*, written by Arthur Patterson in 1903.

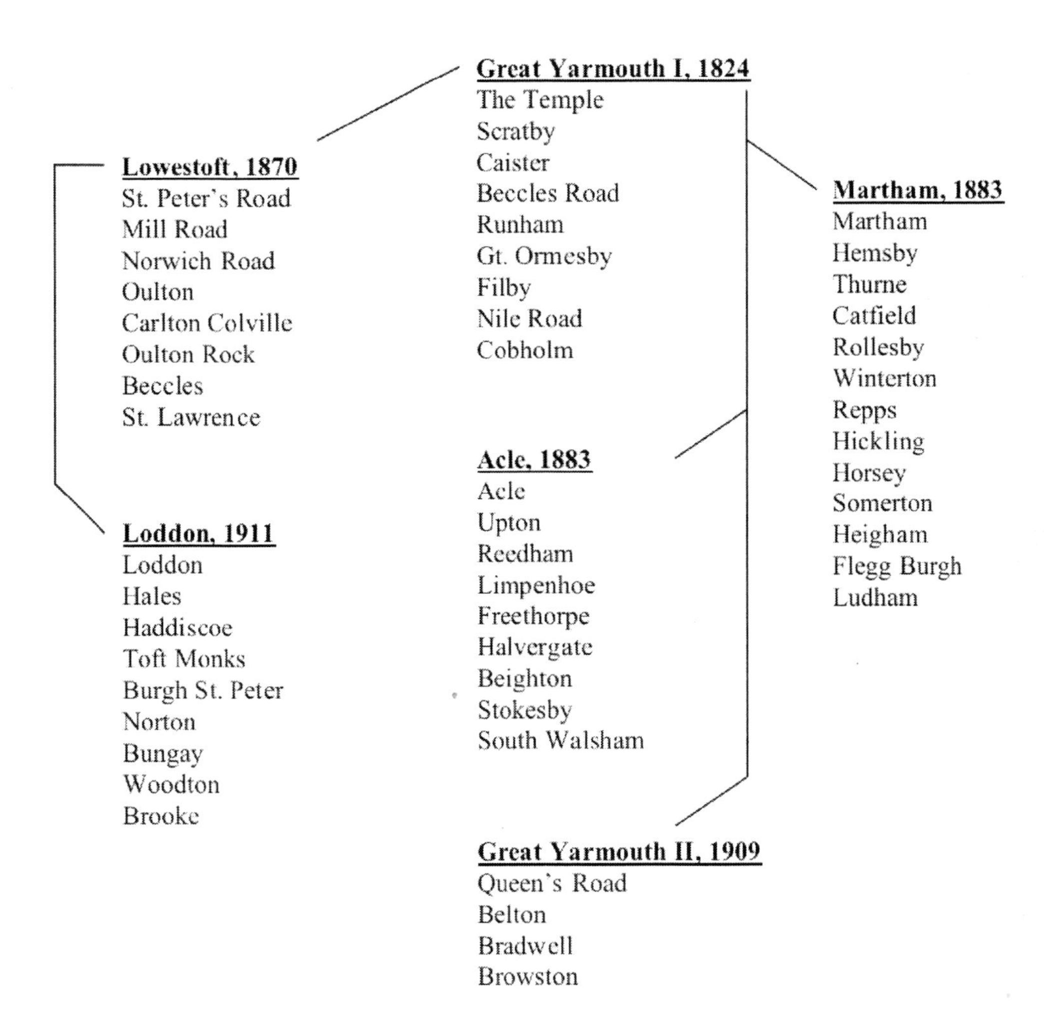

Figure 4.1: The Great Yarmouth Primitive Methodist Circuit and its subsequent division to form circuits based in Lowestoft (1870), Loddon (1911), Acle (1883) and Martham (1883).

Figure 4.2: Primitive Methodist centenary celebration on Sunday 21 July 1907. The group is walking north along Northgate Street in Great Yarmouth, having just passed Frederick Road. The shops in the picture are still shops and on the road can be seen double tram lines.

4.2 Primitive Methodism in Great Yarmouth

In Great Yarmouth, Primitive Methodism had begun in the Hayloft on Priory Plain in the 1820s and soon after was replaced by the First Tabernacle in 1829. From then onwards, Primitive Methodism in Great Yarmouth began to grow rapidly. This led to the First Tabernacle being replaced by the Second Tabernacle in 1850. This was then replaced in 1876 by the much larger Temple. As growth took place, having just a single Primitive Methodist society in the town was not enough. In 1867 a second Primitive Methodist church was opened in the south of Great Yarmouth on Queen's Road. The Cobholm area of Great Yarmouth also began to develop a Primitive Methodist mission which began in a tin chapel in 1905 before being replaced by a brick chapel in 1924. Celebrations were an important part of Primitive Methodism and outings and gatherings were commonplace. Figure 4.2 shows one such event, which shows a Primitive Methodist centenary celebration in 1907 with the group walking along Northgate Street in Great Yarmouth.

Figure 4.3: The Primitive Methodist Second Tabernacle which was located on Priory Plain in Great Yarmouth and built in 1850. To the left of the building is the schoolroom which was added in 1855.

4.2.1 The Second Tabernacle

The First Tabernacle provided an adequate centre for Great Yarmouth's Primitive Methodists for about 20 years until the growing number of members began to cause overcrowding in the building. On 3 July 1849, the trustees, led by Rev T Swindell, decided to embark on a plan to enlarge the Tabernacle as soon as funds could be obtained. Only a year later, in 1850, a second tabernacle was built at a cost of £750. This was considerably larger than the First Tabernacle and measured 57 feet by 52 feet by 25 feet high. At this time the trustees had already raised £433 leaving £317 to be found.

Further expansion of these premises took place in 1855 when a schoolroom was built to the north of the Second Tabernacle at a cost of £460. The photograph in figure 4.3 shows the Second Tabernacle with the new schoolroom at its side.

The Second Tabernacle lasted only 25 years before a decision was made that it was now not large enough and should be replaced by an even larger building. The last meeting at the Second Tabernacle was on 5 April 1875, after which building work for the new church began. The church that replaced the Second Tabernacle was the Temple and this was opened in 1876. The story of the planning and opening of the Temple is described in detail in the next chapter – chapter 5.

4.2.2 Queen's Road

Towards the latter part of the nineteenth century, many members of the Temple lived in the southern part of Great Yarmouth. To cater for these members, open air services in the south of the town had been held for some time. As early as July of 1851 there had been speculation that a new chapel was to be erected in the south of the town to serve these Primitive Methodists. Several years later, in 1866, the Great Yarmouth Primitive Methodist Circuit finally decided to erect a church in the south of Great Yarmouth and a vacant piece of sandy ground was purchased. This cost £150 and was on Queen's Road, opposite the entrance to the Naval Hospital. Several of the local residents were against the building of a new chapel and opposition was raised by a neighbouring house owner. This difficulty was overcome by one of the main supporters of the new church, a Mr George Baker JP, who bought the intervening land between the house and chapel site. On this land Mr Baker built a house which he then moved into. Mr Baker was a generous supporter of the new chapel and made a gift of an organ costing £130.

The foundation stone laying service for the new chapel took place on Thursday 16 May 1867 with the stone being laid by Mr WR Riches of Catfield. Underneath the foundation stone was placed a bottle that contained various items including copies of the *Norfolk News* and *Yarmouth Independent* newspapers, circuit plans, and coins. The stone laying service was led by Rev Seaman and Rev Gunns and people attended from all over the circuit and town. A tea followed the service, and together with other sources of income, £175 was raised. The opening service for the new chapel took place on 26 September 1867 and was taken by Rev Gunns with £12 being raised in the collection.

The cost of building the chapel was £1,680. Early reports state that the seating capacity was for 750 people, although this was later reduced to 600 people. Figure 4.4 shows the Queen's Road Primitive Methodist chapel as it was in about 1900, and also a view taken in 2009 from the same position. The chapel was badly damaged by enemy bombing in the Second World War, which resulted in its demolition in 1954. Two houses now stand on the site, as shown in the lower picture. The closure of the Queen's Road chapel is discussed in more detail in chapter 11.

4.2.3 Cobholm

The Primitive Methodist chapel in Cobholm, also known as the Cobholm Mission, was the last Primitive Methodist chapel to be built in East Norfolk before Methodist unification in 1932. Plans for a Primitive Methodist mission in Cobholm began in 1905, when a temporary tin chapel was rented from the Congregational Church for £12 per year. In 1912 the tin chapel was purchased from the Congregationalists for £50 – the top picture in figure 4.5 shows the old tin Mission Hall. Additional land was also bought at a cost of £320. The Primitive Methodists had planned to construct a new chapel on the site almost immediately, but the start of the First World War in 1914 delayed progress by many years. It wasn't until May 1923 that Mr Swindell and the Superintendent Minister were able to approach architects Olley and Haward for plans for the new chapel. The last service in the old tin chapel was held on 27 July 1923 and the building was subsequently sold for £27.

On 17 September 1923 a stone laying ceremony took place where 14 foundation stones were laid, with a large congregation in attendance. This was followed by tea and a public meeting at the Temple. The day raised a total of £290 for the building fund.

The new Primitive Methodist mission chapel in Cobholm was opened on 10 January 1924 with Mrs F J W Salmon unlocking the door and Rev C H Spivey preaching a dedicatory sermon. Another tea and meeting were held, with Alderman W G Knights presiding, which raised £110 for the building fund. By May 1924 Cobholm had raised

Figure 4.4: Queen's Road Primitive Methodist chapel. The upper picture was taken in about 1900 and the lower picture in 2009. The chapel was badly damaged by enemy bombing during the Second World War and demolished in 1954 to be replaced by two houses.

over £700 towards the £1,400 cost of the chapel. The middle picture in figure 4.5 shows a photograph of the newly built chapel in 1923, just before its opening. This can be compared to a present-day view of the building, which is shown in the bottom picture of figure 4.5, and shows that structurally very little has changed.

As with most Methodist societies, fundraising was an important activity for the Cobholm society and much activity continued in an effort to clear the debt of £700 left after building the chapel. In 1926, two years after the chapel had opened, the debt had been reduced by £142 to £562. More fundraising was needed to reduce the debt and the society also wanted to raise money to build a school hall. At this time the chapel had a Sunday school of 120 children and 16 teachers.

One such fundraising activity was an annual bazaar that was held over two days. In 1926 the bazaar was held on the 5 and 6 of May, and was opened on the first day by the Mayor of Great Yarmouth, Mr AW Yallop JP, and on the second by councillor Mrs F Base. There were ten stalls: two Women's Meeting stalls; Christian Endeavour stall; Sunday school stall, refreshment stall; flower, fruit and vegetable stall; sweet stall; dip and fancy stall; pound stall; and a weighing machine. Other attractions were a fish pond and admission was free!

4.3 Primitive Methodism in Gorleston

Primitive Methodism in Gorleston was established in 1833 in an old chapel on Burnt Lane in north Gorleston. Accounts of the building portray it as a dim and uninspiring place to hold worship. In 1868 the Primitive Methodists of Gorleston purchased land close by on Beccles Road and built a new chapel which was a much better and more attractive building. Thirty years later the population of south Gorleston had increased substantially and a second Primitive Methodist society was formed. This began in a tin chapel on Nile Road, just east of Lowestoft Road. By 1920 the society had grown significantly and occupied a new brick-built chapel.

4.3.1 Beccles Road

The Primitive Methodist "sandpit" chapel on Burnt Lane in Gorleston was used by the Gorleston Primitive Methodists until 1868. By this time the Gorleston Primitive Methodists had decided that they should have a better place to worship in, mainly due to the long flight of stairs that had to be climbed to reach the gallery. The society purchased a piece of land on the corner of Beccles Road and Manby Road and built a much smarter chapel with a small schoolroom. These were built by a Mr Riches at a cost of £386 in 1868 using bricks from the nearby Somerleyton brickworks. The bricks were transported free of charge by Mr William Gosling and Mr Joseph Wright. At the time of opening, £143 had been raised and over the course of the next 30 years the remaining £243 of debt on the chapel was paid off.

In 1898 three cottages were bought in Manby Road alongside the chapel. Two of these were demolished in 1900 to be replaced by a new schoolroom, vestry and extension to the chapel. This work was carried out at a cost of £919 and represented a considerable sum of money to the society. A stone laying ceremony took place on 1 January 1901 with a public tea and meeting afterwards which raised £101. The new schoolroom was opened on 19 May 1901, and during the building work the chapel was lengthened by 14 feet. At

Figure 4.5: The upper picture shows the first Cobholm Mission which was a tin chapel. The middle picture shows the Primitive Methodist Cobholm Mission in 1923, just prior to its opening. The lower picture is a view of the building in 2008 where it is now called The Tabernacle, having ceased to be a Methodist church in 1990.

this time the Beccles Road society had a membership of 57. Electric lighting was installed in 1902. During the First World War, on 25 April 1916, part of a German shell pierced the roof of the chapel, but fortunately no serious damage was done. Figure 4.6 shows the chapel as it was in about 1923 and also as it was in 2008, following conversion into flats after its closure in 1996.

4.3.2 Nile Road

In the southern part of Gorleston much new housing was being built during the end of the nineteenth century. This was some considerable distance from the Beccles Road Primitive Methodist chapel and this prompted Mr George Taylor (a man described as having "sturdy, honest, Christian principles") to begin a Primitive Methodist society in south Gorleston on Nile Road in 1894. This society first met in a corrugated iron building which was established at a cost of £221. In 1913, the Nile Road society was given the organ that had been used in the Temple for the past 32 years, as this had just been replaced with a new organ.

The society in this "tin" chapel prospered and soon put plans in place to replace the structure with a permanent brick-built chapel. The upper photograph in figure 4.7 shows the tin chapel in the background, while in the foreground is a sign that proudly proclaims that the site is soon to become the location of a new Primitive Methodist chapel. This dates the picture to be in the 1910s as the new brick and stone chapel was opened in 1920. The middle photograph in figure 4.7 shows the newly built chapel in about 1923, which had cost £1,459 to build. Below this picture is a photograph of the chapel in 2008, where the building is now the headquarters of the Endeavour Rangers Marching Band.

4.4 Primitive Methodism in villages south of Great Yarmouth

This section looks at the chapels in the Great Yarmouth Primitive Methodist Circuit that were in the villages south of the town. In early circuit preaching plans, the Great Yarmouth Primitive Methodist Circuit extended as far south as Lowestoft in Suffolk, but this falls outside of the East Norfolk area that this book focuses on. Therefore, the villages south of Great Yarmouth are restricted to those shown on Great Yarmouth Primitive Methodist Circuit plans after 1883 when the Lowestoft Circuit had been split off. This leaves the societies in the villages of Belton, Bradwell and Browston for discussion.

4.4.1 Belton

Belton was first put on the Primitive Methodist plan in 1832, although the first purpose built Primitive Methodist chapel was not built until 1859. Prior to this, services were held in the cottages of society members, one of which was a room in a labourer's cottage which is reported to have had a large mangle in it that took up nearly half the space! The chapel that was built in 1859 cost £105, but was reported to be "a poor, barn-like structure, brick floored and ugly."

Thirty years later a second chapel was built to replace the existing chapel and this opened in July 1889 (although some accounts claim the opening was later, in 1896) at a

Figure 4.6: Beccles Road Primitive Methodist chapel. The upper picture shows the chapel in 1923. Below is the building in 2008, looking almost unchanged even though it has been converted into four flats since its closure in 1996.

Figure 4.7: Nile Road Methodist chapel. The upper picture shows the tin hut and a sign advertising this as the site for a new Primitive Methodist chapel. The middle photograph shows the new chapel in about 1923. The lower photograph shows the chapel in 2008, having lost its top section. The chapel was closed because of damage suffered in the Second World War and never reopened.

cost of £500. This was described as a much more handsome building than the previous chapel and was located at the south-west corner of Station Road in Belton, just north of where the railway line crossed the road. The Primitive Methodists worked hard in Belton and the society thrived and it was said that "the village is the warmest hot-bed of Primitive Methodism for miles around." A photograph of Belton Primitive Methodist chapel in 1903 is shown in figure 4.8.

Figure 4.8: Belton Primitive Methodist chapel in about 1903. The chapel was used until about 1970 when it was sold. The building was demolished and bungalows now occupy the site, one of which is named "Chapelfield."

4.4.2 Bradwell

Bradwell was one of the last societies to appear on the Great Yarmouth Primitive Methodist Circuit plan and didn't appear until 1852. The society had begun by holding open-air services in nearby fields around the village and these were led by preachers who travelled from Great Yarmouth. Prayer meetings were established soon after, and these were held in a cottage in Sun Lane. Later, services took place in a building behind the White House on Church Lane in Bradwell. This building had two windows on the left-hand side of the pulpit and some preachers observed that "you might easily lose the thread of your discourse by seeing a stray face peering in at you through the little window!"

A strong Primitive Methodist society soon developed in Bradwell and by the late 1880s plans were formulated to build a chapel in a small field on Church Lane. A foundation stone was laid in 1891 by Mr James Amis whose family were committed Methodists in the village. The chapel opened later in that year at a cost of £400 for the land and building, although £200 had already been raised. A lengthy series of opening services was held and these raised a further £48. The final opening service was held on Thursday 5 November 1891 and was taken by Rev J Smith of Luton, who preached a sermon from Acts, chapter 5, verse 20 "Go, stand in the Temple and tell the people the whole message about this life." A tea took place after the service in a large marquee that had been erected behind the chapel. After the tea a lecture was given by Mr Smith on his recent trip to America. Thanks were given to the speaker and also to Miss Burton for her gift of a harmonium and for undertaking to play it, and to Miss Amis of London for her gift of a bible and hymnal. About ten years later, the building was extended by the addition of a kitchen and toilets. Figure 4.9 shows two pictures of the chapel – the upper picture taken in about 1923 and the lower picture taken in 2009.

4.4.3 Browston

In 1924 the Great Yarmouth Primitive Methodist Circuit opened a new mission chapel at Browston in what was the former Mission Room on Browston Lane. This Mission Room was a corrugated iron building that had been built in 1899 and had been given to the village by Captain Prickett, who lived at nearby Browston Hall. Legal documents record the sale of the Mission Room to the Great Yarmouth Primitive Methodist Circuit as being on 26 September 1923 for the sum of £70. By this time Captain Prickett had died and the Mission Room was sold by his wife, Mrs Caroline Maria Prickett, who had since sold Browston Hall and was living in Weymouth. A Primitive Methodist Church Centenary Celebration souvenir programme of 1924 states that the mission was operated "under most difficult conditions" and that the minister, Rev J Maland, and the officials be commended for their loyalty and devotion.

The Browston society was not particularly successful and struggled to attract members. The chapel remained open for only a few years and was eventually sold in 1939 for £30. The Mission Room still stands today, although it has been unused for many years and is in a poor state of repair, as shown by the photograph in figure 4.10 which was taken in 2009. In recent years the building has come under several threats of being demolished and replaced by housing.

4.5 Primitive Methodism in villages north of Great Yarmouth

This section looks at the formation of societies in the northern part of the Great Yarmouth Primitive Methodist Circuit. Primitive Methodism was particularly well received in many of the small villages to the north of Great Yarmouth and from 1836 to 1884 chapels were built in Runham, Filby, Scratby, Great Ormesby and Caister.

4.5.1 Runham

Primitive Methodism was missioned in Runham in 1833 with services being first held outside on the village green. Worship then moved to an old clay cottage that was in the village. As the society grew, a small chapel was eventually built in 1868 on the corner of what is now Church Lane and Chapel Road, at a cost of £82. The strength of the society

Figure 4.9: Bradwell Primitive Methodist chapel. The upper photograph shows the chapel in about 1923 while the lower picture was taken in 2009.

Figure 4.10: Former Browston Primitive Methodist chapel in 2009. The building was originally opened as a reading room for the residents of Browston in 1899. The building became a Methodist chapel in 1923 but was closed by 1939. As of 2009, the building is in a very poor state of repair and the land is overgrown.

fluctuated during the latter part of the nineteenth century but by the turn of the century it was in a healthy state. This enabled a new chapel to be built in 1902, next to the first chapel, at a cost of £350, with the former chapel becoming the schoolroom. Figure 4.11 shows two photographs of the buildings, one in 1903 and the other in 2007 (following its conversion to a house). In both pictures the much smaller first chapel can be seen on the left and the larger second chapel on the right. The opening service for the new chapel was held on 5 October 1902 and was followed by the Harvest Festival and annual tea. For several years the society was in debt, but at the Harvest Festival service in 1916 the last £15 needed to clear the society's debt was raised.

4.5.2 Filby

Primitive Methodism in Filby began in about 1834 and for some time services were held in a dilapidated old building on Thrigby Road. This was replaced by a new chapel in 1889 which was on Main Road, between the junction with Thrigby Road and Filby bridge, close to Filby Broad. A schoolroom was added later to the south end of the chapel in 1894. Arthur Patterson commented on the Filby chapel that "I should delight to wait, before chapel-time, leaning on the parapet of the low brick bridge watching the crested grebes at play, diving long devious ways between times below the surface of the rippling

Figure 4.11: Runham Primitive Methodist chapel. The upper picture shows the chapel in 1903. The smaller building on the left was the first chapel which was built in 1868. On the right is the larger second chapel that was built in 1902. The lower picture shows the buildings in 2007, having been converted into a private dwelling after the chapel closed in about 1986.

waters, seeking little roach for their sustenance; and sometimes to listen to the reed-bunting and the sedge-warbler trilling in the reed-clump, or to the startled 'quack' of a passing wild-fowl. Pretty Filby!" Figure 4.12 shows the chapel in 1903.

Figure 4.12: Filby Primitive Methodist chapel in 1903. The chapel was built in 1889 and survived for almost 100 years as a Methodist chapel, before being blown down by gales in 1987. No trace remains of the chapel and the site has been replaced by housing.

4.5.3 Scratby

Scratby joined the Great Yarmouth Primitive Methodist Circuit in the winter of 1834 and by 1858 a small chapel had been built on Scratby cliffs at a cost of £90. At the time of its construction the chapel was some distance from the cliff edge. However, the constant erosion of the cliffs by the North Sea quickly left the chapel dangerously close to the cliff edge – separated only by a pathway that ran behind the chapel. Arthur Patterson was a visitor to the chapel on several occasions and reported that "I trembled when my old friend Mayman emphatically accompanied his discourses by appropriate gestures. More than once I pictured him, and the gable-end, going down the cliff, with the sand-martins' nests, all together." The society recognised this danger and in 1894 built a new chapel about half a mile inland, along the coast road from Caister to Hemsby, at a cost of £427. This new chapel is shown in figure 4.13 and has changed very little in over 100 years.

Figure 4.13: Scratby Primitive Methodist chapel. The upper picture shows the chapel in 1903, while the lower picture shows the chapel in 2008. The building is still used as a Methodist chapel.

4.5.4 Great Ormesby

Primitive Methodism in Ormesby began on the village green in 1836. At this time the villagers were not welcoming to religion with one of the villagers quoted as saying "that there was not one person in the parish who professed religion – not even the parson!" However, through the perseverance and work of a few dedicated individuals, the meetings on the green expanded, and Primitive Methodism became accepted. The society was listed on Great Yarmouth Primitive Methodist Circuit plans as Great Ormesby, which distinguished it from the Wesleyan Methodist society which was referred to as Ormesby on the Great Yarmouth Wesleyan Circuit plans. As the society became more established a chapel was hired at a cost of £5 per year. In 1897 land was purchased for £200 and a new chapel was built in 1898 at a cost of £531. This was on North Road, next to what is now Dene Avenue and it is possible that the land purchased was the land that the Great Ormesby society had been renting previously. The new chapel is shown in figure 4.14 in about 1923. By 1913 the debts of the Ormesby society had been reduced to £180.

4.5.5 Caister

Caister was first missioned by the Primitive Methodists in 1833 and shortly afterwards the society began to meet in a chapel that was described as being "shed-like" in its appearance. The precise location of this chapel is unknown, but is reported to have been in a lane in Caister, somewhere close to Yarmouth Road. As the society grew, they decided to build a new chapel. It was built on Yarmouth Road in 1865, almost opposite Bultitudes Loke, at a cost of £373. Figure 4.15 shows the chapel in about 1923. For many years the society used a harmonium to accompany hymn singing, but in 1913 a re-arrangement of the inside allowed an organ to be installed. Caister was also a popular location for camp meetings where a day would be spent outside, with preaching, praying and hymn singing taking place.

Figure 4.14: Ormesby Primitive Methodist chapel. The upper picture shows the chapel in 1923. The lower picture was taken from the same position in 2009, and shows the building to have been converted to a private house after its closure.

Figure 4.15: Caister Primitive Methodist chapel. The upper picture shows the chapel in about 1923. The lower picture is taken from the same position and shows the site in 2008, where the chapel has now been replaced by detached house, after the chapel's closure in 1979.

Chapter 5

The Primitive Methodist Temple – 1876

5.1 Introduction

Chapters 2 and 4 have described how Primitive Methodism became established in Great Yarmouth during the early part of the nineteenth century. This began with outdoor preaching on the Great Yarmouth Denes in 1821 and moved to the rented Hayloft on Priory Plain in 1824. The Primitive Methodists were keen to progress Methodism in the area and soon converted the Hayloft into the first purpose-built Primitive Methodist Tabernacle in Great Yarmouth in 1829. As Primitive Methodism continued to expand, the First Tabernacle soon became too small for the growing congregation, so that in 1850 it was demolished and a larger Second Tabernacle built on the same site. During this time, congregations grew from the relatively small numbers at the first outdoor meetings in 1821 to a membership of 280 at the Hayloft. The First Tabernacle was said to have seating for 625 people and overcrowding there was cited as the reason that the Second Tabernacle was built.

By the time of the Second Tabernacle there were many Primitive Methodist societies throughout East Norfolk. Most of these had small village chapels, perhaps with seating for 50 or so people. The more urban areas tended to have larger churches, such as in Great Yarmouth and Gorleston. The Tabernacle was the largest of these and was generally regarded as the head church of the Great Yarmouth Primitive Methodist Circuit. Growth of the Primitive Methodist movement in Great Yarmouth continued after the Second Tabernacle had been built and because of this plans were drawn up in 1874 to build an even bigger church – the Temple. Of all the churches in all the various branches of Methodism in East Norfolk, the Temple is probably the most renowned, with a long history that stretched 87 years from its opening in 1876 to its closure in 1963. Even now a reminder of the Temple persists, as the main road running through the centre of Great Yarmouth is called "Temple Road." As a result of the Temple's impact on Methodism in East Norfolk, this entire chapter is dedicated to the story of the Temple.

5.2 Planning and building the Temple

Plans for a larger replacement of the Second Tabernacle on Priory Plain in Great Yarmouth were first discussed in 1874. In that year the Primitive Methodist Conference was held in Hull and two of the Great Yarmouth Primitive Methodists, Mr TW Swindell and Mr Robert Bell, attended. During their stay they visited several churches and were impressed with the proportions and exteriors of these buildings. They were particularly impressed with the church on Jarrett Street in Hull. This prompted them, on their return to Great Yarmouth, to propose to the Primitive Methodist trustees that they should build a new church, or as they put it "pull down the old barns and build greater." The trustees were at first apprehensive of this plan as there remained a debt of £150 on the Second Tabernacle. A second meeting was held at Queen's Road Primitive Methodist church where a new trust was formed with responsibility to either renovate the Second Tabernacle or demolish it and erect a new building. It was at this meeting that the name "Temple" was proposed. Initially the new building was going to be called a church. However, one of the elderly trustees, Mr George Bell, cynically remarked "You'd better call it a Temple straight away!" Mr Swindell agreed and the name stayed.

Planning work and fundraising progressed at a rapid pace and it was not long before the trustees were ready to knock down the existing Tabernacle and start building the Temple. The last public meeting held in the second Tabernacle was on 5 April 1875, after which building work commenced. On 22 June 1875 at 2:30pm a foundation stone laying ceremony for the new Temple took place. The stones were laid by Mr John Riches of Catfield, Mr F Salmon, Mr Joseph Neave and Mr AJN Chamberlain. A bottle was placed in Mr Neave's stone that contained various newspapers, Primitive Methodist conference minutes, a circuit plan and various other items. Less than a year later, on 19 April 1876, the keystone of the Temple was laid by Mr George Baker.

Figure 5.1 shows a view of the Temple and schoolroom, which highlights the decorative stonework, arches and columns that adorned the front of the Temple. Nikolaus Pevsner, in his book *The Buildings of England: North-East Norfolk and Norwich*, was not impressed with the Temple and unflatteringly described it as having "Very large facade with attached coupled giant pilaster and a steep all-over pediment. A gross design so near Church Plain." The sheer size of the Temple is also evident in the picture. Comparing the Temple to the two-storey terraced house next to it illustrates just how big the Temple was.

The upper picture in figure 5.2 shows another view of the Temple, taken in 1907, which further highlights the Temple's size. The picture was taken during a gathering of Primitive Methodists on Priory Plain during an anniversary celebration of Primitive Methodism. On the left-hand side of the Temple can clearly be seen the same schoolroom that had previously stood next to the Second Tabernacle – as shown in figure 4.3 on page 57. A row of terraced houses can be seen on the extreme right of the picture. These houses are just to the east of the Fishermen's Hospital on Temple Road and still stand today. To illustrate where the Temple stood, the bottom picture in figure 5.2 shows a modern day photograph taken from the same position. The same row of terraced houses can still be seen on the right-hand side which indicates that the Temple was close to where Temple Road bends right, just before the turn to St Nicholas Road.

Figure 5.1: The Primitive Methodist Temple and schoolroom in about 1910.

5.3 Opening of the Temple

The Temple was dedicated for public worship on Sunday 27 July 1876. Special Sunday services followed that were led by Rev Dr Stoughton. The Temple was much larger than the Second Tabernacle, measuring 72 feet 3 inches by 52 feet 2 inches, and could seat 1,140 people. The basement contained committee rooms and classrooms, storage facilities and heating equipment. On the ground floor were two vestibules and lobbies. At the back were two more vestries and more offices. The inside of the Temple was galleried and these were accessed from the front of the church. The inside was very grand and the height from floor to ceiling was 35 feet. Figure 5.3 shows the inside of the Temple in about 1900, with the galleries clearly visible. The picture also shows a grand rostrum for the preacher and an organ directly above, on the gallery. Figure 5.4 shows two more pictures of the inside of the Temple – the first taken from the top of the gallery and the second showing several ministers and circuit steward, Frank Elliott, standing at the rostrum. More details of the Temple's organ can be found in chapter 14.

The cost of building the Temple was £4,891 which was a considerable sum of money for the Great Yarmouth Primitive Methodists to raise in 1876. At the time of its opening, about £2,000 had been raised, which left the Temple close to £2,900 in debt. The Primitive Methodists worked hard to reduce their debt on the Temple. Twenty years later, in 1896, the debt had been reduced to £1,200.

The Temple survived as a place for Methodist worship in Great Yarmouth for 87

Figure 5.2: The Primitive Methodist Temple on Priory Plain in Great Yarmouth. The upper picture shows the Temple and schoolroom in 1907. The lower picture shows the same scene in 2008. The same row of houses on the extreme right are in both pictures.

Figure 5.3: The inside of the Temple in about 1900. The galleries, raised pulpit and polished pews gave a grand feel to the inside. The organ can just be seen at the top of the picture.

years. For the first 56 of these years it was the head of the Great Yarmouth Primitive Methodist Circuit and for the remaining 31 years it was head of the Great Yarmouth Methodist Circuit. The Temple finally closed in 1963 and was demolished nine years later to make way for the town centre relief road in Great Yarmouth. The story of the Temple is continued in several of the remaining chapters of this book, with chapter 12 dedicated to describing the closure of the Temple.

Figure 5.4: Two views of the inside of the Temple. The upper picture was taken from the top of the west gallery, looking down on to the church. The lower picture shows a close-up of the rostrum inside the Temple, with several ministers and circuit steward, Frank Elliott, present.

Chapter 6

Primitive Methodism around Martham – 1833 to 1932

6.1 Introduction

Primitive Methodism began in the area around Martham soon after it had first been introduced to East Norfolk. Primitive Methodist societies were established at Martham, Hemsby, Thurne, Catfield and Rollesby before 1830. These were soon followed by societies in many of the other surrounding villages, including Fleggburgh (1832), Winterton (1832), Potter Heigham (1833), Repps (1833), Hickling (1834), Horning (1835), Horsey (1836) and Somerton (1850). At the time, these societies were all part of the ever-expanding Great Yarmouth Primitive Methodist Circuit. As has been described in chapter 4, the Great Yarmouth Primitive Methodist Circuit was growing rapidly and covered a large part of east Norfolk and north-east Suffolk. At a meeting of the Great Yarmouth Primitive Methodist Circuit in 1883, a proposal was made by a Mr Whittleton of Hickling that the societies around Martham become a Primitive Methodist circuit in their own right. This was accepted alongside a similar proposal that established a Primitive Methodist circuit at Acle. So, in 1883, the Martham Primitive Methodist Circuit came into existence with 13 societies – Martham, Hemsby, Thurne, Catfield, Rollesby, Winterton, Repps, Hickling, Horsey, Somerton, Potter Heigham, Fleggburgh and Horning. Some years later the circuit was also joined by Ludham Primitive Methodist chapel.

This chapter discuss the evolution of the societies that surrounded Martham in the period from 1833 to 1932. Even though prior to 1883 the societies were in the Great Yarmouth Primitive Methodist Circuit, for ease of discussion, this chapter describes the history of the Martham circuit societies from their beginnings. Table 6.1 lists the societies that have been part of the Martham Primitive Methodist Circuit, together with their membership numbers in the years 1849, 1879 and 1932. Most of these societies went through a similar pattern of evolution. First they were missioned in around 1830 to 1840. Then they saved sufficient funds to build their own chapels, which for many societies was in the period from about 1840 to 1860. Finally, the societies grew to such a level that the early chapels were replaced by new chapels the 1880s or later. In many cases these new chapels remain in use today. Out of all the circuits in the East Norfolk area, those from the Martham Primitive Methodist Circuit have survived the longest. Of the 14 societies that have been members of the Martham Primitive Methodist Circuit, as of 2009, nine still survive.

Table 6.1: List of the societies, and their memberships, that formed the Martham Primitive Methodist Circuit in 1849, 1879 and 1932.

Society	1849	1879	1932
Martham	28	39	53
Hemsby	28	21	24
Thurne	12	7	24
Catfield	23	17	17
Rollesby	18	27	22
Winterton	17	76	28
Repps	6	21	28
Potter Heigham	–	35	26
Fleggburgh	–	7	–
Somerton	–	26	7
Hickling	14	70	–
Horsey	15	11	12
Horning	–	16	–
Ludham (Johnson Street)	–	–	24
Total	161	373	265

6.2 Martham, Hemsby and Winterton

Martham was listed on the Great Yarmouth Wesleyan Methodist Circuit plan as early as 1812 although it was some years later that a Primitive Methodist society was established. Records indicate that the first Primitive Methodist society in Martham was established before 1830. This was probably in the late 1820s, as no society for Martham is listed in the 1823 preaching plan for the Great Yarmouth branch of the Norwich Primitive Methodist Circuit. The first Primitive Methodist chapel in Martham was built in 1852 at a cost of £100. This was used for only 30 years, presumably becoming too small for the growing congregation, after which it was replaced by the current chapel in 1882. Figure 6.1 shows two pictures of the Martham chapel – the first taken in about 1920 and the second in 2009. To the right of the chapel is the minister's manse. The design of the Martham chapel, and the position of the manse next door, is almost identical to the Acle Primitive Methodist church and manse – see figure 7.1 on page 99. This was a sensible design whereby the minister lives next door to the main chapel in the circuit. At Martham, this is still the case in 2009, although at Acle both the church and manse were relocated in the 1980s.

Like Martham, the village of Hemsby was also missioned early on during the Primitive Methodist advance into the more rural parts of East Norfolk. A Primitive Methodist chapel was built in Hemsby in 1852 at a cost of £82. Membership of the society remained quite stable, with between 20 and 30 members up until Methodist unification in 1932. Even so, the society still built a new chapel in 1879 on the corner of Waters Lane and

Figure 6.1: Martham Primitive Methodist chapel. The upper picture shows the chapel in about 1920 while the lower picture shows the chapel in 2009. To the right of the chapel is the manse. Very little has changed in the two pictures, with the exception of the cottage to the left of the chapel, which has had its thatched roof replaced with tiles.

Taylors Loke, even though this was less than 30 years after the first chapel had been built. Figure 6.2 shows two pictures of the chapel, one taken in about 1930 and the other in 2008. The chapel is still in use today.

Figure 6.2: Hemsby Primitive Methodist chapel. The upper picture shows the chapel in about 1930 while the lower picture shows the chapel in 2008. The chapel has changed little in almost 100 years, although new housing is evident.

Primitive Methodist missioning at Winterton began in December 1832. The Wesleyan Methodists had previously established a presence in the village about 20 years earlier and had built a chapel in 1814. However, by the time the Primitive Methodists arrived the Wesleyan society had ended. The first Primitive Methodist chapel in Winterton was built in 1843 for £100 on what is now Old Chapel Road. This building still stands, but was converted into a row of cottages, as shown in figure 6.3. The remains of a date stone can still be seen on the side of the building and reads "P.M. CHAPEL 1843."

Figure 6.3: The first Primitive Methodist chapel that was built in Winterton in 1843. The chapel closed in about 1877 and has since been converted into a row of cottages. On the wall of the cottages that faces the road an outline of a doorway can be seen.

The first chapel was replaced by a newer chapel in 1877 which was built on Beach Road at a cost of £642. The chapel still stands today and is used by the present Winterton Methodist society. Figure 6.4 shows two pictures of the chapel – the first taken in about 1917 and the second taken in 2008. Winterton was a small coastal village with a strong tradition for fishing and had many small fishing boats working on the North Sea. The North Sea is dangerous and a Fishermen's Thanksgiving Service was quite a regular occurrence at the Winterton society to give thanks for the safe return of the fishermen.

6.3 Horsey and Somerton

Methodism was introduced to Horsey through the work of early Primitive Methodist preachers and was missioned in 1836. A society was formed in the village and members met for worship in the kitchen of a Mrs Sarah Watts. Mrs Watts lived in a farm opposite the Nelson's Head public house at Horsey and it is reported that she held services there for many years. Disaster struck in 1859 when Mrs Watts' house was destroyed by fire, leaving the society in need of a new place to meet. One of the highlights of the services that were held at Mrs Watts' house was the visit of Rev Hugh Bourne, who was credited as being one of the founders of the Primitive Methodist movement. During his visit, Rev

Figure 6.4: The second Winterton Primitive Methodist chapel. The upper picture shows the chapel in about 1917 while the lower picture shows the chapel in 2008. The circular stone decoration above the chapel door in the upper picture has been changed at some point and a clock fitted.

Bourne preached in the kitchen of the house and sat in an armchair. This armchair was kept and became an important treasure of the local Methodists.

A chapel was built in 1870 for the society on land owned by Mr William Johnson at Horsey Corner. Mr Johnson was the son-in-law of Sarah Watts, and the building was used by the society until his death in 1909. The building was then sold to a Mr George English who offered the society the option of either buying the chapel for £60 or renting it for £5 per year. Both of these options were considered too expensive by the society and instead they decided to leave the building and seek new premises for worship. The society then used the cottage of a Mr John Pegg as a meeting place until a more permanent place for worship could be found. Mr Pegg was the son-in-law of Mr William Johnson, and meetings were held in the cottage from October 1909 until September 1910.

During the society's stay in the cottage, plans were being developed to build a corrugated iron chapel, along the lines of many of the other smaller Methodist societies both in East Norfolk and further afield. A stone laying ceremony was held for the tin chapel and to the amazement of the Horsey society, a total of £95 was collected. This was much more than had been anticipated and on receiving such an amount the society changed its plans and decided to build a brick chapel. Upon its completion the new chapel had cost £100, with another £40 for seats, the harmonium and various other items. This chapel was opened on Wednesday 28 September 1910 at 3:30pm by the Rev FC Fance and was followed by a public tea and great public meeting. Two years later in 1912, all debts on the new chapel had been cleared. The chapel closed in 1958 when the Horsey society opened a new chapel. Figure 6.5 shows the chapel as it was about 1910 and also as it was in 2008, having been converted into the Old Chapel Guesthouse.

Neighbouring Somerton also had a Primitive Methodist chapel. However, records for Primitive Methodist activities in Somerton are sparse compared to the other societies in the Martham Primitive Methodist Circuit. Somerton was first missioned by the Primitive Methodists in 1850 and shortly afterwards, in 1859, a chapel was built at a cost of £91. The chapel was on Horsey Road although nothing remains of the chapel today, it having been demolished following its closure.

6.4 Thurne, Rollesby and Fleggburgh

Primitive Methodist missioning in Thurne began in the early 1820s, which made it one of the first places in East Norfolk to be missioned. In 1823, Thurne was recorded as being part of the Yarmouth branch of the Norwich Primitive Methodist Circuit and was on the preaching plan for Sunday evening services. Thurne seems to have been a hotbed for Methodism in these early times as it was also one of the first places to be missioned by the Wesleyan Methodists in East Norfolk, having being part of the Norwich Wesleyan Methodist Circuit in 1783. Some records suggest that the Primitive Methodists actually took over the Wesleyan Methodist society, although the date of this, if it occurred, is not clear.

The Thurne Primitive Methodist society was fortunate in the mid 1800s to have a generous benefactor by the name of Mr Henry Dawson Brown, who was a local farmer. In 1852, Mr Brown built a chapel so that the Thurne society would have somewhere to worship after his death. Records indicate that the chapel was sold to the Thurne society in 1873, presumably following Mr Brown's death, for £60. Mr Brown left the society half of the money needed to buy the chapel and the congregation raised the other £30.

Membership of the Thurne chapel fluctuated and in 1879 the society had only seven members. The chapel was enlarged in 1887, which suggests that membership of the society grew considerably over the intervening few years. The chapel was demolished in 1971 and replaced by a new building – see section 13.4.2 on page 181 for details. However, the stone plaque from the 1852 chapel still survives and is used as the step for the north door of

Figure 6.5: Horsey Primitive Methodist chapel. The upper picture shows the chapel in about 1910. The lower picture shows the building as it was in 2008, having been converted into the Old Chapel Guesthouse and extended much further to the left.

Figure 6.6: The stone plaque from the original chapel at Thurne. Following the chapel's replacement in 1971, this stone now serves as a step outside the north door of the new chapel.

the new chapel. The stone is shown in figure 6.6 and is inscribed "Primitive Methodist Chapel – enlarged 1887."

A strength of the Thurne society was the success of its Sunday school work. In the early 1900s Sunday school anniversary services attracted up to 150 people and these were very popular, being held in a barn at Villa Farm. The children who came to the services were given oranges and some cloth – for the boys to make a shirt and for the girls to make a night-dress.

The village of Rollesby was missioned by the Primitive Methodists before 1830 and their first chapel was opened in 1837 at a cost of £61. The chapel was on Back Lane in Rollesby and next door to it was the minister's house. The building still stands today and was converted to a private house many years ago. Membership of the society grew and a new chapel was subsequently opened in 1866 along Main Road in Rollesby, backing on to Rollesby Broad, at a cost of £156. This chapel was used for 135 years by the Rollesby Methodists, before closing in 2001. The chapel building still stands and, like its predecessor, has also been converted to a private house. Figure 6.7 shows the chapel in 2008. Interestingly, in 2009 the building was for sale with an asking price of £275,000.

The Sunday school was a big part of the Rollesby society and each year a Sunday school anniversary service was held. Records show that the society held their Eighth Sabbath School Anniversary on Sunday 20 June 1886 which was taken by Mr W Pratt of Hickling. This would have been a big day for the society as services were held at 10:45am, 2:30pm and again at 6:30pm, with the children singing hymns and giving recitations. Mr Pratt seems to have been popular at Rollesby. In 1889 he returned to lead the Eleventh Sunday School anniversary, again preaching in the morning, afternoon and evening ser-

Figure 6.7: The former Rollesby Methodist chapel in 2008, having been converted to a private house. The chapel opened in 1866 and was in regular use for 135 years until its closure in 2001.

vices. Interestingly, between 1886 and 1889 the name was changed from Sabbath School to Sunday School.

Fleggburgh was another of the villages that the Wesleyan Methodists had established a society in during the 1820s and 1830s. However, Primitive Methodism was strong in this rural area and much missioning work was being carried out in the villages to the north of Great Yarmouth. Even though Fleggburgh was a small village, it is reported to have been missioned the Primitive Methodists in 1832, as well as having a Wesleyan Methodist society. By 1853, the Primitives had also built a chapel in the village at a cost of £81.

The society seems to have found difficulty establishing itself in Fleggburgh, perhaps due to the close presence of the Wesleyan society. Membership of the Primitive society in 1883 was 10, which made it the second smallest society in the Martham Primitive Methodist Circuit and it had less than half of the membership of the Wesleyan society in the village. Preaching plans for the Martham Primitive Methodist Circuit in 1936 do not list the Fleggburgh society which indicates that it was closed sometime between 1883 and 1936. After the chapel was closed, the pews were bought by the Methodist society at Thurne.

6.5 Catfield and Hickling

Catfield was one of the earliest places to establish a Methodist society in the area covered by the Martham circuit. As early as 1826 various houses were being used in Catfield for worship "by an assembly or congregation of Protestants." It is speculated that this was the beginning of the Primitive Methodist society in Catfield. By 1836, confirmation exists that Primitive Methodist worship was taking place in Catfield through a certificate which gave permission to premises in Catfield for the "holding and occupation of the Primitive Methodist ... as a place of worship by an assembly or congregation of Protestants."

In 1838 land was purchased in Catfield for a Primitive Methodist chapel to be built. This cost £150 and on 5 September 1838 the new chapel was certified for use as a place of religious worship. In 1842 a mortgage of £86 was taken out on the chapel and in around 1879 a further loan for £149 was also taken out. Alterations were made to the chapel building in 1877 that cost £159, and it is likely that this second loan was to cover these costs. A piece of land was given to the society by Mr Hudson Barber in 1912 for a new schoolroom to be built. The cost of the new schoolroom was £130 and this money was raised by two bazaars and a further funding event which raised £50, £80 and £60, respectively. By about 1933 all the society's debts were paid. Figure 6.8 shows the chapel in about 1900 and also in 2008.

The chapel underwent modification in 1938 when the inside was changed from having a single central aisle to two side aisles. This was carried out as it was found that the ends of the pews joining the chapel walls were rotten. These modifications cost £130 with £120 of this being borrowed from the Chapel Committee and the remaining £10 given as a grant by the Special Extension Fund. To repay some of this loan an auction was held which included the sale of pigs and calves and raised £100. In 1939 a further plot of land was given to the society and this now forms the chapel car park.

Hickling was missioned by the Primitive Methodists in 1834 and their first chapel was built in 1844 at a cost of £183. The Hickling Primitive Methodists had to compete with Wesleyan Methodists who also had a chapel in the village, although this society was part of the Cromer and North Walsham Wesleyan Methodist Circuit. The Primitive Methodists seem to have prospered, as by 1879 the Hickling society had a membership of 70 and in 1882 built a new chapel on Heath Road. This chapel is still in use today by the Hickling Methodists, although at the time of Methodist unification the Hickling society left the Martham circuit and transferred to the North Walsham Methodist Circuit. Figure 6.9 shows Hickling Methodist chapel in 2008.

6.6 Potter Heigham, Repps and Ludham

The Primitive Methodists missioned Potter Heigham in June 1833 and began holding cottage meetings and prayer meetings in various parts of the village. The first Primitive Methodist chapel was opened in 1863 on Chapel Lane and cost £137 to build. The chapel survived for over 90 years before being closed in 1956 when a new chapel was opened close by on Green Lane. Nothing remains of the old chapel today, although one of the memorial stones was retained and this is now set into the brickwork of a garage belonging to one of the houses on Chapel Lane, close to where the chapel once was. Figure 6.10 shows the stone set into the garage wall.

At nearby Repps, Primitive Methodist missioning started in September 1833 and this early society met in a cottage belonging to one of the villagers. The 23 June 1852 was recorded as a great day for the Repps society as it was on that day that the great Primitive Methodist, Robert Key, visited. Records report his visit as follows:

June 23rd 1852. Robert Key the Ranting Preacher in Haddon's Barn. 300 people. I

Figure 6.8: Catfield Primitive Methodist chapel. The upper picture shows the chapel in about 1900 while the lower picture shows the chapel in 2008. In the 2008 picture the schoolroom can be seen at the rear of the chapel, while in the upper picture no schoolroom is present. (The top picture has been included by kind permission of Norfolk County Council Library and Information Services).

Figure 6.9: Hickling Methodist chapel in 2008, which was built in 1882.

laid on my straw stack and heard all. The groaning and Hallowing (Hollering) out was tremendous.

The Repps society opened a chapel soon after Robert Key's visit in 1858. The chapel survived for about 50 years before being replaced by a new chapel in 1907 that was on High Road, which runs through the village. In the 54 year history of the Martham Primitive Methodist Circuit, Repps was the only new chapel to be built. Building work began for the chapel and schoolroom with a foundation stone laying service that was held on April 1 1907. The stone laying began at 3pm with the following stones laid:

- R.J. Price, Esq.
- Edwin Tildesley, Esq.
- Mr J Balls and family
- Mr J Watts
- Mr Harry Dean
- Mr W H Guyton
- Rev F C France
- Trustees' Stone
- Circuit Official Stone

Figure 6.10: The former memorial stone at Potter Heigham Primitive Methodist chapel. The chapel was closed in 1956 and the stone set into the wall of a brick garage on Chapel Lane in the village.

- Repps and Circuit C.E. Stone
- Sunday School Stone.

After the stone laying a public tea was held at 5pm and this was followed by an evening meeting which had Rev W A Hammond, from Hull, and RJ Price, Esq. as speakers. The chapel was opened later in 1907. Figure 6.11 shows the chapel on its opening day with a large group of people from the Martham circuit in attendance. Also shown in the figure is a picture of the chapel in 2009, two years after its closure.

The village of Ludham was one of the last places in the Martham circuit where the Primitive Methodists opened a chapel. The chapel was built on Johnson Street and was almost a mile out of the village, on the road towards Horning. Some accounts suggest that the chapel was built by the owner of nearby Horning Hall for his workers to attend – which was supposedly compulsory! Figure 6.12 shows a picture of the Ludham Johnson Street chapel on the day of its opening.

Figure 6.11: Repps Primitive Methodist chapel. The upper picture shows the chapel on its opening day in 1907, while the lower picture shows the chapel in 2009, two years after its closure in 2007.

Figure 6.12: Ludham Johnson Street Primitive Methodist chapel on the day of its opening.

Chapter 7

Primitive Methodism around Acle – 1833 to 1932

7.1 Introduction

The Acle Primitive Methodist Circuit was formed at the same time as the Martham Primitive Methodist Circuit in 1883. The societies in both of these circuits had previously been part of the Great Yarmouth Primitive Methodist Circuit which prior to 1883 encompassed 33 societies. At a meeting of the Great Yarmouth circuit in 1883, proposals were made that Acle and Martham become circuits in their own right. These proposals were accepted in the meeting and a letter was then sent to the District Meeting and Conference of 1883 which read:

> Dear Brethren,
> By a large and unanimous vote of the Quarterly Meeting of this Circuit held on March 5 1883 it was resolved to divide this Circuit into the Yarmouth, Acle and Martham Circuits; and we hereby ask the District Meeting and Conference to sanction the division of the Circuit as resolved upon by the Quarterly Meeting. With this application is sent information respecting Old and New Stations as rule requires.
> Minute 21: That Reedham, Limpenhoe, Beighton, Freethorpe, Halvergate, Stokesby, Upton, South Walsham, Panxworth and Acle shall be formed into a Circuit to be called the Acle Circuit, the division to take place next July; and that we apply to the Connexional Courts in the usual way for sanction thereto.
> Mr Samuel Wright, local preacher, is appointed to represent the proposed Acle Circuit on this matter in the District Meeting.
> The Acle Circuit will receive:
>
> 1 Travelling Preacher
>
> 31 Local Preachers
>
> 9 Chapels and one other Preaching Room

374 Members; and there is on this Circuit a number of men who have long been active circuit officials and are duly qualified to conduct the business of the Circuit.

Signed on behalf of the Quarterly Meeting held March the 5 1883.
Albert Hebblethwaite, President
George William Turner, Secretary

Missioning by the Primitive Methodists in some of the villages around Acle had started before 1830, such as at Upton and Reedham. In the first few years of the 1830s, the Primitive Methodists worked hard and missioned many more villages in the area, including Limpenhoe (1832), Acle (1833), Halvergate (1833), South Walsham (1833), Freethorpe (1833), Stokesby (1833) and Beighton (1837). By the time that the Acle Primitive Methodist Circuit was formed in 1883, ten societies had been established, nine with their own chapels. Over the next 50 years, up to the time of Methodist unification in 1932, eight of these societies would remain, while two would close. A few other societies also opened and closed in this period, such as at Clippesby and Hassingham. Table 7.1 lists the societies in the Acle Primitive Methodist Circuit in the years 1849, 1883, 1912, 1922 and 1932, and also shows their memberships. The remainder of this chapter describes the missioning and development of these societies around Acle in the period from 1833 to Methodist unification in 1932. Even though the Acle circuit wasn't established until 1883, the societies that were to subsequently belong to the Acle Primitive Methodist Circuit are discussed in this chapter.

Table 7.1: List of the societies, and their memberships, that formed the Acle Primitive Methodist Circuit in 1849, 1883, 1912, 1922 and 1932.

Society	1849	1883	1912	1922	1932
Acle	–	21	40	40	45
Upton	35	30	38	35	29
Reedham	25	54	25	22	21
Limpenhoe	9	23	20	18	21
Freethorpe	23	48	77	70	85
Halvergate	17	60	66	51	70
Beighton	–	66	25	21	30
Stokesby	6	28	13	7	–
South Walsham	–	25	25	21	28
Panxworth	–	19	–	–	–
Clippesby	–	–	2	–	–
Hassingham	–	–	–	–	–
Total	115	374	331	285	329

7.2 Acle, Halvergate and Beighton

Acle was missioned by the Primitive Methodists in 1833 and for many years used a rented chapel for its services. Holding worship in a rented chapel was unusual for the Primitive

Methodists in East Norfolk, as most societies built their own chapels relatively soon after they were formed. Eventually, in 1883, the Acle society did build their first chapel which was on Reedham Road in the village. The design was similar to Martham Primitive Methodist chapel, which had been built two years before, and both had their minister's manse conveniently next door to the chapel. Figure 7.1 shows the chapel in the early 1900s.

Figure 7.1: Acle Primitive Methodist chapel and manse on Reedham Road in the early 1900s. The chapel was built in 1883 and survived until the late 1980s when the Acle Methodist society moved to a new chapel in the village on Bridewell Lane.

Halvergate was missioned in the same year as Acle and the society built a chapel in 1878 on Chapel Road for £425. For such a small place, the Halvergate society had the second largest number of members in the Acle Primitive Methodist Circuit, having a membership of 70 in 1932. Figure 7.2 shows two pictures of the chapel – first in around 1920 and then in 2008, where the chapel is still in use.

The village of Beighton was missioned by the Primitive Methodists slightly later than Acle, in 1837. A Primitive Methodist chapel was first built in Beighton in 1862 on Chapel Road at a cost of £184. The Beighton chapel was in use until its closure in 2005, whereupon it was sold for conversion into a private house. Figure 7.3 shows two pictures of the chapel – the first taken in about 1930 and the second taken in 2008, after its closure.

Figure 7.2: Halvergate Primitive Methodist chapel. The upper picture was taken in about 1920 and the lower picture in 2008. The pictures show that very little has changed in almost 100 years, apart from the removal of the chimney from the schoolroom.

Figure 7.3: Beighton Primitive Methodist chapel. The upper picture shows the chapel in about 1930, while the lower picture was taken in 2008. The chapel closed in 2005 and is being converted to a house.

7.3 Upton and South Walsham

The village of Upton was missioned by the Primitive Methodists before 1830 and a chapel was first built in there 1852 at a cost of £136. This was replaced by a new chapel in about 1878 on Marsh Road in the village. Three years later, in 1891, a larger chapel was built and the 1878 chapel then became the schoolroom. Figure 7.4 shows the Upton chapel in the early 1900s and also in 2008. The 1878 chapel can be seen in the upper photograph, behind the larger 1891 chapel.

South Walsham was missioned by the Primitive Methodists in 1833 and a chapel was built in 1869 on Wymers Lane for £138. Strictly speaking, the chapel is in neighbouring Pilson Green, although the society was always listed as South Walsham. Figure 7.5 shows the South Walsham chapel in 2009, it having been converted into a private house since its closure in 1986.

7.4 Reedham, Freethorpe and Limpenhoe

Reedham was one of the first villages to missioned by the Primitive Methodists in the area around Acle. This was before 1830 and by 1851 the Reedham society had built a chapel at a cost of £156. Thirty years later, in 1881, a second chapel was built on The Hills in Reedham. Figure 7.6 shows the inside of that chapel in 1931 during a jubilee celebration service for the chapel. The chapel continued serving Reedham for another 70 years after its jubilee, before closing in 2001. Figure 7.7 shows the Reedham chapel in the early part of the 1900s and again in 2008.

Freethorpe was missioned slightly later than Reedham by the Primitive Methodists in 1833. The Freethorpe society built its first chapel in 1865 for £241. This was replaced by the current chapel in 1896 which was built on The Common. The number of members at the Freethorpe society grew significantly from its formation and reached a peak in 1932 with a membership of 85. This made the Freethorpe society the largest in the entire Acle Primitive Methodist Circuit and accounted for a quarter of the circuit's members. Figure 7.8 shows two pictures of the Freethorpe chapel – the first taken in the early 1900s and the second in 2008.

Limpenhoe was missioned in 1832 and a chapel opened in 1878 at a cost of £264. The chapel was built on a piece of land at the side of a farmer's field on Reedham Road and was in a very remote location. Even so, the Limpenhoe society had a membership of 23 at the time of the formation of the Acle Primitive Methodist Circuit in 1883 and maintained a good membership through to Methodist unification in 1932. Figure 7.9 shows the Limpenhoe chapel in 2009, looking very overgrown since its closure in 1993.

7.5 Stokesby, Panxworth, Clippesby and Hassingham

The societies at Stokesby, Panxworth, Clippesby and Hassingham were shorter-lived than the other societies that made up the Acle Primitive Methodist Circuit. In fact, none of these societies survived to the time of Methodist unification in 1932.

Wesleyan Methodism had been introduced to Stokesby many years before Primitive Methodism and a Wesleyan chapel was built in 1811. Primitive Methodism was not introduced to Stokesby until 1833, although by the time of the formation of the Acle

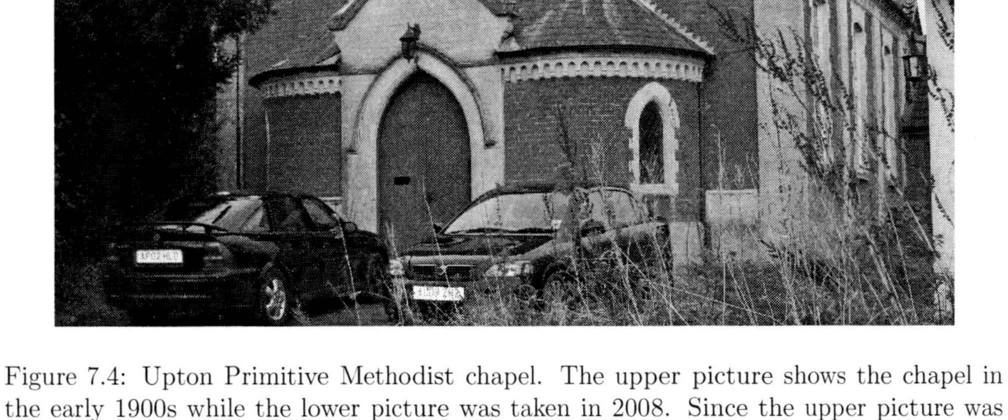

Figure 7.4: Upton Primitive Methodist chapel. The upper picture shows the chapel in the early 1900s while the lower picture was taken in 2008. Since the upper picture was taken, much housing has been built around the chapel. The chapel closed in 2001 and has since been converted into a private house.

Figure 7.5: South Walsham (Pilson Green) Primitive Methodist chapel in 2009, having been converted to a house since its closure in 1986.

Figure 7.6: Jubilee celebration service at Reedham Primitive Methodist chapel in 1931.

Figure 7.7: Reedham Primitive Methodist chapel. The upper picture shows the chapel in the early 1900s while the lower picture was taken in 2008. The chapel has been unoccupied since its closure in 2001.

Figure 7.8: Freethorpe Primitive Methodist chapel. The upper picture shows the chapel in the early 1900s while the lower picture was taken in 2008. The large window at the front of the chapel, seen in the early picture, has been largely bricked up. A side porch has also been added.

Figure 7.9: Limpenhoe Methodist chapel in 2009. The picture shows the remoteness of the Limpenhoe chapel which closed in 1993.

Primitive Methodist Circuit, membership had reached 28. In 1900, the Stokesby society made a request to the Acle Primitive Methodist Circuit for donations to a building fund for a new chapel. By 1907, sufficient funds had been raised and a new Primitive Methodist chapel was built in Stokesby on Mill Road. However, membership at the chapel was in decline and by 1922 had fallen to just seven members. In 1925 the chapel closed. Meanwhile, the Wesleyan Methodists in Stokesby were prospering, although their own chapel was in need of major repairs. Instead of repairing their chapel, the Wesleyans bought the now closed Primitive Methodist chapel from the Acle circuit in 1925 at a cost of £250 and transferred their worship to the building.

The village of Panxworth had a small Primitive Methodist society of 19 members at the time of the formation of the Acle Primitive Methodist Circuit in 1883. However, by the early 1900s services were discontinued at Panxworth and the society was removed from the preaching plan. The Primitive Methodist society at Clippesby seems to have had a similar fate. No society at Clippesby was reported on the opening of the Acle Primitive Methodist Circuit, although a very small society, with a membership of just two, was reported for 1912. The society was short-lived and by 1931 plans were in place to dispose of the chapel at Clippesby. The small village of Hassingham was another place that the Acle Primitive Methodist Circuit had limited success. The Hassingham society was added and removed from the preaching plan several times and at times only offered summertime services.

Chapter 8

United Methodism – 1833 to 1932

8.1 Introduction

United Methodism came into existence in 1907 through the merger of the Methodist New Connexion, Bible Christian Society and United Methodist Free Churches. The United Methodist Free Churches was itself the result of an early merger in 1857 of the Wesleyan Reformers and Protestant Methodists. This chapter groups together the activities of all these branches of Methodism and discusses their operations in East Norfolk in the period from 1833 to 1932. Primarily, for East Norfolk, this concentrates on the Methodist New Connexion and the Wesleyan Reformers, as the other branches of Methodism were not active in the area. The United Methodist Church was not as big a branch of Methodism as either the Wesleyan Methodists or the Primitive Methodists were in East Norfolk. At its peak in the early 1900s, the Great Yarmouth United Methodists had five societies and about 250 members. This was considerably smaller than either the Wesleyan or Primitive Methodist circuits in Great Yarmouth, which were both well over twice this size.

The Methodist New Connexion first arrived in Great Yarmouth in 1806 at the invitation of a Mr Sewell, who was a disgruntled member of the Wesleyan Methodist society in the town – see section 2.3. Within a few years the Methodist New Connexion had built chapels in Great Yarmouth, Gorleston and Lound. These societies did not survive for long and within a few years they had closed and the Methodist New Connexion no longer had a presence in East Norfolk. However, as will be explained in this chapter, the Methodist New Connexion did return to East Norfolk in 1833 and once again began to establish societies in the area.

The Wesleyan Reform Movement began in around 1849 and was an attempt to reform the way that Wesleyan Methodism was being run. Several Wesleyan ministers believed that too much power was held by too few people and they attempted to bring in reforms. The proposals failed to gain approval and as a result these minsters were expelled from the Wesleyan Methodist Conference and they then established their own Wesleyan Reform Movement. The Reform Movement caused a lot of problems for the Wesleyan Methodists and divided many congregations. In many cases, Wesleyan members left and set up Reform societies close by. The effect of this was disastrous for the Wesleyan Methodists. In the period just after 1849 they experienced big reductions in their membership and several societies were forced to close, having lost too many members to the Reform movement be able to continue. However, the Reform movement only remained popular for a few years, after which many of its members returned to their original Wesleyan societies. Some Reform societies did survive and by 1857 the Reform movement merged with the Protestant Methodists and renamed itself the United Methodist Free Churches.

The activities of these branches of Methodism that collectively created United Methodism is not as straightforward as the history of the Wesleyan and Primitive Methodists in East Norfolk. The approach taken to describe these activities in this chapter is first to describe the Methodist New Connexion's activities and then those of the Wesleyan Reform movement. Finally, the two societies are looked at collectively in terms of them being part of United Methodism, which they merged to form in 1907.

8.2 Methodist New Connexion

Following their failed earlier attempt to establish societies in Great Yarmouth, the Methodist New Connexion returned to East Norfolk in 1833. Within a few years they had managed to establish a few societies in areas around Great Yarmouth. By the time of their merger to become part of the United Methodist Church in 1907, they had opened chapels in Great Yarmouth, Burgh Castle and Lound.

8.2.1 Great Yarmouth

The Methodist New Connexion returned to Great Yarmouth in 1833 and began to hold preaching services in a large room in a building on South Quay. Over time, the number of people attending these services grew and eventually the society decided to move into larger premises. The society purchased some old offices on King Street that had been used in the fishing industry. These were demolished and replaced by a new chapel. It was opened on Christmas Day in 1835 by the Rev Samuel Hulme, who was one of the leading ministers in the Methodist New Connexion.

At first, large numbers of people attended the new chapel and services were crowded with the volume of people worshipping. However, it was not long before the congregation began to diminish. The decline continued and by 1842 membership had fallen to such a level that the chapel was closed. A further attempt was made in 1846 to establish a Methodist New Connexion society in Great Yarmouth. A chapel, which was known as the Brunswick Chapel, was opened for services by the Methodist New Connexion although congregations remained small.

Records of Methodist New Connexion activities in Great Yarmouth are quite sparse in comparison with the information available for other branches of Methodism. However, a further Methodist New Connexion church was opened on the southern part of King Street, close to St Peter's church. Records indicate that the chapel was open in 1896, although it had ceased being a Methodist New Connexion chapel by the 1930s. The building was subsequently taken over by St Peter's church and used as their church hall. Latterly, the building was the showroom for Goldstar fireplaces – as shown in figure 8.1.

Figure 8.1: Former location of the Methodist New Connexion church on King Street in Great Yarmouth. After closing as a Methodist church the building became the church hall for St Peter's church and finally a shop selling fireplaces.

8.2.2 Burgh Castle

The Methodist New Connexion did not venture north of Great Yarmouth into the more rural areas, but instead they concentrated their efforts to the south of the town. The village of Burgh Castle, to the south-west of Gorleston, was one of the first more rural areas where the Methodist New Connexion established a society. A small Methodist New Connexion chapel was built in Burgh Castle in 1864. This was on Butt Road, just to the north of the junction with Mill Lane, and was designed to accommodate up to 50 people.

8.2.3 Lound

Lound was one of the villages where the Methodist New Connexion had established a society during its first visit to East Norfolk in the early 1800s. A Methodist New Connexion chapel had been built in Lound as early as 1807 but the society came to nothing and the chapel was closed. During the efforts to re-establish the Methodist New Connexion in Great Yarmouth, a second chapel was built in Lound in 1883, with its foundation stone laid by SR Nockolds in September of that year. The chapel was built at Bunker's Hill which was almost a mile north of Lound and located alongside a footpath following the southern side of the reservoir at Lound waterworks.

The positions of these two chapels can be seen on the two maps shown in figure 8.2. The first map is from the late 1800s and shows a Wesleyan Methodist chapel (this chapel

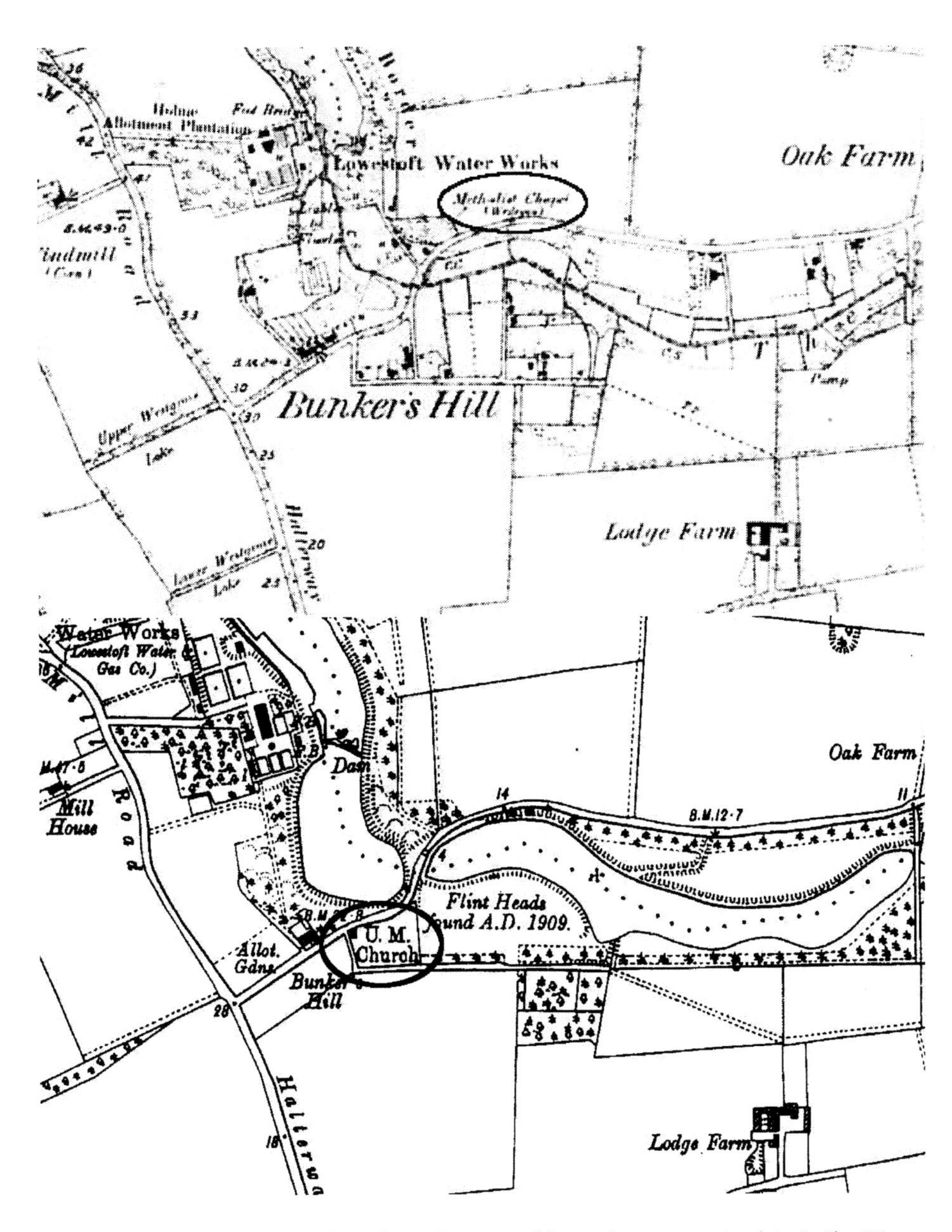

Figure 8.2: Location of Methodist chapels around Lound waterworks (circled). The upper map is from the late 1800s and shows a Wesleyan chapel to the north of a much smaller reservoir than exists today. The bottom map shows the same location but in 1928 where it can be seen that the reservoir has been significantly expanded. The position of the Wesleyan chapel from 1891 is now under water, while a new United Methodist chapel is on the south of the reservoir at Bunker's Hill.

could even have been the former Methodist New Connexion chapel that had been built in 1807). The second map is from 1928 and shows a United Methodist church (labelled U.M. Church on the map). The road passing through the area is the same on both maps. However, the size of the reservoir has increased significantly in the second map. In fact, it has increased so much that the Wesleyan chapel has gone, presumably because it would have been under water following expansion of the reservoir. The second map shows the Methodist New Connexion chapel (labelled as a United Methodist chapel on the map as this was after unification in 1907) on the south side of the reservoir. The doors of the chapel faced north and opened out overlooking the reservoir. Figure 8.3 shows a picture of this view, taken from the inside of the chapel looking out over the reservoir – what a view this must have been for worshippers leaving after a service!

Figure 8.3: The view looking outwards from the entrance of Lound Methodist chapel, overlooking one of the reservoirs of Lound waterworks.

Just under 20 years after its opening, the 1883 Lound chapel was compulsorily purchased by the Lowestoft Water and Gas Company on 12 March 1902 for £350. The reason for this is not entirely clear, but it is assumed that water company had planned to further expand the reservoir at Lound. The chapel was literally on the edge of the reservoir, so any expansion would have required the location of the chapel to be flooded. After taking over the chapel, the water company allowed the trustees of the Lound society a period of time in which to find alternative premises to hold services. However, by 1903 the trustees had not been able to find another site on which to build a new chapel. During this time, services had continued to be held in the chapel. Having no premises to move to, the trustees made a request to the water company that they be able to continue to use the chapel until they could find new premises. The water company agreed, and on 20 March 1903 a formal contract was signed stating that the rent would be £5 per year. The company also stated in the contract that as soon as a suitable site was found the building should be vacated. Interestingly, expansion of the reservoir never took place and the chapel was never needed by the water company. The Lound society continued to use the chapel under the same lease contract until its closure in the early 1970s. Figure 8.4 shows two pictures of the Lound chapel – the first in 1953 during a wedding and the second in 2007, many years after its closure and looking very overgrown.

8.3 Wesleyan Reformers

The Wesleyan Reform movement began in about 1849 and very quickly established a network of societies in East Norfolk. Most of the members of these new Reform societies were people who had left the traditional Wesleyan societies in favour of the reforms. By 1851, a Great Yarmouth branch of the Wesleyan Reform movement had been set up and its January preaching plan included societies at Great Yarmouth, Gorleston, Hopton, Ormesby, Filby, Fleggburgh, Clippesby and Martham.

Many of these societies were very short-lived and existed for only a few years. In many cases members tended to leave the Reform society and return to their original Wesleyan chapel. Alternatively, some Reform societies joined with the original Wesleyan society that their members had originally left – this happened at Caister. A few Reform societies were strong enough to survive for longer. At Gorleston, the Reform society survived until the merger of the Wesleyan Reformers with the Protestant Methodists in 1857 to become part of the United Methodist Free Churches. This society was relatively strong and continued until it became a United Methodist chapel in 1907 when the United Methodist Free Churches merged with the Methodist New Connexion and Bible Christians.

8.3.1 Great Yarmouth

A large Methodist church was built on the southern side of Regent Road in 1856 that had a seating capacity of 600. Records of 1896 state that this church was part of the United Methodist Free Churches, which would suggest that it was originally opened as a Wesleyan Reform church. The church was situated near to the corner of Alexandra Road, between numbers 108 and 109, with 109 Regent Road being the manse. The church was enlarged in 1877 and was particularly popular with Scottish people who were working in Great Yarmouth in the herring fishing industry. The church survived into the 1930s and for many years was the main church in the Great Yarmouth United Methodist Circuit. Figure 8.5 shows the church as it is now, having been converted into a gift shop.

8.3.2 Gorleston

In Gorleston the Wesleyan Reformers caused a lot of disruption to the Wesleyan Methodist society that was based on the High Street. By the start of the 1850s a large split had developed in the society, which was caused by the contradicting views of traditional Wesleyan Methodists and Wesleyan Reformers. This led to many members of the Wesleyan society leaving to join the Reform movement. Membership of the Wesleyan Methodist society had fallen from 79 members in 1844 to 23 by 1851 and was continuing to fall. This

Figure 8.4: The upper picture shows the wedding of Miss Iris Beare to Mr John Hawkins at Lound chapel in 1953. The lower picture shows the chapel in 2007, having been closed for over 35 years and in an overgrown state.

Figure 8.5: The former Regent Road Methodist church and manse. The large building on the left, which is now Martyn's gift shop, was originally the Regent Road Methodist church. To its right, the Orchid Nails boutique was the manse.

made it difficult to keep the society viable, with the eventual result that the chapel was sold at the end of 1851 for £260. It was bought by two former members of the Wesleyan Methodist society, Mr James Lawn and Mr Michael Field, who had left to join the Reform movement. They opened the chapel as a Wesleyan Reform chapel and in 1865 sold the chapel to the Wesleyan Reform movement for £300. The chapel was later sold to the United Methodist Free Churches in 1873 for £322. When the United Methodist Free Churches merged with the Bible Christian Society and Methodist New Connexion in 1907, the High Street chapel became a United Methodist church, which is shown in figure 8.6.

A second Wesleyan Reform church was also established in Gorleston on Palmer Road, which is just off the southern part of the High Street. This seems to have operated quite independently and even during the 1960s was referring to itself as a Wesleyan Reform chapel – over 100 years after the Wesleyan Reform movement had merged to become the United Methodist Free Churches in 1857. Figure 8.7 shows a picture of the entrance to the chapel during a wedding in 1962, where a notice can be seen clearly that states that the chapel was Wesleyan Reform. The chapel closed sometime in the 1970s and then became an Ebenezer Pentecostal church. From 1995 to 2005 the building became the

Figure 8.6: The United Methodist chapel on the west side of the High Street in Gorleston. The chapel was situated where GT Motors now is, just south of Gorleston shopping precinct.

Kings Church before their move to a new purpose-built church in Southtown – see figure 8.8. The building was subsequently demolished and a row of town houses now occupies the site.

8.3.3 Caister

The West Caister Wesleyan Methodist chapel was another society to be affected badly by the Wesleyan Reform movement. The society was in a healthy state in 1844 with a membership of 43. However, by 1851 almost all of the members had left to join a local Wesleyan Reform society, leaving just seven members at the Wesleyan society. The Reform society grew quickly and by 1855 had started to rent a chapel on the High Street in Caister. However, by the late 1860s the society had lost many members and those remaining decided that the best course of action would be to merge with the Wesleyan Methodists in Caister. This they did, with the result that an East Caister Wesleyan Methodist society was established. Ultimately, the East Caister and West Caister Wesleyan Methodist societies joined and opened a new chapel on Beach Road in 1886. Section 3.4 gives further details of this society.

8.3.4 Newtown

The first church building on the Newtown Methodist church site was a school chapel that was opened on 8 October 1891. The building measured 60 feet by 25 feet and was based on designs by Mr G Springall and built by Mr TG Leggett and Mr B Springall. The total cost of the building, including furnishings, was almost £500 and by the time of its opening the trustees had raised £200 towards this cost. The opening ceremony of the chapel began with a sermon preached by Rev T Ferrier Hulme and was followed by a tea. In the evening a public meeting was held with Mr G Baker presiding. Fundraising during the day raised £10 of which £5 was given by Mr Baker himself. Further celebrations were held on the next Sunday afternoon when the choir from the United Methodist Free Church on Regent Road gave a service of song, entitled "Rhoda." This original chapel still stands today at the rear of the present church and is used as a schoolroom and kitchen.

The idea for building a larger church at Newtown began at the annual assembly of the United Methodist Free Churches which was held in Sheffield at the start of the twentieth century. During the assembly it was agreed to establish a "Twentieth Century Fund" with the aim of developing and extended the work of God in connection with churches at home and abroad. A target of raising 100,000 guineas was set. From these monies, not less than half would be allocated to the annual assembly, with two-fifths earmarked for extension work at home. The remaining money would be available for local extension work.

The inauguration of the fund in Great Yarmouth took place at the United Methodist Free Church on Regent Road with Rev Dr Brook of Bristol (General Secretary of the Fund) and Rev ED Cornish of Manchester (former President of the United Methodist Free Church) explaining the aims behind the fundraising. A public meeting and tea were held afterwards and each member of the circuit was asked to make a contribution to the fund which could be paid over a period of two to five years. The minister commented that the people of the circuit were not wealthy, but they were very loyal. Two objectives of the fund were agreed: first, to assist the United Methodist Free Church in Gorleston,

Figure 8.7: Photograph of the entrance to the Palmer Road Wesleyan Reform chapel, taken during a wedding in 1962. The sign inside the entrance can be seen to still refer to the building as being a Wesleyan Reform church.

Figure 8.8: Palmer Road chapel as the Kings Church. From 1995 to 2005 the Palmer Road chapel was used by the Kings Church before their move to Queen Anne's Road in Southtown.

and second, to add to the circuit's building fund with the aim of building a new church at Newtown.

To encourage members to partake, the minister likened the giving of money to "taking a cold bath on a cold morning, where it is easy to look at the water for a moment or two and shrink from plunging in. But when the plunging was over, and after a good rub down, the world would seem a better and brighter place!" The analogy seems to have been successful as by the end of the meeting promises totalling £155 had been made, including 25 guineas from Rev Walkden himself. Nationally, more prosperous areas were expected to raise more money. For example, Norwich raised 900 guineas, but as Great Yarmouth was a poorer area it was not expected to raise as much.

By 1907 sufficient funds had been raised by the Newtown trustees to enable the present-day church to be built. The church is quite characteristic in appearance and has a stout-looking clock tower on the front corner of the building, which is shown in figure 8.9. In 1912 the trustees purchased an organ from St John's church in Great Yarmouth and had to make several modifications to their building in order to accommodate the instrument, including demolishing the southern vestry and adjusting the choir stalls. The organ had been built by Mr William Christmas Mack who was a respected organ builder in Great Yarmouth. Mr Mack had also built the organs at the United Methodist Free Church on Regent Road and at the Dene Side Wesleyan Methodist church.

Figure 8.9: Newtown Methodist church in 2008. Adjoining the church is a clock tower which is a rare feature for a Methodist church. One hundred years after its opening, the church is still in regular use, holding Sunday services and a range of weekday events.

Table 8.1: Great Yarmouth United Methodist Circuit in 1933.

Church	Membership
Great Yarmouth, Regent Road	101
Gorleston, High Street	78
Newtown	38
Lound	17
Burgh Castle	15
Total	249

8.4 United Methodist Church – 1907

In 1907 the merger of the United Methodist Free Churches with the Methodist New Connexion and the Bible Christian Society led to the formation of the United Methodist Church. For East Norfolk, this created the Great Yarmouth United Methodist Circuit which had five churches: Regent Road and Newtown in Great Yarmouth, High Street in Gorleston, Lound and Burgh Castle. The head of this new United Methodist circuit was the Regent Road church as it was the largest of the five societies in the circuit. This circuit survived until the 1930s when Methodist unification took place. Table 8.1 lists the five societies and their memberships in 1933, just prior to unification with the Wesleyan and Primitive circuits.

Chapter 9

Methodist Unification in East Norfolk – 1932 to 1938

9.1 Introduction

The year 1932 was a historic time for Methodism as the Wesleyan Methodist Church, the Primitive Methodist Church and the United Methodist Church joined to become the Methodist Church of Great Britain. The various factions of Methodism had started to merge in 1907 when the Methodist New Connexion, Bible Christians and United Methodist Free Churches came together to form the United Methodist Church. A few years later the idea to have a single Methodist Church came about. There was not much difference theologically between the Wesleyans, Primitives and United Methodist Churches. However there were class differences. Wesleyan Methodists tended to belong to the middle classes and were professional people or well-to-do tradesmen. United Methodists, as a generalisation, belonged partly to these classes but more often they were skilled manual workers. The Primitive Methodists, nationally, tended to be from mining, industrial and agricultural communities. To some extent these class divisions did cause some practical problems with unification, with some societies regarding others as either "inferior" or "snooty."

The Primitive and United Methodists were in favour of the union, partly as their finances had become stretched since the time of the First World War and also because they were keen to join so that a larger and stronger Methodist Church could be formed. The Wesleyans were not so convinced about the advantages for union, although they were generally in agreement that unification would be a good thing for Methodism as a whole. Unification took place at the Uniting Conference which was held in September 1932 after which there were no, officially, separate Wesleyan, Primitive and United Methodist Churches, just a unified Methodist Church.

Although unification took place in 1932, no changes to the structure of the Methodist circuits in East Norfolk took place until 1938. Having such a long delay before local unification took place was not uncommon nationally, as the issues of closing Methodist societies or merging them with other societies was a highly emotive subject that required considerable debate. However, it was inevitable that some societies would have to close simply due to the amount of over-provision that existed following unification. In

Great Yarmouth and Gorleston alone, there were three former Wesleyan societies (Dene Side, Tower Street Mission and Lowestoft Road), five former Primitive societies (Temple, Queen's Road, Beccles Road, Nile Road and Cobholm) and three former United societies (Regent Road, Newtown and High Street). This made a total of 11 societies which was not efficient nor was it any longer economical. Even in the wider East Norfolk area, several small towns and villages had two Methodist chapels – Acle, Caister, Ormesby and Ludham all had both Wesleyan and Primitive societies.

This chapter discusses the state of Methodism in East Norfolk just prior to the 1932 Uniting Conference and then goes on to explain the process of unification which finally took place in 1938. Several societies closed during this period, some merged and some moved to different circuits. However, by 1938 the number of Methodist societies in East Norfolk had only reduced to 43, from 47 societies before unification in 1932. This still was a considerable over-provision of societies, but, as is discussed in chapter 11, the damage caused by the Second World War would have an even larger effect on the closure of societies than Methodist unification.

9.2 Methodism in East Norfolk prior to 1932

Prior to the 1932 Methodist Uniting Conference there were five Methodist circuits in East Norfolk. Great Yarmouth had three Methodist circuits – the Wesleyan circuit, the Primitive circuit and the United circuit. There were also Primitive Methodist circuits at Acle and Martham. An immediate effect of the Uniting Conference was that the names Wesleyan, Primitive and United were dropped from the names of the circuits. In Great Yarmouth, to avoid having three circuits all with the same name, the circuits took their names from the principal church in the circuit. Therefore, the Great Yarmouth Wesleyan Methodist Circuit became the Dene Side Methodist Circuit, the Great Yarmouth Primitive Methodist Circuit became the Temple Methodist Circuit and the Great Yarmouth United Methodist Circuit became the Regent Road Methodist Circuit. In Acle and Martham renaming was more simple, with the word 'Primitive' simply deleted from the name, resulting in the Acle Methodist Circuit and the Martham Methodist Circuit.

The societies making up the Dene Side, Temple and Regent Road circuits in Great Yarmouth are listed in tables 9.1, 9.2 and 9.3. At the time of Methodist unification much information was being gathered about individual circuits, with a view to devising a plan for merging circuits and societies where this was possible. The tables also list some of the information that was collected during the survey, which includes for each society their membership, value of the building and their yearly assessment.

The Dene Side and Temple circuits were similar in both their membership numbers and assessments, although Dene Side had fewer societies. The Dene Side circuit had a membership of 591 and collected a yearly assessment of £798 from its ten churches. The Temple circuit had a membership of 548 and collected an assessment of £817 from its 13 churches. The value of the churches in the Dene Side circuit was considerably higher than those of the Temple circuit. Dene Side's properties were valued at £37,500 which was almost twice the value of the Temple circuit's properties which were valued at just under £20,000. Many of the buildings in the Temple circuit were village chapels that were quite small and in many cases valued below £1,000. The Temple circuit did have some more urban churches, such as the Temple, Queen's Road and Beccles Road, although these were

Table 9.1: Dene Side Methodist Circuit (former Great Yarmouth Wesleyan Circuit) in 1933.

Church	Membership	Value	Assessment
Dene Side	285	£20,000	£474
Tower Street Mission	34	£1,000	£10
Lowestoft Road	134	£11,000	£227
Caister (Beach Rd.)	42	£1,500	£27
Ormesby	17	£1,000	£17
Stokesby	25	£800	£16
Ludham (High Street)	14	£1,000	£9
Fleggburgh	11	£500	£4
Wickhampton	20	£700	£8
Acle	9	–	£6
Total	591	£37,500	£798

Table 9.2: Temple Methodist Circuit (former Great Yarmouth Primitive Circuit) in 1933.

Church	Membership	Value	Assessment
Temple	170	£8,000	£341
Queen's Road	56	£2,000	£100
Scratby	22	£450	£26
Caister (Yarmouth Rd.)	30	£600	£45
Beccles Road	54	£1,000	£71
Belton	44	£850	£40
Runham	11	£400	£13
Ormesby	31	£500	£28
Filby	20	£600	£12
Bradwell	31	£1,000	£31
Nile Road	41	£2,000	£69
Cobholm	35	£2,300	£35
Browston	3	£110	£6
Total	548	£19,810	£817

Table 9.3: Regent Road Methodist Circuit (former Great Yarmouth United Circuit) in 1933.

Church	Membership	Value	Assessment
Regent Road	101	£4,000	£284
High Street	78	£2,500	£139
Newtown	38	£5,000	£117
Lound	17	Rented	£16
Burgh Castle	15	£260	£16
Total	249	£11,760	£572

smaller compared to the urban churches of the Dene Side circuit, with the exception of the Temple. In comparison, the Dene Side circuit had two large and prominently positioned churches – Dene Side and Lowestoft Road in Gorleston, which were valued at £20,000 and £11,000, respectively.

The Regent Road Circuit was smaller than the Dene Side and Temple circuits and had only five societies with a total membership of 249. The value of the properties was also much less than the other two circuits, being just £11,760. In fact, one of the five chapels in the Regent Road circuit was rented from Lound waterworks and another at Burgh Castle was valued at only £260. Interestingly, the Newtown church had a higher valuation than the Regent Road church.

Tables 9.4 and 9.5 show the churches that made up the Acle Circuit in 1932 and the Martham Circuit in 1936, along with their membership numbers and assessments. These circuits were smaller in membership than the Dene Side and Temple circuits. The Acle Circuit had a membership of 329 spread across eight churches while the Martham Circuit had a membership of 265 spread over 11 churches. Both of these circuits also had only one full-time minister appointed to them.

Table 9.4: Acle Methodist Circuit (former Acle Primitive Circuit) in 1932.

Church	Membership	Assessment
Acle	45	£59
Upton	29	£33
Reedham	21	£29
Limpenhoe	21	£23
Freethorpe	85	£84
Halvergate	70	£52
Beighton	30	£29
South Walsham	28	£20
Total	329	£329

Table 9.5: Martham Methodist Circuit (former Martham Primitive Circuit) in 1936.

Church	Membership	Assessment
Martham	53	£71
Hemsby	24	£32
Thurne	24	£30
Catfield	17	£24
Rollesby	22	£20
Winterton	28	£40
Repps	28	£38
Horsey	12	£15
Somerton	7	£10
Heigham	26	£34
Ludham (Johnson Street)	24	£26
Total	265	£340

The five circuits overlapped quite substantially in terms of the locations of their respective societies. Great Yarmouth had most overlap, with the combined Dene Side, Temple and Regent Road circuits having seven churches in the town. Gorleston also suffered from overlap, having four churches from the same three circuits. Even some of the smaller towns and villages had two churches from different circuits – Acle, Caister, Ormesby and Ludham all had two Methodist chapels in 1932. The three former Primitive circuits (Temple, Acle and Martham) had no overlap with each other, which was due to their evolution, having been created by successive splitting from the original Great Yarmouth Primitive Methodist Circuit in 1883. Overlap came primarily from the more rural societies that belonged to the former Wesleyan (now Dene Side) circuit.

With these five circuits all now belonging to a single Methodist Church, having so much duplication of churches in these areas was unnecessary. Ultimately this would have to lead to mergers between societies and the closure of some societies would be necessary, although this would not be an easy task to carry out. As history has shown, many of these relatively small villages did manage to maintain two Methodist chapels for many years – the longest being Caister, which retained two Methodist chapels until 1979 when the former Primitive chapel closed leaving just the former Wesleyan chapel.

9.3 Plans for Methodist unification in East Norfolk

From the start of Methodist unification in 1932, plans began to be developed to explore possibilities for uniting the three Methodist circuits in Great Yarmouth. Having three separate circuits was not seen to be an effective way to operate Methodism in Great Yarmouth and therefore changes would need to be made. Methodist unification had much more of an effect in Great Yarmouth than it did in the surrounding areas, because of the large over-provision of churches in the town. However, the effects of unification would also be felt in the surrounding circuits of Acle and Martham, but to a lesser degree. The unification process started by taking the statistics gathered from the three circuits in Great Yarmouth and from the Acle and Martham circuits, and forming a team of ministers from the five circuits to consider them in detail. The team of ministers then produced a series of recommendations that suggested five different options for bringing unification to Methodism in East Norfolk:

- *Option A* – Merge the Regent Road Circuit with either the Dene Side Circuit or Temple Circuit. A merged circuit comprising Regent Road and Dene Side would have 14 churches and three ministers, while the Temple circuit would have 13 churches and three ministers. Merging the Regent Road and Temple circuits would give a circuit of 18 churches and four ministers, while the Dene Side circuit would have nine churches and two ministers.

- *Option B* – Merge all three Great Yarmouth circuits into one circuit. This would give a circuit with 27 churches and six ministers.

- *Option C* – Merge all three Great Yarmouth circuits into one circuit and move eight of the country churches north of Great Yarmouth into the Martham Circuit. The chapels moving to the Martham Circuit would be Stokesby, Fleggburgh, Ludham, Runham, Filby, Scratby, Ormesby (ex-Primitive) and Ormesby (ex-Wesleyan). In lieu of these additional chapels, Martham would benefit from the appointment of a probationary minister. The would leave the Great Yarmouth Circuit with 19 churches.

- *Option D* – Temporarily merge the three Great Yarmouth circuits, the Acle Circuit and Martham Circuit and subsequently make adjustments according to need.

- *Option E* – Create a separate Gorleston Circuit from the Great Yarmouth Circuit. The Gorleston Circuit would comprise Beccles Road, High Street, Lowestoft Road, Nile Road, Burgh Castle, Bradwell, Belton, Browston and Lound. This would be supported by one minister and a probationary minister. The remaining 18 churches would form the Great Yarmouth Circuit which would have four ministers.

The recommendations also stated that some modifications of these options may be necessary.

A meeting was held by the Methodist Council on 9 March 1934 which voted 23 to four that the three circuits in Great Yarmouth should be united. This result was to be sent to the next Quarterly Meetings of the circuits involved, with a request that any alternatives to these options be submitted. The Methodist Council also recommended that amalgamation should take place at the Methodist Conference of 1934. The council also requested that the position of a probationary minister be relieved and at the first change of a circuit minister this vacancy should be replaced by a probationary ministerial position. In effect, this amounted to the new circuit losing one circuit minister. The churches would maintain their current quarterly assessment payments with the exception of the Regent Road and Newtown churches which would have their assessments reduced by £125 per year. The minister stationed at the Regent Road church would also look after the Newtown church. This would leave the two ministers based in Gorleston to look after the Gorleston churches.

9.4 Church closures prior to unification

Although the proposal that the Methodist circuits in Great Yarmouth should unite was made in 1934, it wasn't until 1938 that unification actually took place. In the intervening time several of the Methodist societies in the East Norfolk area closed. The Regent Road Methodist Church, which was the principal society of the Regent Road Circuit, was the biggest casualty, although for several years it had been suffering from both a declining membership and financial problems. The former Wesleyan chapel at Acle and the former Primitive chapel at Browston were in similar situations with both societies in serious decline which led to their closures in the period between 1934 and 1938. The remainder of this section examines these three closures in more detail. The closures actually helped the unification process of the societies in Great Yarmouth.

Another major closure in Great Yarmouth in this same period was that of the Dene Side church. Although Dene Side closed in 1937, and the building subsequently sold, this was only temporary as the society moved to form the new Central Hall in Great Yarmouth in 1938. This is a significant piece of Methodist history in Great Yarmouth and the next chapter (chapter 10) is dedicated to describing this move which relates to some of the discussions in this chapter.

9.4.1 Closure of Regent Road church

During the debates into the unification of Methodism in East Norfolk, the Regent Road church in Great Yarmouth was suffering serious financial problems. By 1934, a falling congregation and debts approaching £1,000 led to the full-time minister appointed to Regent Road being withdrawn. This was a serious blow to the Regent Road church, which was the principal society of the Regent Road Circuit, and highlighted the seriousness of its problems.

In 1936, the trustees of the Regent Road church were approached with an offer to buy their premises and were asked how much they would sell them for. They responded with a price of £10,000 but were told that this was much too high. Instead they were offered £6,000 for the church and associated house which had been the manse. In a trustees meeting on 14 October 1936 the offer of £6,000 was accepted. At the same meeting the trustees also decided that Newtown Methodist church should be given the communion clips, communion table and chairs and the pulpit chairs. The pulpit bible was given to Lound and the schoolroom clock to Burgh Castle. These churches had all been in the same former United Methodist circuit as the Regent Road church prior to unification, and it was deemed appropriate that they should receive these items. Regent Road Methodist church closed on the last Sunday of 1936 with many of the remaining congregation, including the choir, transferring to Newtown Methodist church. Ultimately the sale of premises did not go through as the buyers mistakenly thought that they were buying Dene Side Methodist church which was 150 metres to the west, on Regent Road!

At a trustees' meeting in October 1937, with the minister Rev T Banks presiding, sale prices of £5,000 for the church and £1,500 for the associated house were agreed. From any sale, the trustees decided that two-fifths of the proceeds should go to the Regent Road Circuit, another two-fifths should go to the Temple and the remaining one-fifth should go to the circuit Quarterly Meeting. However, a subsequent letter from the Department for Chapel Affairs stated that the proposed proportioning of the proceeds of any sale was not acceptable. The department was concerned mainly with the two-fifths allocated to the Temple which they considered going towards running expenses and not further extension of the circuit which was against Methodist rules.

It appears that in 1945 the trustees were considering signing a Deed of Waiver which would allow intoxicating liquor to be sold on the site after its sale. For this the trustees were to be paid £200. However, in September 1945 a forceful letter was sent from the Department of Chapel Affairs telling the trustees that they were not empowered to sign any such waiver and in any case this was contrary to Methodist law!

Several organisations expressed an interest in taking over the Regent Road premises, although most came to nothing. At one point the Salvation Army discussed either leasing or buying the premises, but again nothing came of this. The premises were eventually sold in early 1946 to the Toby Motor Garage for £6,250. From the proceeds of the sale the Regent Road church debt of £1,165 was cleared, £150 was given to Lound Methodist chapel (formerly of the Regent Road Circuit), £189 was paid as commission to estate agents Gambling and Duffield and £81 was paid in legal fees. This left a balance of £4,665 from which £836 was given to the Temple to clear the debts on their building. From the remainder of the proceeds from the sale, consideration was given as to making donations to the other churches in the Regent Road Circuit (High Street, Lound, Burgh Castle and Newtown). Some money was given to Newtown for an extension and the possibility of transferring the organ from Regent Road was also considered. The organ never did make it to Newtown, as instead it was bought by the Cobholm Methodists for £115 and installed there.

Since its closure, the former Regent Road church building has undergone considerable change. It was first used as a motor garage and is now Martyn's gift shop and unrecognisable as a former Methodist church. However, viewing the building from the rear, from Albion Road, much of the original structure remains unchanged and a large curved roof and arches are clearly visible. The former manse, at 109 Regent Road, still stands although the ground floor has been converted into a retail outlet that is currently a nail boutique. Figure 8.5, on page 115, shows a picture of the former church and manse, taken in 2008.

9.4.2 Closure of Acle (ex-Wesleyan) chapel

The Wesleyan Methodist chapel at Acle had been experiencing difficulties for many years, even before the unification of Methodism, and had only a small number of members attending services. In 1928, the Acle Methodist society considered closing the chapel, but this was opposed by some of the local preachers who agreed to try and increase the number of people attending. A year later some improvement in numbers had been achieved, although this was short-lived. In 1933 the chapel steward at Acle resigned which led to services being discontinued. At a trustees' meeting in 1934, taking all these circumstances into account, it was agreed to close the Acle former Wesleyan Methodist chapel and for the society to join with the former Primitive Methodist society in Acle.

Following its closure, the Acle chapel was leased to various groups including the police. In 1941, the Ministry of Labour took over the lease of the building, for which they paid £1.18.6 per week which included lighting, heating, decorating and cleaning. The lease was later changed, in 1960, to £1 per week but without the cleaning and lighting. The annual rent of over £50 per year was a very good deal for the Acle Methodists. Local estate agents had suggested that a more realistic rent of £25 per year would be likely, should the Ministry move out. They also valued the building to be worth between £50 and £150, which made the £50 annual rent appear exceptional. The Department for Chapel Affairs was not so pleased. It was their policy that redundant chapels should be sold and the money used for extension schemes within circuits.

As the years went on, the condition of the former Wesleyan chapel deteriorated and the Ministry of Labour became less and less satisfied. In 1961 they complained of rot in the floor. This had still not been repaired by 1963 and the Ministry was having to put filing cabinets over the rotten parts of the floor to cover them up and prevent people falling through! In 1962, the heating failed because of electrical problems and cost £126 to put right. In 1963 the roof was reported as being faulty, although the building had been decorated internally.

9.4.3 Closure of Browston (ex-Primitive) chapel

At the time of Methodist unification, the Browston society was in serious decline and had only three members. Since its opening in 1924 the society had never really prospered and a decision to close the chapel was taken. This was prior to the 1938 merging of Methodist societies in Great Yarmouth and so Browston never actually became part of the new unified circuit. Records indicate that the chapel was sold in 1939 for £30 with restrictions put in place over future uses of the building. The building is still standing in 2009 but is in a poor state of repair.

9.5 Methodist Circuits in East Norfolk after unification

At the beginning of 1938 the unification of the Methodist circuits in Great Yarmouth that had been proposed in 1934 had still not occurred. The Dene Side, Temple and Regent Road circuits still operated as independent circuits as they had done before Methodist unification. These three circuits had each lost one of their societies through closure – the Dene Side Circuit had lost Acle, the Temple Circuit had lost Browston and the Regent Road Circuit had lost the Regent Road church. This left 25 churches across the three Great Yarmouth Methodist circuits. The circuits between them had a total of five ministers and one pastor, who were allocated as follows:

- *Dene Side*
  - Rev Clement Harpur, 45 Wellesly Road, Great Yarmouth
  - Rev C. Wesley Parry, 104 Lowestoft Road, Gorleston
- *Temple*
  - Rev Thomas Banks, Holmwood, Hamilton Road
  - Rev Harry Harrison, 44 Middleton Road, Gorleston
  - Pastor J.E. Townson, 32 South Beach Parade, Great Yarmouth
- *Regent Road*
  - Rev W.R. Britton, 221 Beccles Road, Gorleston

The Dene Side Circuit had two ministers, Rev Clement Harpur and Rev C Wesley Parry, who were based in Great Yarmouth and Gorleston respectively. The Temple Circuit had two ministers and a pastor, two based in Great Yarmouth and the other in Gorleston. The Regent Road circuit was considerably smaller, especially since having just lost the main Regent Road church, and had just one minister.

It wasn't until 7 April 1938 that Methodist unification in East Norfolk finally took place with the new circuit named the Great Yarmouth and Gorleston Methodist Circuit. This coincided with the opening of the new Central Hall in the town which had replaced the Dene Side church. Most of the members of Dene Side transferred to the Central Hall which was operated independently as a central mission and was not part of the new circuit. Details of the closure of Dene Side and the opening of the Central Hall are discussed in the next chapter – chapter 10.

Geographically, the Dene Side Circuit, which had formerly been the Great Yarmouth Wesleyan Circuit, covered a larger area than either the Temple or Regent Road circuits. The Dene Side circuit had several former Wesleyan chapels that were some distance from Great Yarmouth, such as Wickhampton, Ludham, Stokesby and Fleggburgh. Following unification to a single Methodist circuit in Great Yarmouth, these more rural chapels would now be closer to either the Acle or Martham circuits than to the new Great Yarmouth and Gorleston Circuit and it made sense to transfer them to these other circuits. However, these societies were not keen to move out of the Dene Side circuit and into different circuits.

The members at Ludham were very much against joining the Martham circuit and wrote a strongly worded letter to Rev Heap, who was Chairman of the East Anglia District, saying so. The Superintendent Minister of the Great Yarmouth circuit was dispatched to Ludham to pacify the situation, but reported back after having tried to persuade them to join the Martham circuit, that "in their present temper we shall probably have to leave them where they are for the present." However, they did eventually relent and joined the Martham circuit. This left the Martham circuit with two societies in Ludham – High Street (the former Wesleyan society) and Johnson Street (the former Primitive society). At the same time the former Wesleyan society at Fleggburgh also joined the Martham circuit, but with more willingness than the Ludham society.

The Wickhampton society was initially in opposition to joining the Acle circuit but they did come to accept the recommendation. In fact, they were made very welcome by Acle circuit, who wrote in their circuit plan at the time:

"At the request of the Great Yarmouth (Dene Side) Circuit, the Quarterly Meeting agreed to take over the Wickhampton society as part of our circuit from 5th September 1937. We take this opportunity of giving a hearty welcome to our Wickhampton friends, and assuring them that the full resources of the this circuit are gladly accorded to them. After certain alterations and repairs to the building have been completed, special re-opening services will be arranged, the date of which will be announced later. Our staff of local preachers will realise that the addition of another church to the circuit will necessitate extra services on their part, but this I know, will be cheerfully given."

The Methodist society at Stokesby also stated that they did not wish to join the Acle circuit and they also said that they expected that Acle would not want them either! They, however, did remain in the Great Yarmouth circuit.

Taking into account the closures of the Regent Road and Browston churches, the transfer of the Ludham, Wickhampton and Fleggburgh societies, and the creation of the independent Central Hall from the Dene Side society, this left the new Great Yarmouth and Gorleston Circuit with 21 churches and 925 members, the details of which are shown in table 9.6. The loss of the Regent Road and Dene Side churches left the Temple as the largest church, and so it became the head of the new circuit. Although the Temple was now the principal church in the new circuit, it was not in a particularly healthy state, either structurally or financially. The stonework on the Temple had deteriorated badly and was becoming dangerous and in need of repair. The Temple's debt had also increased to £400 which was a significant increase over its debt of £251 only four years previously in 1934. The estimate for the stonework repairs was £360 and the Temple needed to raise this money urgently to prevent further damage and expense. The minister at the Temple, Rev Banks, appealed to the General Chapel Committee for help with these costs, based on the fact that the Temple was now the principal Methodist church in the town. The committee could not provide the funds directly, but were able to help with securing a loan for the repairs. The loan was ultimately approved and the repairs carried out. It was also hoped that the reorganisation of Methodism in the town would allow the Temple's debt to be relieved somewhat.

Table 9.6: Churches in the new Great Yarmouth and Gorleston Methodist Circuit, formed on 7 April 1938.

Church	Membership	Previous circuit
Temple	152	Ex-GY Primitive
Queen's Road	54	"
Scratby	24	"
Caister (Yarmouth Road)	29	"
Beccles Road	54	"
Belton	29	"
Runham	12	"
Ormesby (former Primitive)	24	"
Filby	17	"
Bradwell	37	"
Cobholm	51	"
Nile Road	35	"
High Street	74	Ex-GY United
Newtown	58	"
Lound	21	"
Burgh Castle	18	"
Tower Street Mission	38	Ex-GY Wesleyan
Lowestoft Road	128	"
Caister (Beach Road)	34	"
Ormesby (former Wesleyan)	14	"
Stokesby	22	"
Total	925	

Table 9.7: Churches in the new Acle Methodist Circuit in 1938.

Church	Membership	Previous circuit
Acle	36	Ex-Acle Primitive
Upton	39	"
Reedham	18	"
Limpenhoe	18	"
Freethorpe	88	"
Halvergate	67	"
Beighton	29	"
South Walsham	20	"
Wickhampton	23	Ex-GY Wesleyan
Total	338	

Table 9.8: Churches in the new Martham Methodist Circuit in 1938.

Church	Previous circuit
Martham	Ex-Martham Primitive
Hemsby	"
Thurne	"
Catfield	"
Rollesby	"
Winterton	"
Repps	"
Horsey	"
Somerton	"
Heigham	"
Ludham Johnson Street	"
Ludham High Street	Ex-GY Wesleyan
Fleggburgh	"

The Acle and Martham circuits had both changed slightly following unification when they each took over societies from the former Dene Side (Wesleyan) circuit – Ludham and Fleggburgh transferred to the Martham circuit and Wickhampton to the Acle circuit. Tables 9.7 and 9.8 show the societies that made up the Acle and Martham circuits in 1938, along with their memberships.

At the initiation of the new Great Yarmouth and Gorleston Circuit an examination was made of the finances of its 21 churches. Table 9.9 summarises the income and expenditure of these churches. The new circuit had a staff of four full-time ministers and a lay pastor who was stationed at Queen's Road. At the time, the cost of a full-time minister was reckoned to be £340 per year, while the lay pastor cost £200 per year. Half of the cost of the lay pastor was paid by the circuit, while the remaining £100 came from the Home Mission Committee. Following the deduction of the circuit's contribution towards the lay pastor, this left the circuit with an income of £1,170. The cost of the four full-time ministers was £1,360, which, when deducted from the circuit income, left a deficit of £190. This could not be sustained and so it was proposed to reduce the number of full-

Table 9.9: Income and expenditure of the Great Yarmouth and Gorleston Methodist Circuit churches in 1938.

Income		Expenditure	
Former Temple Circuit	£640	Stipends	£960
Queens Road	£100	Levy	£140
Lowestoft Road and Caister Beach Road	£260	Manse rates	£90
High Street, Newtown, Lound, Burgh Castle	£270	Lay Pastor at Queen's Road	£100
Total income	£1,270	Total expenditure	£1,290

time ministers to three and appoint a probationary minister. The cost of a probationary minister was under £150 which allowed the circuit to continue without operating at a loss.

As table 9.6 shows, the new Great Yarmouth and Gorleston Circuit still had two villages that had two separate Methodist societies in them – Ormesby and Caister. This rather defeated the purpose of Methodist unification and so these societies were asked to consider how to join together to form single societies in Ormesby and Caister.

9.5.1 Merger of Ormesby societies

The ex-Wesleyan and ex-Primitive chapels in Ormesby were both relatively strong societies in their own right, with the ex-Wesleyan society having 14 members and the ex-Primitive society having 24 members in 1938. However, the two Ormesby societies were quite forward thinking and shortly after the formation of the new Great Yarmouth and Gorleston Circuit the two chapels amalgamated to form one society. The new society met at the ex-Wesleyan chapel for Sunday morning worship and at the ex-Primitive chapel for Sunday evening worship. At a meeting held in June 1938 a resolution was passed to make one set of trustees for the two chapels in Ormesby. Recommendations had also been made that the ex-Primitive chapel should become the single Ormesby Methodist Church. The choice of adopting the ex-Primitive chapel was based on four reasons:

1. The ex-Primitive society had a larger membership than the ex-Wesleyan society
2. The ex-Primitive chapel was larger and could hold both congregations
3. Moving to the former Primitive chapel would cause the least dislocation in terms of sentiment
4. The ex-Wesleyan chapel could become the school hall.

In 1942, an offer was made to buy the ex-Wesleyan chapel. However, the trustees declined this offer at their September meeting. This seemed to signal a revival of the ex-Wesleyan chapel, as by 1946 the trustees decided to re-open it for Sunday services, with the ex-Primitive chapel used by the Sunday school and for social events. A year later the trustees decided to raise funds to restore the ex-Wesleyan chapel. This continued through into 1949, culminating in a re-opening ceremony which was held on 27 October 1949. The photograph in figure 9.1 shows a Mrs Whitby re-opening the chapel and Rev Hughes

Figure 9.1: The re-opening ceremony at Ormesby (former Wesleyan) Methodist chapel on 27 October 1949. Mrs Whitby opened the chapel with Rev Hughes and Rev Newby presiding. (This picture has been included by kind permission of Archant)

and Rev Newby presiding. The ex-Primitive chapel was now no longer in use and was subsequently sold a few years later in March 1950 for £900. It is now a private house – see figure 4.14 on 73.

9.5.2 Proposed merger of Caister societies

At the time of Methodist unification, Caister had both ex-Primitive and ex-Wesleyan societies. These two societies entered into discussion of how to amalgamate and a recommendation was made to make the ex-Primitive chapel on Yarmouth Road the single Methodist church in Caister. This was based on its better location in the village, being situated along the main road, in comparison to the ex-Wesleyan chapel which was considered too far out of the way at its site near to the beach. It was also advised that £1,000 would be needed to pay for improvements to the ex-Primitive chapel. These recommendations were not adopted and it wasn't until 1979 that the two chapels actually joined – see chapter 13 for more details.

Chapter 10

The Closure of Dene Side and the Central Hall – 1938

10.1 Introduction

The 1930s were a difficult time for Methodism in Great Yarmouth. Two of the largest churches in the town, Dene Side and Regent Road, were facing severe financial problems. Coupled with this, the Methodist Uniting Conference that took place in 1932 had resolved to merge the Wesleyan, Primitive and United Methodist churches into a single Methodist Church. At this time, Great Yarmouth and the wider East Norfolk area had five circuits that this would ultimately affect. Both of these problems would lead to major changes to the structure of Methodism in East Norfolk, particularly in Great Yarmouth.

This chapter focuses on the problems faced by Dene Side Methodist church which eventually led to its closure in 1937. The story continues, however, with the building of a new Central Hall in the town centre to replace Dene Side. This played a major role in Great Yarmouth Methodism for over 50 years.

10.2 Closure of Dene Side Methodist Church

The prosperity of Dene Side Methodist church had been in decline for many years and by the mid 1930s the society was in severe financial difficulties. The church had debts of £2,000 and was being financed by just a few of its elderly members. The seriousness of this financial position was reported formally by the Superintendent Minister of the Dene Side Circuit, Rev Harper, in a letter to the Chairman of the East Anglia District, Rev Heap, in November 1936. Rev Harper considered Dene Side's problems to be so severe that he raised the possibility that the church might have to be sold. An offer of £25,000 for the church had been made by developers who had plans to demolish the building and replace it with a retail development.

The 1932 Methodist Uniting Conference further complicated Dene Side's situation. Four years after the conference, in 1936, Great Yarmouth still had three separate circuits as no local unification had yet taken place. This issue of unification also needed to be considered when deciding on the future of Dene Side, which was the main church of the Wesleyan Methodists in Great Yarmouth.

10.2.1 Mr Joseph Rank and options for Dene Side

One proposal, made in 1936, was that the three Methodist circuits in Great Yarmouth should merge to form a single circuit and that Dene Side be used as a Central Mission, independent from the merged Great Yarmouth circuit. In late 1936, Rev Heap approached Mr Joseph Rank, the cinema mogul and generous Methodist supporter, about a scheme to convert Dene Side into a Central Mission. This would cost approximately £10,000. Mr Rank was not very supportive of the scheme, commenting that he thought the days of missions were past – in his words "brought about by the modernist ideas of many ministers!" However, he did say that he was not familiar with the Great Yarmouth area. Mr Rank offered an alternative suggestion, which was to sell the Dene Side church building and build a new church close to where the people of Great Yarmouth were based. This formed a second proposal which was to sell Dene Side and use the money to build up a new merged circuit. A third proposal was to sell Dene Side and use the proceeds to buy the Congregational church that was on King Street in the town centre. This church had been built in 1855 and could seat 825 people, making it large enough to accommodate the Dene Side congregation. At this time there were two Congregational churches in the town, the other being on Middlegate Street. The King Street Congregationalists were planning to join with their Middlegate brothers, and selling their church to the Methodists would give them an ideal opportunity to do this. Figure 10.1 shows the former Congregational church on King Street in about 1900.

The suggestion made by Mr Rank of building a church near to where the people lived had been considered a few years earlier in 1934. A lease had been taken out on a building plot in the new suburbs in the northern part of Great Yarmouth. This was known as plot number 4,437 and was on the north-west corner of Beatty Road and Beresford Road. It appears that some of the Methodist societies in the town would not make a formal commitment to develop the site. This led to the Town Hall sending several letters enquiring as to whether building work on the proposed new chapel would ever be started. Eventually, a final letter was sent on 12 October 1934 to Rev G Jackson stating that this was the last day building work could start before the lease would expire. Clearly no building work ever took place and plot number 4,437 was subsequently developed for housing.

The favoured scheme of the trustees was the first option which was to convert Dene Side into a Central Mission and correspondence was entered into with the Department for Chapel Affairs to do this. They, however, were not supportive of the proposal and in a letter sent by them in January 1937 they questioned "whether there is enough power in Great Yarmouth Methodism to build a Central Hall and use it as a Central Mission." The department also preferred using Dene Side as the Central Hall, and they considered moving to the Congregational church a "poor second best." A further letter, sent by the department in February 1937, raised more concerns as they thought that the proposed scheme had fallen through. They advised not to lose Dene Side, but stated that "the people of Great Yarmouth cannot have everything done for them and need to take action."

Figure 10.1: The upper picture shows the former King Street Congregational church in about 1900. The lower picture was taken in 2008 and shows the building as Christchurch, which it has been since 1990. (The top picture has been included by kind permission of Norfolk County Council Library and Information Services).

10.2.2 King Street Congregational Church

The high costs of converting Dene Side into the Central Mission eventually led to the proposal being abandoned. Preference was now given to the third option, which was to sell Dene Side and move to the Congregational church. By early 1937 the Deacons at the King Street Congregational church had agreed on a purchase price of £10,000. The scheme could now be finalised and this involved selling Dene Side and the associated school rooms to a developer for £25,000. This provided funds to buy the Congregational church, the Gourlay School on Dene Side and the house adjoining the church. The total cost of the scheme, which included liquidating Dene Side's debts, was expected to be about £23,000. The remaining £2,000 from the sale was to be devoted to consolidating Methodism in Great Yarmouth following unification.

The last service at Dene Side was held on 26 September 1937 and was conducted by Rev Stanley Parker. After its closure, the church was soon demolished to make way for the new retail development. Figure 10.2 shows two pictures of the church being demolished. Many artefacts from the closed Dene Side church were given to other churches in the area with Lowestoft Road Methodist church in Gorleston benefiting most, largely as this was also a former Wesleyan Methodist church. The pews from Dene Side replaced the old wicker-style chairs at Lowestoft Road and the communion table, chairs and the Wesley pulpit were also transferred and are still in use there today.

Figure 10.2: Demolition of Dene Side Methodist church in about 1937. The men are working high up on the walls and are using pickaxes to demolish the church – a scene long gone since the introduction of health and safety laws! The site was soon to become a retail development and is now the location of the Great Yarmouth branch of BHS.

10.3 Building the Central Hall

Although Dene Side closed in September 1937 it would be six months before the new Central Hall was completed and ready for worship. During this time the Dene Side congregation used both the Regent Road Methodist church and the cinema on Regent Road for worship, as they were both only a short walk away. The Regent Road Methodist church had closed only a year earlier and made an ideal temporary location for worship – chapter 9 describes this in more detail. Congregations were huge at this time and it was not uncommon for 1,400 people to attend, which led to "Church Full" notices having to be placed outside!

Figure 10.3 shows an early illustration of the proposed front of the new Central Hall. The plan differs very little from the original Congregational church with the exception of a new porch over the main entrance doors.

Figure 10.3: Illustration of the proposed new Central Hall, based on the existing King Street Congregational church.

The transformation work to convert the Congregational church into the new Central Hall was extensive. The building was re-seated with modern tip-up seats that were upholstered in blue. This gave the interior a cinema-like appearance although the inside was finely decorated. Figure 10.4 shows an advertisement for the seating contractors, WW Turner and Co. of London, who appear proud to have been awarded the contract to install their seats in the new Central Hall.

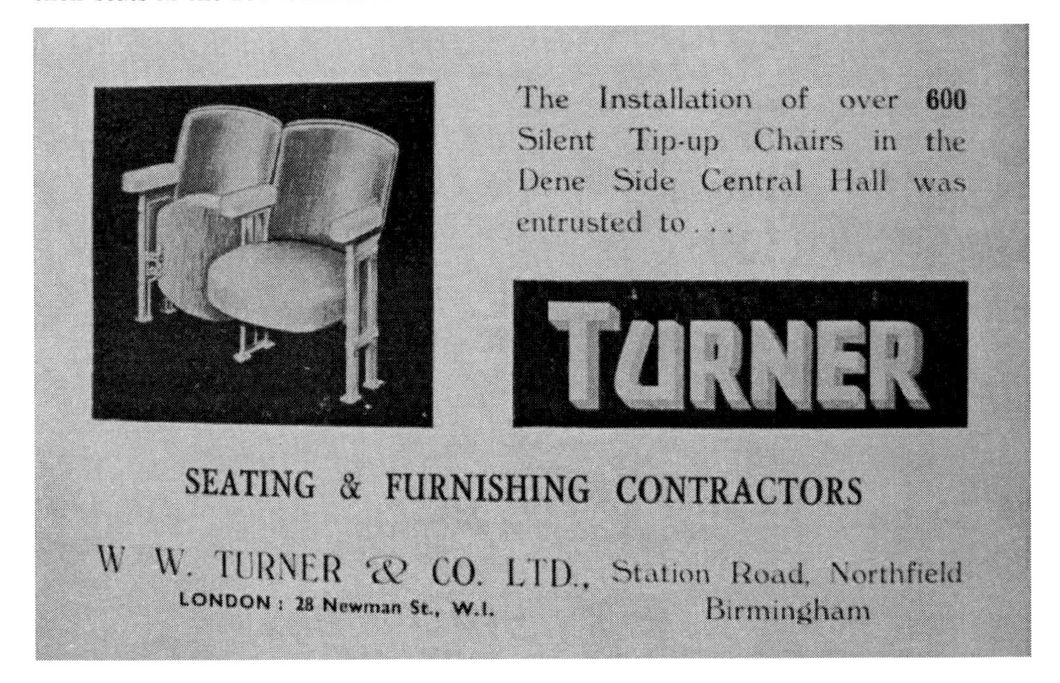

Figure 10.4: An advertisement for the tip-up seats installed in the new Central Hall by WW Turner and Co.

The original pulpit in the Congregational church was replaced with a new platform which could accommodate about 40 choir members. The original oak choir seats in the Congregational church were made redundant as they were also replaced by the new tip-up seats. The pews were removed and installed at Ormesby Methodist chapel, as a gift from the Congregational church trustees. Figure 10.5 shows the choir seats after their removal from the church, ready for installation at Ormesby.

A new Compton organ was installed which was the latest of its kind and said to be the most up-to-date organ in Great Yarmouth. The pillars and railings of the old church remained, but the railings were lowered by five inches to give the congregation a better view of the hall and platform. In total the new Central Hall could accommodate about 700 people, which was slightly less than the 825 seats that had originally been fitted when the Congregational church was built. Figure 10.6 shows the inside of the building in its three guises – as King Street Congregational church, as Central Hall and finally as Christchurch which it became in 1990. In all three pictures parts of the grand central arch at the back of the church are visible, although the layout of the inside is very different in all three incarnations.

The newly acquired Gourlay School was only a short walk away along Dene Side and this was converted into a large building to hold the Sunday school, young peoples' meetings and other social and fellowship activities. The building was extensively redeveloped and had a complete new storey added for billiards, table tennis and other indoor games. Rooms

Figure 10.5: The original oak choir seats from the King Street Congregational church. These were removed during the conversion to Central Hall and were replaced by cinema-style tip-up seats. The original seats were installed at Ormesby Methodist chapel as a gift from the Congregational church trustees.

were also furnished for the Sunday school with each room having a piano. A service lift was even added to connect each floor with the ground-floor kitchen to make tea parties less difficult for the helpers. The main Sunday school room could hold over 100 people.

The total cost of acquiring the Congregational church, adjoining house and Gourlay School, and the conversion work came to £26,056. The fund for developing the new Central Hall contributed £25,147 which represented the vast majority of the money. Other sources of income contributed £810 while a "Chair Fund" contributed a further £78. The Chair Fund was the idea of Mr Bedford, who was a director of Arnolds department store in Great Yarmouth. Mr Bedford suggested that as the members of the Central Hall had not been asked to contribute towards the conversion, it would be reasonable to ask them to make donations towards the chairs.

10.4 Opening of the Central Hall

The new Central Hall opened on 7 April 1938 and the souvenir programme proclaimed "We hope to make the Central Hall the spiritual home of the multitudes in Yarmouth. It will indeed be 'the Church of the Happy Welcome.' " The opening of the new Central Hall was a momentous occasion for Great Yarmouth and during the day three ceremonies were held with dignitaries attending from across the circuit, district and connexion. Figure 10.7 shows the newly completed Central Hall.

The opening ceremony began in the Sunday school rooms where the crowd was so large that Dene Side was blocked. The main doors were unlocked by Mr E Ernest Palmer who was presented with a golden key by Mr A Brocklehurst, who was at the time a leading

Figure 10.6: Three views of the inside of the Central Hall building showing the grand arch at the back. The upper picture is from the King Street Congregational church taken before 1937. The middle picture is of the Central Hall in about 1960. The lower picture shows it as Christchurch in 2008.

Figure 10.7: Dene Side Central Hall pictured in about 1938 after the opening celebrations.

Methodist architect. Mr H W Larke, the senior superintendent of the Sunday school, introduced Mr Palmer and declared "We are making history here, and if our young people put their backs into it I believe we will accomplish a great deal."

The crowd then moved to the new Central Hall where the door was unlocked by Mr A Phillips of Cromer who was introduced by Mr E F Keable. Mr Keable also praised Mr Brocklehurst and the building contractors Moore and Son. In his address, Mr Phillips praised "these courageous people" for their decision to sell Dene Side and purchase a new building. A dedication service was then preached by Rev Dr F L Wiseman (who was a Doctor of Divinity and a Doctor of Letters) who was one of the most prominent Methodists in the country and a member of the Chapel Committee which was responsible for the organisation of Central Missions. Also present were Rev Colin A Roberts, the Chairman of the East Anglian District, and Rev A Stanley Parker, the Minister of the Central Hall.

In the evening the Deputy Mayor, Mr H T Greenacre, presided at a meeting and gave an address where he paid tribute to the work done by Mr Keable. Mr Coleman, the chapel steward, praised Mr Keable for being the driving force behind the whole scheme. In response, Mr Keable said, "Whatever I have done has been a thank offering to Dene Side, for everything I have I owe to Dene Side."

Coinciding with the opening of Central Hall, the three Methodist circuits in the town united to form a single circuit. This was with the exception of the new Central Hall which operated separately as a central mission. Figure 10.8 shows Rev A Stanley Parker along with trustees and circuit stewards from Central Hall.

Figure 10.8: The trustees, circuit stewards and Rev Stanley Parker from the Central Hall, taken sometime between 1938 and 1941.

Chapter 11

The Second World War and its effects – 1939 to 1960

11.1 Introduction

The Second World War caused huge disruption to Methodist life in East Norfolk. The urban nature of Great Yarmouth and Gorleston, combined with their closeness to mainland Europe, made them a frequent target for enemy bombing. During 1941, bombing raids were taking place on average every two days, making Great Yarmouth and Gorleston one of the most heavily attacked parts of the country. Much damage to property was inflicted on the two towns and a large number of Methodist churches suffered substantial bomb damage. In the wider East Norfolk area, attacks were less concentrated, although several chapels outside of Great Yarmouth and Gorleston were damaged and forced to close temporarily whilst repairs were carried out.

This disruption forced many congregations to move to other churches or into temporary buildings for worship. In many cases the moves were short-term and the congregations returned once repairs had been made, either during or after the war. However, for four Methodist churches –Queen's Road and the Tower Street Mission in Great Yarmouth, and Nile Road and High Street in Gorleston – the damage was so severe that they never did re-open after the war. Combined services between churches also became common practice, particularly when one of the churches was damaged and had limited facilities.

The effect of bombing was devastating for both individuals and congregations. However, the permanent closure of some Methodist churches did in some ways help Methodism. Just before the war in 1938, Great Yarmouth had three separate circuits. Following their merger into a single circuit, there was much over-provision of churches. For example, in Great Yarmouth alone there were five Methodist churches which was many more than needed, given the number of people attending services. This spread very thinly the limited number of ministers and funds that were available to such an extent that it became difficult to operate effectively. Closing some of these churches, to consolidate Methodism in the area, would not have been an easy task given the emotive attachment that members had to their own churches. However, the permanent closure of several churches as a result of enemy bombing helped to focus Methodism into a more compact circuit in Great

Table 11.1: The 18 churches in the Temple Circuit and the three churches in the Central Hall Circuit, first in 1938 and then in 1943. Note – by 1943 the two societies at Ormesby had united to form a single society. Symbol * is used when membership information is not known.

Temple Circuit	1938	1943	Central Hall Circuit	1938	1943
Temple	152	171	Central Hall	*	*
Queen's Road	54	52	Tower Street	38	30
Newtown	58	*	Cobholm	51	40
Scratby	24	*			
Great Ormesby	38	*			
Runham	12	*			
Filby	17	*			
Stokesby	22	*			
Caister Yarmouth Road	29	*			
Caister Beach Road	34	*			
Lowestoft Road	128	129			
Nile Road	35	34			
High Street	74	75			
Beccles Road	54	51			
Belton	29	29			
Bradwell	37	34			
Lound	21	20			
Burgh Castle	18	14			

Yarmouth. In Great Yarmouth and Gorleston, a benefit that the war had on Methodism was that it indirectly provided funds to build the Magdalen Way Methodist church. War damage insurance payments from several of the damaged churches were collected together and this formed the majority of the money needed to establish a Methodist church on the new Magdalen Estate in Gorleston.

The church at Magdalen Way wasn't the only new church to be opened in the post-war period. At both Potter Heigham and Horsey the societies moved from their old chapels into new church buildings that were designed to be more functional.

The remainder of this chapter tells the story of Methodism in East Norfolk during the Second World War and the effects of this after the war.

11.2 Damage and closure of churches during the war

One of the first changes to the organisation of Methodism during the war was that both the Cobholm Mission and the Tower Street Mission were moved out of the Temple Circuit linked with the Central Hall. This created a Central Hall Circuit which comprised three churches and reduced the size of the Temple Circuit to 18 churches. Table 11.1 shows the churches, and their memberships, that made up the two circuits in 1943. For comparison, membership numbers from 1938 are included.

Enemy bombing during the Second World War caused disruption to over ten Methodist churches in East Norfolk, leading to either their temporary or permanent closure. The damage sustained by four churches, two in Great Yarmouth and two in Gorleston, was so severe that they never did re-open. Towards the end of 1941 the Tower Street Mission was damaged by enemy bombing. This rendered the building unsuitable for worship and services were suspended. Most of the congregation continued worshipping at the Central Hall which was only a short walk away and also in the same circuit. The Queen's Road church also suffered severe bomb damage. This, combined with the fact that many of the members of Queen's Road had been evacuated, meant that services were no longer viable and so the church was closed. Originally this closure was planned to be temporary, but as section 11.3.2 explains, this was not the case and the church never did re-open. In Gorleston, both Nile Road Methodist church and the High Street Methodist church were badly damaged by bombing and were forced to close. The congregation at Nile Road had already been having joint services with Lowestoft Road Methodist church, which was only about a quarter of a mile away. After the closure of Nile Road, the congregation continued worshipping at Lowestoft Road. A similar arrangement was made by the High Street members, who joined with the nearby Beccles Road Methodist church for joint services.

Many other churches also suffered damage during the Second World War and were forced to make alternative arrangements. Many different solutions were tried and these included temporarily moving into their schoolrooms or to another building elsewhere. Newtown Methodist church was badly damaged early on in the war and services there were suspended by the middle of 1941. Services did resume in the adjacent schoolroom shortly afterwards and joint services were also held with the Temple church, where morning services were held in one church and evening services in the other. In addition to the Newtown church being rendered inoperable, the organ was also damaged by the bombing. Cobholm was another Methodist society that experienced similar bomb damage and associated problems during the war.

Further away from Great Yarmouth, some village churches were also affected by bombing. In Caister, the Beach Road Methodist chapel was badly damaged by bombing which caused some of its windows to be blown out and also damaged its ceiling. The Sunday school was able to continue operating at the premises, although for worship, the Beach Road congregation attended the Yarmouth Road Methodist chapel (former Primitive society) in Caister. The Yarmouth Road chapel was itself damaged by bombing, but the damage was less serious than at the Beach Road chapel. Further out into the country, Runham Methodist chapel was damaged by enemy action. Although there were no direct hits to the chapel, several bombs exploded nearby and caused some structural damage to the building.

By the end of the war, the two circuits in Great Yarmouth (Temple and Central Hall) had both seen some of their churches permanently closed. The Temple Circuit was reduced from 19 churches in 1938 to 15 churches in 1945 (although the chapel lost at Ormesby was not lost as a result of war damage, but from the two Ormesby societies merging). The Central Hall Circuit was reduced from three churches in 1938 to two churches in 1945. For the two rural circuits in East Norfolk – Acle and Martham – whilst having chapels that experienced bomb damage and disruption, neither lost any chapels and their lists of societies remained the same. In fact, the Martham Methodist Circuit actually benefited from some effects of the war. The airfield at Ludham was missioned by the Martham circuit and a society known as Ludham Airfield appeared on preaching plans. Figure 11.2 lists the societies in the Martham circuit in 1949 where the airfield society is seen to have

Table 11.2: List of societies and membership in the Martham Methodist Circuit in 1949.

Society	Membership
Martham	54
Hemsby	29
Thurne	27
Catfield	26
Rollesby	18
Winterton	29
Repps	20
Potter Heigham	27
Fleggburgh	9
Horsey	16
Ludham High Street	26
Ludham Johnson Street	19
Ludham Airfield	6
Somerton	9
Total	315

a membership of six. This meant that, at the time, Ludham actually had three Methodist societies – High Street, Johnson Street and Airfield. Another link with the war occurred at Catfield, where prisoners of war would regularly come to the chapel and perform duets for the congregation!

11.3 Closures after the war

Once the war ended, plans were introduced to start the process of repairing and re-opening the damaged churches. Many of the societies were fortunate in that the damage sustained to their buildings was not too severe and they could be repaired and opened in a relatively short time. However, for some of the other buildings the damage proved to be so serious that the societies were never to be re-opened. This was the case for the Tower Street Mission and Queen's Road churches in Great Yarmouth, and for the Nile Road and High Street churches in Gorleston.

11.3.1 Tower Street Mission

Towards the end of the war, in February 1945, the trustees of the Tower Street Mission held a meeting at the Central Hall in Great Yarmouth. The meeting heard that there was no possibility of the building being used as a mission at the present time because of the seriousness of damage to the building. As an alternative use for the building, a suggestion was made that the premises could be used as a youth centre. However, later investigations into seeking a war damage insurance claim revealed that payments would only be available if the premises were to be used for religious worship and not as a youth centre. This put an end to the consideration of developing a youth centre with the existing building.

In 1951 an estimate of £1,849 was provided by builders R Carter for repairing and restoring the mission building. This was submitted to the War Damage Commission to seek an insurance claim, but they stated that not enough first-aid repairs had been carried out after the initial bomb damage. Their insurance offer reflected this and was only for the sum of £1,013. At a later trustees' meeting in 1951, the trustees decided that raising the deficit of £836 to restore the building would not be possible and so it was decided to permanently close the Tower Street Mission.

By 1952 the building had deteriorated and was in a very poor state of repair, with several complaints having been made about its unsightly appearance. The only option now left for the building was to demolish it and this was carried out by a Lowestoft firm free of charge. However, in clearing the site they left a large hole where the building had stood. A letter was sent by Great Yarmouth's Borough Engineer saying that the site was dangerous and needed filling in. To avoid having to devote any more effort and money to the site, it was sold to Great Yarmouth Borough Council for £10. The trustees made a request that the war damage insurance money be ported to the new church being built at Magdalen Way in Gorleston. At the final trustees' meeting for the Tower Street Mission, on 8 July 1955, the Superintendent Minister, Rev Trevithick, reported that the War Damage Commission would not port the money to Magdalen Way, but they would allow it to be spent on new toilets at Central Hall. In light of this strange decision, Rev Trevithick agreed to speak to the War Damage Commission to see if this decision could be changed. Records suggest that this decision stood.

11.3.2 Queen's Road

The Queen's Road church in the southern part of Great Yarmouth had been badly damaged during the war and was closed. After the war, in September 1946, plans were drawn up by Norwich architect Mr Clifford Dann for rebuilding the Queen's Road church. The plans were for a church that could hold 247 people, which included provision for a 25 person choir. This was considerably less than 550 person seating capacity of the original church, but the new building was also planned to contain a hall, classrooms, vestry and toilets. At a trustees' meeting held in early 1948 it was decided not to proceed immediately with the scheme, but instead wait for war damages insurance payment and also to consider moving the church to another site. The estimated cost of repairing the Queen's Road church was £6,600. However, the financial situation at Queen's Road was not strong and the society had a debt of £310 on which £123 of interest had accumulated. No repayments on the debt had been received since 1941. Suggestions were made that the debt could be paid from the money raised from the sale of the Regent Road Methodist church in Great Yarmouth, although this was subsequently not sanctioned by the Department for Chapel Affairs. At a trustees' meeting early in 1950 it was agreed that the church should be re-established in that part of Great Yarmouth and also provide a Sunday school, a women's meeting and other fellowship activities. However, only 12 members remained from the original church. The majority of these were at least middle-aged and concerns were raised as to whether these remaining members could establish a new church there by themselves.

By 1950 no progress had been made on the scheme and the building was becoming dangerous, with slates falling from the roof. The situation deteriorated further and on 31 October 1950 a police constable was called to Queen's Road by local residents who reported hearing the roof collapse. Neighbours Mr Palentine and Mr Tate, who lived on either side of the church, also complained that masonry was continually falling from the building. The Great Yarmouth Borough Engineers' Office sent a report to the minister saying that the noise heard previously was in fact part of the plaster ceiling falling down, rather than the roof collapsing. The Borough Engineer did, however, report that the front gable was loose. In December 1950 further problems with the building were reported in a letter from the Borough Engineer to Mr Clifford Dann. The letter requested that the front of the church be fenced off to safeguard the public. If not, the church authorities would be served with a Dangerous Buildings Notice, which the Borough Engineer wished to avoid. Another letter was sent to Mr Clifford Dann by the Borough Engineer in May 1951 as the ceiling was beginning to fall in, causing considerable noise and disturbance to the neighbours. Although the fencing around the church had prevented danger to the public, it was claimed that the noise had caused a loss in revenue for some of the local residents who ran guest houses.

Negotiations with the War Damage Commission at the end of 1953 resulted in a good-size settlement for the church. Although the seating capacity had previously been for 550 people, in recent times that size of congregation had not been seen at Queen's Road. Instead, the War Damage Commission offered to provide money to rebuild a church capable of seating 250–300 people, in addition to providing for facilities such as toilets, a vestibule and organ. They also agreed that this new church did not have to be built on the Queen's Road site. The resulting insurance payment went towards the new Methodist church at Magdalen Way in Gorleston.

As time went on, the structural condition of the building deteriorated still further and by early 1954 the main wall of the church was found to be unsafe. This left no option other than to demolish the building. This had costs associated with it, but with no funds at Queen's Road, the Gorleston area was asked to pay for these initial expenses and told that they would be reimbursed later, once the settlement from the War Damages Commission was received. The building was demolished later in 1954 and two houses now occupy the site – see figure 4.4 on page 59.

11.3.3 Nile Road

Following the closure of Nile Road Methodist church in Gorleston during the war, many members of the congregation transferred their membership to Lowestoft Road Methodist church. After the war, the congregation didn't return to Nile Road and no plans were put in place to repair and re-open the church. In October 1948 a group from the Gorleston Baptist Church enquired about buying the Nile Road church as the former Baptist church in Gorleston had been damaged during the war. A valuation was made by Great Yarmouth estate agents Gambling and Duffield (now Aldreds), who valued the building at £8,000 but suggested that a fair price to the Baptists would be £6,500. In November 1948 a letter was sent to the Department for Chapel Affairs that requested permission to sell the building to the Baptists. The sale never went through, with the Baptists subsequently building a new church at the northern end of Lowestoft Road. In 1949 the Church of England also enquired about buying the building, with plans to set up a new church in the southern part of Gorleston. Nothing became of this enquiry, although later in that same year the Baptists moved in temporarily while their new church was being built.

In November 1951 organ builders William Hill and Sons enquired into the purchase of the organ at Nile Road. They claimed that this had originally been at the Temple in Great Yarmouth and was moved to Nile Road in 1913. It appears that no sale took place, as a letter from the Department of Chapel Affairs in February 1955 expressed disappointment that the organ at Nile Road had been neglected. In May of 1958 the trustees of Nile Road were approached by the Elim Pentecostal Church with a request to rent the church for £150 per year for three years with an option to purchase the building for £2,200. The Department for Chapel Affairs responded to this request rather negatively, saying that it was not happy to sell the building to a "lesser sect!" Nevertheless, the building was leased to the Elim Pentecostal Church from 1958.

In 1961, the trustees for Nile Road met and decided once again to try to sell the building. They also proposed to have the lettering saying "Primitive Methodist Chapel" removed from the front of the building and from the foundation stones. As before, they were unsuccessful in selling the building but they were able to secure a lease to the commercial artists Repro Arts under the same agreement as proposed in 1958. At a trustees' meeting in April 1963 it was agreed to donate £500 to Lowestoft Road Methodist church which was to go towards their new heating system. The cost of this was estimated to be between £1,000 and £1,200, of which Lowestoft Road had only been able to raise £507.

On Sunday 13 January 1964 the premises were badly damaged by fire. Fortunately the buildings were insured for £4,500 and this was paid to have them repaired. In April 1966 Repro Arts approached the trustees and said that they wished to take up the option to buy the premises for £2,200, which was in the original lease agreement of almost ten years previously. This was now considerably less than the building was worth, given the repairs after the fire, but also, as stated by Repro Arts, from improvements that they had made to the building. The Department for Chapel Affairs was not pleased with the Nile Road trustees and sent them a letter in April 1966 saying that they had entered unwisely into the lease and option arrangement using the much earlier, outdated, figures. They were now in a deal that they could not get out of, with the result that the building was being undersold by about £4,000. The buildings were sold to Repro Arts in December 1967 for £2,200.

The building changed hands once again in 1978 when it was bought for £5,000 and leased to the Endeavour Rangers Marching Band. The building was opened for this purpose in June 1978 by the Mayor of Great Yarmouth, Mr George Scott. Several years later, in 1986, the Endeavour Rangers took out a loan of £4,500 from the Great Yarmouth Corporation and, combined with £3,000 of their own money, bought the building outright for £7,500. The building today remains the permanent home of the Endeavour Rangers, but is also used by other community groups.

As with so many Methodist churches that have now closed, many of their artefacts have been passed on to other churches. Two such items from Nile Road that are still in regular use are their communion jug and font, both of which were given to Lowestoft Road Methodist church. The communion jug is used regularly to dispense the wine when preparing for communion and the font is central to all baptisms at Lowestoft Road. Figure 11.1 shows the jug with the inscription "Nile Road Church, Gorleston-on-Sea, 1914" and beneath that, the font.

Figure 11.1: The communion jug and font from Nile Road Methodist church which are both now at Lowestoft Road Methodist church, since Nile Road's closure in the 1940s.

11.3.4 High Street

The High Street Methodist church in Gorleston was in a very poor state of repair after the war and a subsequent fire left the circuit very concerned over the future of the building. The structure soon became so weak that it had to be shored-up to prevent it from collapsing. Just after the war a decision had been made to build a new Methodist church in Gorleston on the new and expanding Magdalen Estate. To the High Street trustees, moving to this new church seemed a much better proposition than trying to rebuild the High Street church. A subsequent war damage insurance payment of £2,000 for the High Street church was put towards the new Magdalen Way Methodist church rather than rebuilding the High Street church. In 1959 the church, associated cottages and land were sold for £700. Part of this money was used to clear the debt outstanding on the building of Caister Methodist church. Following the sale, the High Street church was demolished and the site is now partly occupied by Gorleston Shopping Precinct. Figure 11.2 shows the damaged building, with the shoring-up necessary to keep the building standing clearly visible on the left-hand side. Outside the church, a sign directs people to the temporary church at Peterhouse School, prior to the opening of the new church on Magdalen Way.

11.4 Repairs and re-openings after the war

Many of the churches that had been damaged by bombing were not in such serious conditions as those described in the previous section that were forced to close. For these less damaged churches, following suitable repairs, they were able to be re-opened a few years after the end of the war in the late 1940s or early 1950s. Often, additional improvements were carried out during the repair work and the re-opening services were times for great celebration.

At Newtown Methodist church, which was damaged in 1941, much repair work was carried out. During the bombing the organ had been damaged and this was subsequently cleaned and repaired and the old hand-operated organ pump was replaced with a new electric pump. The original coloured windows were also replaced by clear glass. The restoration work was completed in 1949.

After the Second World War, the Temple also underwent considerable building work and redecoration and was in the hands of builders for some time. During this period the ceilings were renewed and moulded cornices were added, electric circuits were re-wired, the organ was renovated and cleaned and the whole church redecorated. When the work was complete, a rededication service was held at the Temple on Thursday May 25 1950 with the Rev Thomas Banks preaching.

At Cobholm Methodist church the cost of repairs and redecoration was £750, of which the members were expected to raise £300. This was a large amount of money for a relatively small society of 40 members and represented over £7 for each member. However, funds were raised and the work was completed. The church re-opened in May 1951.

War damage insurance was received by the Caister society but, in addition to this, a decision was made to increase the money in their Restoration Fund. Several local choirs were invited to perform at special events to raise money. These included the Martham Methodist Choir, the Lowestoft Road Choir and the Hickling Male Voice Choir. A rededication service was held at the Yarmouth Road chapel in 1949, with the Superintendent Minister asked to conduct the service and Rev William Howard of Acle invited as a special

Figure 11.2: High Street Gorleston Methodist church after its closure. The picture shows the shoring-up necessary to support the weakened structure. A sign can be seen hanging down from the front of the church – from the other side it reads "This church is closed. Services now held at Peterhouse Infants School every Sunday". This was just before the opening of Magdalen Way Methodist Church.

speaker.

The damage incurred by Runham Methodist chapel was repaired after the war and a re-opening and rededication celebration was held on Thursday 7 July 1949, led by the minister, Pastor Leonard G Jones. The re-opening ceremony was held in the afternoon and taken by Rev W Eastwood, who was the Superintendent Minister in the Great Yarmouth circuit. This was followed by a public tea in the schoolroom and a Grand Public Meeting. A similar event took place at Filby Methodist chapel where a re-opening and rededication service was held on Thursday 6 September 1951.

11.5 Three new churches

In the late 1950s three new Methodist churches were opened in East Norfolk – Potter Heigham in 1956, Magdalen Way in Gorleston in 1957, and Horsey in 1958. The new churches at Potter Heigham and Horsey were relocations of societies from earlier chapel buildings that had become outdated and lacked facilities, such as a schoolroom and vestry, and were generally not able to support the needs of more modern worship. Magdalen Way represented, in part, a relocation of previous societies, namely High Street and Queen's Road, both of which had lost their buildings – but was also an opportunity to establish a Methodist presence in the new Magdalen Estate in Gorleston.

The styles of the three buildings are similar, even through their respective sizes and shapes are quite different – see figures 11.3, 11.5 and 11.6 for pictures of the churches. The architect of all three was Mr Clifford Dann from Norwich, who also advised on the possible rebuilding of the Queen's Road Methodist church in Great Yarmouth. The design of the buildings is more functional than inspirational – presumably funds were limited in this post-war period, which prevented elaborate designs from being considered. The very fact that three societies were able to build new churches at this time is a credit to their leaders. It is interesting that in the space of 50 years the design of chapels had changed considerably. For example, the Methodist chapel at Repps had been built in 1907 and had a classic "chapel" look and was broadly the same as chapels that had been built many years before. The three new chapels built in the 1950s were very different. They had lost the chapel look and were less stylish, but they were more practical and offered the advantages of schoolrooms, less maintenance and easier access.

11.5.1 Magdalen Way

Housing in Great Yarmouth and Gorleston was undergoing significant change by the end of the Second World War. The war-damaged housing in the centre of Great Yarmouth, particularly the row houses, was being demolished and large housing estates in Gorleston were being built to accommodate the displaced occupants. One of the first housing estates to be built was the Magdalen Estate, which was built on land bought from Magdalen College, Oxford. To the Methodists of Great Yarmouth and Gorleston, this new estate would be an ideal location for a new Methodist church.

The scheme of building a new church on the Magdalen Estate replaced some of the earlier plans for rebuilding the bombed Queen's Road church in Great Yarmouth and the High Street church in Gorleston. The scheme gathered pace with the result that Methodism began on the Magdalen Estate in 1954. This took the form of a Methodist Sunday school which was opened at Peterhouse School and had upwards of 200 children

Figure 11.3: Magdalen Way Methodist church in 2007, which was opened on 26 September 1957.

in attendance. The scheme to build a church got underway when land was purchased on 11 June 1956 in an agreement between Rev Harry Harrison, and 19 other trustees, and the County Borough of Great Yarmouth. A plot of land was sold for £715 to the Great Yarmouth circuit that had a 110 foot frontage to Magdalen Way and a 90 foot frontage to Pembroke Avenue. The land had previously been bought by the County Borough of Great Yarmouth from the President and Scholars of the College of St Mary Magdalen of the University of Oxford on 1 July 1936.

The estimated cost of building this new church was stated as being £24,000 in a letter sent in October 1956 by the Department for Chapel Affairs. The cost of this development was met largely by the war insurance payments that the circuit had received for the Queen's Road and High Street churches, which amounted to £17,000. The Joseph Rank Benevolent Trust also made a generous donation of £3,000 and the Methodist War Damage and Rebuilding Fund agreed a grant of £2,000. Other donations were also received, including £200 from the Matthes family who were prominent bakers in the town.

The new church was designed by Mr Clifford Dann, the Norwich architect who had been involved in some of the plans to rebuild the Queen's Road church. The Magdalen Way church was designed to seat 150 people and to be connected by a wooden partition to a larger hall that could increase the seating capacity to 400. Two schoolrooms and a kitchen were also included in the design to support Sunday school activities. Figure 11.3 shows the church in 2007, taken from Magdalen Way.

Construction of the Magdalen Way Methodist church was completed in 1957 and an opening service was held on 26 September 1957. Figure 11.4 shows the opening ceremony taking place, with the key to the new church being handed over by architect Mr Clifford Dann. The church was dedicated by the Rev HJ Martin who was the newly appointed chairman of the East Anglia district and an address was given by Rev CL Tudor who was the secretary of the Methodist Home Mission department. At this time about £400 still needed to be raised in order to meet the target of £2,500 that had to be raised locally.

Figure 11.4: Opening ceremony of Magdalen Way Methodist church, Gorleston, on 26 September 1957. Mr Frank Spencer, who opened the new church, is handed the key by architect Mr Clifford Dann. Also present are Rev HJ Martin (Chairman of the East Anglia District), Rev CL Tudor (Methodist Home Mission Department), Rev H Harrison (minister of the new church) and Mrs KM Adlington (Mayor of Great Yarmouth). (This picture has been included by kind permission of Archant)

11.5.2 Potter Heigham

The first Methodist chapel in Potter Heigham was built in 1863 and this remained in use for many years. However, by about 1940 discussions were begun into building a new church that would be better suited to worship and a building fund was started. Through perseverance and faith, the Potter Heigham society had raised sufficient funds so that on Whit-Monday in 1955 a stone-laying ceremony was held for the new church. It was to be built on a large plot of land on Green Lane, about a quarter of a mile from the existing chapel. The architect for the new church was Mr Clifford Dann, who was also responsible for the design of Magdalen Way Methodist church in Gorleston.

Only one year later on May 16 1956 the new chapel was opened by Mrs DK Greenacre from Stalham. The opening ceremony was held at 4pm and was followed by a Dedicatory Service with the Chairman of the East Anglia District, Rev Alan Roughley, and Rev Deryck Collingwood from Birmingham. At 5:30pm a public tea was held and this was followed at 7pm by a Great Public Meeting, chaired by Mr Hubert Meadows from Old Brampton Hall. Figure 11.5 shows two pictures of the Potter Heigham church – the first taken during its construction in 1955/1956 and the second in 2009.

Mr WJ Playford, who was the Potter Heigham society's treasurer, gave an account of the fundraising. The new church had cost £5,600 to build and so far £4,750 had been raised. In addition to local fundraising the Joseph Rank Benevolent Fund had contributed £1,750 and the Chapel Committee £300. The Chapel Committee had also promised to pay the last £200 which left £650 to be raised. It only took two years to raise the remaining money and clear the debt on the new church. In celebration of this great achievement, Mr Playford wrote a 148-line poem, entitled "A church goes free."

11.5.3 Horsey

Towards the end of the Second World War the society at Horsey began to think that the current chapel was lacking some of facilities that they would like to have, such as a schoolroom and vestry. A piece of land adjacent to the chapel was subsequently bought to accommodate the proposed extension to the chapel. Plans were drawn up, but before building work started, the trustees decided that the scheme may not have been the best way forward. This was followed by much deliberation and delay before the Chapel Committee suggested that a better scheme might be to build a new chapel on a new site.

Land for the new chapel was acquired just off the B1159 road running through the village and close to the Anglican church. Building work began in June of 1958 and a stone-laying ceremony was held on 1 July of the same year. Building work progressed well and an Opening and Dedication Service for the new chapel was held on Wednesday 14 November 1958. The opening ceremony began at 4pm and the chapel was opened by Mrs J. Roughley of Norwich and dedicated by Rev Hubert J Martin who was the Chairman of the East Anglia District. A sermon was then preached by Rev William G Fielder of Lincoln. Following the opening ceremony a public tea was held at 5:30pm, followed by an evening rally at 7pm.

The chapel was designed by Mr Clifford Dann and built by JG Chase builders. Interestingly, one of the builders was the father of Mr Ken Saul who is currently (2009) a Methodist local preacher in the East Norfolk circuit. Figure 11.6 shows a picture of the chapel at Horsey in 2008. The following amounts were raised towards the cost of the new chapel:

- £2,000 Joseph Rank Benevolent Trust
- £500 Methodist Department for Chapel Affairs
- £500 offered for the old chapel and land
- £1,700 raised by members and friends of the society.

Figure 11.5: Potter Heigham Methodist chapel. The upper picture shows construction of the chapel in 1955/1956 while the lower picture shows the building in 2009. The chapel was opened on 16 May 1956.

Figure 11.6: Horsey Methodist chapel in 2008 which was opened on 14 November 1958.

Chapter 12

Closure of the Temple and a new Great Yarmouth and Gorleston Circuit – 1963

12.1 Introduction

By the early 1960s Great Yarmouth still had two separate Methodist circuits – the Temple Circuit and the Central Hall Circuit. Of more concern was the fact that both circuits had a large church in the centre of Great Yarmouth, namely the Temple on Priory Plain and Central Hall on King Street. These churches both had large memberships (98 at the Temple and 265 at Central Hall) but were located less than half a mile apart. The Methodist Conference did not think this was good for Great Yarmouth and proposed various plans to merge the two churches and circuits. This chapter describes the discussions that took place and the options presented to the two circuits for merging, with the result that, in 1963, the Temple closed and the two circuits merged to become the Great Yarmouth and Gorleston Methodist Circuit.

12.2 Proposed amalgamation of the Temple and Central Hall circuits

In 1961 a Methodist Conference Commission examined the situation of Methodism in Great Yarmouth and raised concerns that two large societies existed in the centre of the town. The Commission requested that immediate consideration be given to the making of "one strong, consolidated witness in the centre of town." In practical terms this meant a union between the Temple and Central Hall societies and ultimately the closure of one of these two churches. Matters were made more complicated by the fact that the two churches were in different circuits, with the Temple being the main church of the Temple Circuit and the Central Hall being the main church of the Central Hall Circuit. The East Anglia Methodist District also contributed to the discussion by advising that the union should extend beyond just the two churches and look to form a single circuit in Great

Table 12.1: The 16 churches in the Temple circuit (taken from the August 1963 plan), just prior to the closure of the Temple. The table also shows memberships and quarterly assessments of the churches.

Church	Membership	Assessment
Temple	98	£100.0.0
Newtown	67	£50.0.0
Scratby	20	£23.0.0
Great Ormesby	16	£18.0.0
Runham	17	£12.0.0
Filby	12	£10.0.0
Stokesby	11	£15.0.0
Caister Yarmouth Road	24	£17.10.0
Caister Beach Road	41	£32.10.0
Lowestoft Road	122	£130.0.0
Beccles Road	27	£25.0.0
Belton	12	£7.0.0
Bradwell	24	£25.0.0
Lound	12	£10.0.0
Burgh Castle	8	£8.0.0
Magdalen Way	116	£70.0.0
Total	627	£552.20.0

Table 12.2: The two churches in the Central Hall Circuit in 1961, just prior to the closure of the Temple, and their memberships.

Church	Membership
Central Hall	265
Cobholm	38
Total	303

Yarmouth. At the time of these discussions, the Temple Circuit comprised 16 churches and 627 members while the Central Hall Circuit had just two churches and 303 members. Tables 12.1 and 12.2 list the churches that made up the Temple and Central Hall circuits at that time. The tables also show the membership of each church and circuit and, for the Temple circuit, their quarterly assessment.

The Temple Circuit had a total membership of 627 which made it considerably larger than the Central Hall Circuit which had 303 members. The Temple Circuit had three full-time ministers as opposed to just one minister in the Central Hall Circuit. Below are listed the ministers of the two circuits, along with the churches that they looked after, and the location of their manses.

- *Central Hall Circuit*
  - Rev Eric Bilton, 12 Osborne Avenue, Great Yarmouth - *Central Hall, Cobholm*
- *Temple Circuit*

- Rev John Jackson, 6 Windsor Avenue, Great Yarmouth – *Temple, Newtown, Caister Beach Road, Caister Yarmouth Road, Scratby, Ormesby, Stokesby*
- Rev John White, 3 Clarence Road, Gorleston – *Lowestoft Road, Belton, Bradwell, Burgh Castle, Lound*
- Rev F Alan Cliff, 17 Exeter Road, Gorleston – *Magdalen Way, Beccles Road, Runham, Filby*

Rev Bilton at Central Hall only had two churches to look after and spent a sizeable majority of his time at Central Hall, preaching there most Sundays. In comparison, the ministers of the Temple Circuit had considerably more churches to look after, albeit with smaller memberships.

Representatives from the two circuits met many times, both informally and formally, over the next two years to try to work out how best to merge the two churches and circuits. The issue of closing either the Temple or the Central Hall was a highly emotive subject and led to much disagreement between the two circuits and churches. Eventually, to resolve the issues, a meeting of the District Redundancy Commission was called and this met in Great Yarmouth on 27 February 1963. After considering carefully all the viewpoints from the two circuits, the Commission recommended the following three proposals for consideration:

- *Proposal 1.* That the Temple Circuit and Central Hall Circuit amalgamate at the Methodist Conference in 1963.
- *Proposal 2.* That the two churches in the centre of Great Yarmouth, namely the Temple and Central Hall, unite and worship at the Central Hall.
- *Proposal 3.* That the Temple site be retained and that discussion should be commenced with regard to the building of a new church on a site unspecified.

These recommendations were to be reported to the District Synod in May 1963. In addition, the Redundancy Commission requested that the three proposals be discussed at the March Quarterly Meetings of the Temple Circuit and the Central Hall Circuit and the outcomes be reported at the May Synod.

12.2.1 Temple Circuit Quarterly Meeting

The Temple Circuit Quarterly Meeting was held on 6 March 1963. At this meeting, the circuit was in favour of the three proposals made by the District Redundancy Commission. For the first recommendation, 73 votes were in favour of the two circuits amalgamating, with no votes either against or neutral. Even the second recommendation of the Temple joining with the Central Hall and worshipping at Central Hall was largely approved, with 57 votes for and 16 against. This is rather surprising, given that this would mean the members of the Temple leaving their own church and worshipping elsewhere. The final recommendation of retaining the Temple and building a new church was again strongly supported, with 68 in favour and only five against. One of the reasons for the popularity of the third proposal was that the Temple could hold a congregation of 1,000 people while Central Hall had a much smaller capacity of 600. If the Temple site was lost it was thought that potential problems could arise with this reduced capacity when holding circuit rallies.

12.2.2 Central Hall Circuit Quarterly Meeting

The Central Hall Circuit Quarterly Meeting was held on 4 March 1963. The Central Hall Circuit was much less keen on amalgamation than the Temple Circuit had been. The Central Hall Circuit was very keen on remaining a separate central mission. They insisted that they could not carry on as central mission if they became part of an amalgamated circuit. Instead, they suggested that they remain a Central Hall and that a separate circuit be formed which covered the Gorleston area and the surrounding villages. Proposals were also considered which included joining with some or all of the Martham Methodist Circuit.

At the end of the meeting the Central Hall Circuit agreed on the second proposal which was to unite with the Temple and worship at Central Hall, and so form a strong consolidated church in the centre of Great Yarmouth. However, they were unable to accept the first proposal of amalgamating with the Temple Circuit and preferred to remain a central mission. The consensus of the meeting was that they wanted their ideas for amalgamation to go forward, but if not they wished to continue as they had been doing previously.

12.3 Closure of the Temple

The Temple Circuit's agreement of the Redundancy Commission's proposal of merging the Temple and Central Hall circuits had major implications for the Temple church. In a meeting at the Temple on 26 April 1963, the Temple trustees were resigned to the fact that the changes to the Temple and Central Hall circuits would mean closure of the Temple. In the meeting Mr J Duffield made the following proposal which was seconded by Mr Wagg:

"The Trustees of Temple Church, whilst regretting the necessity of closure, resolve in the light of all the circuits and in the interests of Methodist unity in Great Yarmouth, that Temple Church be closed for worship as from the end of October 1963, in accordance with the recommendation of the Circuit Quarterly Meeting, if the Synod approves the amalgamation of the circuits."

The following amendment to the proposal was then proposed by Mr Storey and seconded by Mr Brown:

"The Trustees of Temple Church resolve that, if the amalgamation of circuits takes place, Temple shall remain open for the time being, pending a decision concerning the building of a new church in central Yarmouth."

The trustees voted on both of these proposals with the result that the first proposal was carried five votes to two, with one neutral. The amendment proposed by Mr Storey was, however, rejected five votes to three. This officially signalled the end for the Temple. The Temple actually closed slightly earlier than proposed and held its final service on Sunday 27 September 1963.

After the Temple closed, the trustees received requests from several Methodist churches in the area for items from the church. A Temple trustees' meeting on 14 January 1964 agreed on the following distribution of items within the circuit:

- *Central Hall*
  - choir music, table cloths, plates and cutlery

- *Newtown*
  - 30 stacking chairs, communion table and chairs, pedestal, offertory plates, chest of drawers, BBC hymn books, four folding tables, Sunday school hymnals, piano, polished table
- *Lowestoft Road*
  - communion rail, children's chapel, notice board
- *Beccles Road*
  - chairs
- *Cobholm*
  - 30 stacking chairs, cross from communion table, two folding tables
- *Scratby*
  - small communion table, 23 stacking chairs, piano

The communion rail from the Temple is still in use at Lowestoft Road Methodist church, although not as a communion rail any more. The rail is shown in figure 12.1 along with a photograph of a small brass plaque which commemorates the fact that it came from the Temple.

The trustees 'meeting also discussed offers concerning future uses of the Temple. Bretts Furnishing had made a request to lease the Temple but this was rejected by the trustees. The Mobil Oil Company had also approached the trustees with a view to acquiring the building. It appears that the Temple had only a leasehold on the site and Mr Duffield was tasked with approaching the council to seek to purchase the freehold, presumably to allow it to be sold to the Mobil Oil Company.

The proposed sale did not go through and the Temple remained unsold for many years, gradually deteriorating. It was finally sold in 1972 to the Great Yarmouth Corporation for £12,500. The corporation had already taken possession of the Temple and begun to demolish it before the legal formalities of the sale had been completed, due to the dangerous condition of the building. The Rev Hammond supervised the sale of the Temple and, after expenses, the proceeds of the sale were shared as follows:

- £11,700 Circuit Advance Fund
- £710 Connexion Advance Fund
- £8 Grant refund

The new town centre relief road scheme, which was opened in 1982, passes through the site of the Temple. A competition was held in local schools to give a name to this new road. The name chosen was "Temple Road" which keeps memories of the Temple alive even today, many years after its closure.

Figure 12.1: The upper picture shows the former Temple communion rail which is now kept at Lowestoft Road Methodist church. Below is shown a brass plaque which commemorates the fact that the rail came from the Temple.

12.4 The new Great Yarmouth and Gorleston Circuit

Coinciding with the Temple's closure was the amalgamation of the Temple Circuit and Central Hall Circuit to form the new Great Yarmouth and Gorleston Methodist Circuit. This was formed on 1 September 1963 and was made up of the remaining 17 churches, which are listed in table 12.3 along with their membership numbers in 1965. The four ministers, Revs Bilton, Jackson, White and Cliff, who made up the ministerial team of the Temple and Central Hall circuits, now became the ministers of the new circuit, with Rev Eric Bilton the superintendent. The total membership of the new circuit in 1965 was 883. This was a sizable number and made the circuit the third largest in the East Anglia District

In addition to showing church memberships in 1965, table 12.3 also shows the memberships of the churches just before the merger and the resulting change in numbers. By 1965, after the Temple had been closed for two years, only 14 former Temple members had not yet transferred their membership. The remaining 84 former Temple members had either transferred their membership to a new church, or in some cases moved away,

Table 12.3: List of the 17 churches, and their memberships, in the Great Yarmouth and Gorleston Methodist Circuit in 1963 and 1965.

Church	Membership 1963	Membership 1965	Change
Ex-Temple	98	14	-84
Central Hall	265	232	-33
Cobholm	38	50	12
Newtown	67	92	25
Scratby	20	21	1
Great Ormesby	16	16	0
Runham	17	15	-2
Filby	12	13	1
Stokesby	11	11	0
Caister Yarmouth Road	24	25	1
Caister Beach Road	41	43	2
Lowestoft Road	122	126	4
Beccles Road	27	25	-2
Belton	12	12	0
Bradwell	24	25	1
Lound	12	6	-6
Burgh Castle	8	7	1
Magdalen Way	116	150	34
Total	930	883	-47

or died. The changes in membership numbers in the table suggests that the majority of members from the Temple transferred to Cobholm, Newtown or Magdalen Way. These churches all witnessed large increases in their membership shortly after the Temple closed – Cobholm increased from 38 to 50, Newtown increased from 67 to 92 and Magdalen Way increased from 116 to 150. The Gorleston churches (excluding Magdalen Way) and the village churches experienced only small changes in membership which suggests the former Temple members did not transfer to them. The drop in membership at Central Hall following the merger is rather surprising, as it would have been expected that some former Temple members would transfer there. This, apparently, was not the case.

To celebrate the formation of new Great Yarmouth and Gorleston Circuit, a circuit rally took place on Thursday 19 September 1963. The rally started in the Market Place at 7pm and progressed to the Central Hall for 7:30pm. Circuit buses were laid on to transport people from both Gorleston and Filby. The Chairman of the East Anglia District addressed the rally and a choir led the singing with Eldred Webster at the organ.

The Great Yarmouth and Gorleston Circuit remained in this form (albeit with several churches being closed – see chapter 13) until September 2007 when it merged with the Acle and Martham Methodist circuits to become the East Norfolk Methodist Circuit (see chapter 15).

Chapter 13

Centenaries, Closures and Christchurch – 1963 to 2007

13.1 Introduction

The period of Methodist history in East Norfolk from 1963 to 2007 can be characterised by three main events. First is centenaries. Many chapels in East Norfolk were built towards the end of the nineteenth century, making the period from 1963 to 2007 a time when they celebrated their centenary. For a chapel to survive for 100 years is a great event and worthy of celebration. The second major event was closures. Sadly, this period was also a time when a great many chapels were closed. From a total of 38 Methodist churches in East Norfolk in 1963, 19 had closed by 2007. Third, this period also saw the conversion of the Central Hall in Great Yarmouth into Christchurch. This was possibly the largest development in Methodism in East Norfolk since the Dene Side church closed and was replaced by the Central Hall in 1938. Several other building schemes also took place in this period and included new churches at Thurne and Acle, as well as smaller-sized building works.

Another development was the addition of several Methodist societies to the Acle circuit. The Methodist society at Lingwood joined the Acle circuit having previously been part of the Norwich Methodist Circuit. In 2003 the Loddon Methodist Circuit also joined with the Acle circuit. This brought three further societies into the Acle circuit – Loddon, Norton Subcourse and Broome.

In 1963 the Great Yarmouth and Gorleston Methodist Circuit had 17 societies, the Acle Methodist Circuit had nine societies and the Martham Methodist Circuit had 12 societies, making a total of 38 societies in the East Norfolk area. Tables 13.1, 13.2 and 13.3 list the societies that made up these three circuits and show how their memberships changed over the period 1963 to 2007. For societies that closed, the final column of the table shows their year of closure. Possibly the main feature of this period was the closure of so many of the smaller rural chapels. These were not just societies belonging to the Acle and Martham circuits, but also societies from the Great Yarmouth and Gorleston circuit. Out of a total of 28 rural societies in East Norfolk in 1963, only 12 remained by 2007. These more rural societies tended to have Primitive Methodist origins, which,

Table 13.1: List of churches and membership in the Great Yarmouth and Gorleston Methodist Circuit in 1965, 1974, 1996 and 2006.

Church	1965	1974	1996	2006	Closed
Central Hall/Christchurch	232	208	111	108	Open
Cobholm	50	36	x	x	1990
Newtown	92	79	65	28	Open
Scratby	21	12	8	7	Open
Great Ormesby	16	8	x	x	1979
Runham	15	10	x	x	1986
Filby	13	10	x	x	1987
Stokesby	11	6	6	x	2002
Caister Yarmouth Road	25	17	x	x	1979
Caister Beach Road	43	52	42	36	Open
Lowestoft Road	126	91	40	26	Open
Beccles Road	25	24	17	x	1996
Belton	12	9	x	x	1971
Bradwell	25	40	31	28	Open
Lound	6	x	x	x	1971
Burgh Castle	7	x	x	x	1972
Magdalen Way	150	124	70	74	Open
Total	869	726	390	307	

proportionally, experienced the greatest number of closures. Methodist societies from more urban places fared better than the rural societies. In 1963 the more urban areas of Great Yarmouth, Gorleston, Caister, Acle and Martham had a total of ten societies between them. By 2007, seven of these still remained. The three that closed (Cobholm, Beccles Road and Caister Yarmouth Road) were also all former Primitive societies, which again further reduced the number of ex-Primitive societies. In fact, of the 38 Methodist societies in East Norfolk in 1963, 26 were ex-Primitive. In 2007, only 12 former Primitive societies remained out of the 20 societies remaining.

The period also saw the demise of the ex-United Methodist societies to just one – Newtown – following closure of the societies at Lound and Burgh Castle in the early 1970s. The ex-Wesleyan societies fared much better. Out of six ex-Wesleyan societies in 1963 (Dene Side/Central Hall, Lowestoft Road, Caister Beach Road, Fleggburgh, Wickhampton and Ludham High Street) only one had closed by 2007 – Wickhampton. The reason for the longevity of the ex-Wesleyan societies is not easily explained. However, the Wesleyan chapels did tend to be situated in more prominent locations than the Primitive chapels, which may have made it easier for them to recruit new members and therefore keep going. The Wesleyan chapels were also, in general, better built than Primitive chapels, which may have led to them being retained rather than ex-Primitive chapels when it came to closing a society. In fact, several ex-Primitive chapels closed primarily because of problems with the fabric of the building. Beccles Road had problems with its roof, Belton had woodworm and Filby was blown down!

Table 13.2: List of churches and membership in the Acle Methodist Circuit in 1963, 1973, 1983 and 2007. Note – the societies of Lingwood, Loddon and Norton Subcourse joined the Acle circuit after the year 2000.

Church	1963	1973	1983	2007	Closed
Acle	39	50	56	57	Open
Upton	33	27	19	x	2001
Reedham	16	12	15	x	2001
Limpenhoe	20	14	9	x	1993
Freethorpe	82	66	56	37	Open
Halvergate	72	47	39	10	Open
Beighton	17	15	6	x	2005
South Walsham	25	18	10	x	1986
Wickhampton	16	10	5	x	1987
Cantley	–	4	12	x	1996
Lingwood	–	–	–	15	Open
Loddon	–	–	–	112	Open
Norton Subcourse	–	–	–	7	Open
Total	320	263	227	238	

Table 13.3: List of churches and membership in the Martham Methodist Circuit in 1967, 1979, 1986 and 2007.

Society	1967	1979	1986	2007	Closed
Martham	44	36	35	32	Open
Hemsby	36	25	21	9	Open
Thurne	31	38	44	31	Open
Catfield	36	36	36	17	Open
Rollesby	12	7	5	x	2001
Winterton	24	19	12	7	Open
Repps	17	11	10	x	2007
Potter Heigham	39	20	21	17	Open
Fleggburgh	7	2	12	6	Open
Horsey	22	16	12	8	Open
Ludham High Street	36	31	29	19	Open
Ludham Johnson Street	14	10	x	x	circa 1984
Total	318	251	237	146	

13.2 Centenaries

The period from 1963 to 2007 saw many Methodist centenary celebrations in East Norfolk. At the circuit level the year 1983 represented the centenary of both the Acle Methodist Circuit and Martham Methodist Circuit, both having been established in 1883 when they separated from the Great Yarmouth Primitive Methodist Circuit. Many chapels also celebrated their centenaries too, or had celebrations of even greater anniversaries. Catfield, for example, celebrated its 150th anniversary in 1986. Other societies celebrated other events, such as redecoration or other such happy occasions. This section describes a few of these celebrations that took place in East Norfolk.

13.2.1 Circuit centenaries

The Acle Methodist Circuit and the Martham Methodist Circuit had both become circuits in their own right in 1883, following proposals made at a meeting of the Great Yarmouth Primitive Methodist Circuit on 5 March of that year. This made the year 1983 the centenary of both of these circuits and both engaged in extensive activities to celebrate that fact.

When the Acle circuit was formed in 1883 it had nine chapels – Acle, Upton, Reedham, Limpenhoe, Freethorpe, Halvergate, Beighton, Stokesby and South Walsham – and three preaching places – Panxworth, Clippesby and Hassingham. One hundred years later the character of the circuit had changed little. Nine chapels still made up the circuit, albeit not exactly the same nine – Acle, Upton, Reedham, Limpenhoe, Freethorpe, Halvergate, Beighton, South Walsham and Wickhampton. Stokesby had been sold to the Wesleyan Methodists in the 1920s and Wickhampton moved into the Acle circuit from the Great Yarmouth Wesleyan circuit in the 1930s following Methodist unification. The original three preaching places had all gone, but a new preaching place at Cantley had been established more recently.

The Martham Primitive Methodist Circuit began in 1883 with 13 societies – Martham, Hemsby, Thurne, Catfield, Rollesby, Winterton, Repps, Hickling, Horsey, Somerton, Potter Heigham, Fleggburgh and Horning. One hundred years later, similar to the Acle circuit, the Martham circuit had changed little, now having 12 societies. Out of the original 13 societies, ten remained, with Hickling moving to the North Walsham Methodist Circuit and the Somerton and Horning societies closing. Two new societies joined, both at Ludham – Ludham High Street and Ludham Johnson Street. The Johnson Street chapel was built post-1883 and the High Street chapel was inherited from the former Great Yarmouth Wesleyan Methodist society during Methodist unification.

Acle began its centenary celebrations in 1983 by publishing a "Circuit Centenary Brochure." This included greetings and messages from several Methodist ministers who had been associated with Acle, and included Rev Norwyn Denny, President of the Methodist Conference, Rev G Eddy, Chairman of the East Anglia District, Rev Robert Austin, Superintendent of the Acle Circuit and other former ministers of the circuit – Rev Howard, Rev Deeks, Rev Cooper, Rev Nunnerley and Rev Jones. The year included many celebratory events, beginning in January with a United Circuit Service at Beighton. This continued with a concert by the Norfolk Male Voice Praises Choir, a celebratory dinner at Freethorpe, a flower festival at Acle and a United Centenary Service at Acle.

The Martham Circuit also began its centenary year with a "Centenary Celebration

Souvenir Programme" that contained various messages of goodwill. Three main celebratory events were planned for the year. First was a visit by the President of the Methodist Conference at Potter Heigham in May. Next was a circuit flower festival at Martham in July. Last was a circuit festival of praise at Horsey in August.

13.2.2 Chapel centenaries

The late nineteenth century was a time when the Wesleyan, Primitive and United Methodist movements were witnessing large numbers of people attending their services. To accommodate these big congregations many new churches were built, while others were enlarged. One of the results of this growth was that the period from 1963 to 2007 was a time when many chapels celebrated their centenaries. Each society celebrated in its own way, but all were common in their rejoicing, having made it to their centenary year. East Norfolk was no different from the rest of the country and the societies in this area held many centenary celebrations.

Lowestoft Road Methodist church in Gorleston was one of the first to celebrate its centenary in the period from 1963 to 2007. A centenary service was held on 20 April 1966 and was taken by Rev John Banks. A souvenir programme was produced with messages of greeting from various people including the President of the Methodist Conference, Rev W Walker Lee, and six ministers who had connections with the church. One of the messages was from Rev Jack Elliott who began worshipping at Lowestoft Road as a young boy and later became a Methodist minister. Rev Elliott wrote:

"Lowestoft Road Methodist Church was the location of my 'spiritual launching pad.' I was sent into the orbit of Christian service through the caring ministry of successive ministers and members. I learned to pray, play and say at Lowestoft Road and was never made to feel unhappy. My wife Edna and I were married there. We love the place and the people. Our good wishes for an outstanding Centenary celebration. We hope to be present."

'Use the present opportunity to the full, for these are evil days. So do not be fools, but try to understand what the will of the Lord is . . . and in the name of the Lord Jesus Christ give thanks every day for everything to our God and Father' (Ephesians 5, v 17–20 NEB).

Figure 13.1 shows the inside of Lowestoft Road Methodist church during what looks to be a flower festival, probably during the early 1960s.

A week after Lowestoft Road's centenary, the chapel at Rollesby had its centenary. This was held on 27 April 1966 and began with a gift service in the evening, followed by a circuit rally with Mr H Starkings of Catfield acting as chairman. Gifts were collected for the Rollesby Methodist Church Trust Fund. Easter of 1967 saw the High Street Ludham Methodist society celebrate its centenary, having originally opened as the Ludham Wesleyan chapel in 1867. The service was taken by Rev George Nunnerly who was superintendent minister of the Martham Circuit. As the years went on, society after society held its centenary celebration. In fact, a few chapels were able to celebrate even longer anniversaries, such as 125 years or even 150 years.

Hemsby Methodist chapel celebrated 125 years of worship in 2004 with an evening of praise, song and strawberries. A celebratory service was also held with Rev Stephen Yelland returning to take the service. Rev Yelland had previously been superintendent minister of the Martham circuit from 1985 to 1993. In 1986 the society at Catfield

Figure 13.1: The inside of Lowestoft Road Methodist church during what looks to be a flower festival. The precise date of the picture is unknown but it is probably from the early 1960s.

celebrated its 150th anniversary. This was a time for great celebration and a year-long programme of events was held. In March of that year the President of the Methodist Conference, Rev Christopher Hughes Smith, visited the chapel, and concerts, special services and a flower festival were also held.

13.3 Chapel closures

At the beginning of the period 1963 to 2007 East Norfolk had 38 active Methodist societies, but by 2007 19 had closed leaving just half of the original number. Rural areas were worst affected, although closures did also occur in some of the larger villages and towns. From 17 chapels in the Great Yarmouth and Gorleston circuit in 1963, ten chapels were to close by 2007. Eight of these were from the surrounding villages – Belton, Lound, Burgh Castle, Caister Yarmouth Road, Ormesby, Runham, Filby, Stokesby – and two were in towns – Beccles Road in Gorleston and Cobholm. The rate of closure in the Acle circuit was even worse, with seven out of ten societies closing in the same period – Upton, Reedham, Limpenhoe, Beighton, South Walsham, Wickhampton and Cantley. Closures in the Martham circuit were not as severe, with only three chapels closing out of 12 – Rollesby, Repps and Ludham Johnson Street.

For almost all the societies that closed, the main reason for closure was a declining membership. For an individual chapel this caused two problems. First, having fewer members reduces the income into the society which makes paying for the upkeep of the chapel more difficult as well as paying other bills, such as quarterly assessments. Second, it becomes more and more difficult to find people to take on important positions in the society – such as stewards, treasurer, organist and so on. The remainder of this section examines the closures of those societies in East Norfolk that closed between 1963 and 2007.

13.3.1 Belton, Lound and Burgh Castle

The late 1960s and early 1970s were bad times for several of the smaller Methodist societies to the south of Great Yarmouth. At Belton, in the mid 1960s, the membership of the society had fallen to 12, with only six members attending regularly on Sundays. Given no other choice, the superintendent minister responsible for Belton, Rev Povey, signed an Application to Close form on 21 November 1965. The form declared that those still worshipping would be able to transfer to the nearby Methodist chapels at either Burgh Castle or Bradwell. The building was sold in 1971 to Chartervale Properties Ltd for £600. Bungalows now occupy the site, one of which takes the name "Chapelfield."

The Methodist chapel at Lound experienced a declining membership in the 1960s and by 1968 the membership had reduced to just two brothers who were both in their eighties. Faced with a similar position to that at Belton, no other option was realistic, other than to make a request to close the chapel. On 22 October 1968 the District Home Missions committee accepted the request for closure of the chapel. The chapel closed in 1971 and by 1972 the chapel had been cleared and the key returned to the Water Board, from whom the chapel was rented. The pews from the chapel were sold for £21.50 and the proceeds were used to buy chairs for Bradwell Sunday school. The building still stands today and is used for storage, with a large, metal roller door installed at the rear.

A similar decline in membership happened at Burgh Castle Methodist chapel and this was closed on 2 January 1972. Later in that year a Mr Dowling offered £1,500 for the building on the condition that planning permission be granted to demolish it and build a house on the site. Unfortunately, planning permission was turned down by East Suffolk Planning Department and the sale did not go through. In October of the same year a Mr Hole sent a proposal to the circuit for converting the building into a DIY shop. This was again refused by East Suffolk Planning Department on the grounds that the building was too far in front of the building line and the road too narrow. They suggested the only future for the site would be to demolish the building and for the land be incorporated into the gardens of the neighbouring bungalows. Mr Hole then offered £250 for the building to use it for storage before its demolition. It was sold in 1972.

13.3.2 Caister Yarmouth Road and Great Ormesby

In the 1960s Caister still had two Methodist churches – the former Wesleyan chapel on Beach Road and the former Primitive chapel on Yarmouth Road. Discussions took place between the two societies in 1969 to consider amalgamating, but at that time no decision could be reached and the plan was left unresolved. This was an ongoing matter of discussion for the two societies, as similar discussions had been held in the 1950s, again to no avail. The matter resurfaced in the late 1970s and on 21 September 1978 a joint church council meeting, chaired by the Superintendent Minister, Rev Hoar, was held. The two societies were again asked to consider the future of Methodism in Caister. Amalgamation and moving to Beach Road was considered unsuitable due to the inaccessibility of Beach Road. Moving to Yarmouth Road was ruled out because of the small size of the chapel's grounds. Instead, two alternatives were proposed. The first was for the two societies to merge, sell their respective buildings and move to a new site in the village. Estimates put the cost of buying a site and building the new church at about £100,000. The second proposal was a joint scheme with Caister Parish Council. A new community centre would be built and the Methodist society would share this with the Parish Council, with some of the rooms used for worship. This scheme was estimated to cost between £25,000 and £30,000.

Neither of these options was ultimately implemented as in 1979 the former Primitive Methodist chapel on Yarmouth Road was closed, with most of its members transferring to the Beach Road society. The proposal of moving to a new site and building a joint church failed to materialise as it proved difficult to find a suitable site and also the funds associated with buying such a site. The proposal of a joint Methodist church and community centre was also pursued, with an old school on Beach Road considered a likely location. After lengthy discussions, Caister Parish Council decided against the scheme. The Yarmouth Road chapel was demolished in the following year and the site sold for £9,000. A new house now stands on the site.

Ormesby had been in a similar position to Caister in that it too once had both Wesleyan and Primitive Methodist chapels. However, these societies had merged much earlier than Caister, in 1938. By the 1970s, the remaining Ormesby society was in decline, and in the years from 1965 to 1974 had seen its membership halve from 16 to eight. This left few options for the Ormesby society, other than to close. Following closure, the chapel remained empty for several years until it was bought by the Ormesby Baptists in the early 1980s for £4,000. A more modern porch has been added to the front of the chapel, and the building is still used by the Ormesby Baptists – see figure 3.13 on page 50.

The money raised from the sale of the Ormesby chapel, together with proceeds from the sale of the Yarmouth Road chapel in Caister, were used to pay for an extension to the Beach Road chapel in Caister. A foundation stone for the new extension was laid in 1980, the stone having previously been a foundation stone at the Yarmouth Road chapel. The extension was completed in 1981 and opened by Mrs Rosa Russell and Mrs Bertha Would.

13.3.3 Filby, Runham and Stokesby

For eight years, following the closure of the chapel on Yarmouth Road in Caister, no Methodist chapels in the Great Yarmouth and Gorleston circuit were closed. However, this changed unexpectedly during the gales of October 1987 when the chapel at Filby was blown down. This was a particularly severe shock to the society, and to the wider Great Yarmouth circuit, as insurance payments on the chapel had not been paid. This left the circuit with very little to salvage from the ruins. Rebuilding the chapel was not a viable possibility due to the high costs involved. This left no alternative but to sell the land. A house now occupies the site.

At Runham, the chapel was quite remote and small. Membership at Runham had remained reasonably level for many years, fluctuating between about ten and 15 members. However, it became more and more expensive to operate the chapel, and with a decline in members it was decided to close. The chapel was closed in 1986 and it was converted into a private house.

Stokesby Methodist chapel was the last society to close in the Great Yarmouth and Gorleston circuit. By the early 2000s, Stokesby's congregation had reduced to less than ten members and the society's trustees decided that the best course of action was to close the chapel. Closure took place in 2002 and most of the remaining congregation then transferred to the Acle Methodist church. The final service at Stokesby was taken by Rev John Fenn on 25 August 2002. The building was subsequently sold and converted into a private house.

13.3.4 Cobholm

In 1989 the Central Hall in Great Yarmouth was undergoing substantial redevelopment and being converted into Christchurch – as described in section 13.5 of this chapter. During the building work it was not possible to hold services at the Central Hall and so the congregation moved temporarily to the Cobholm Methodist church and shared worship with the Cobholm society. The plan was that when building work was finished, the Central Hall congregation would move back into the newly developed Christchurch. During this period of shared worship with the Central Hall congregation, the members at Cobholm found that they enjoyed being part of a larger congregation. The Cobholm society held a meeting on 13 March 1990 where they decided unanimously to join with Christchurch and close the Cobholm society.

The last service held at the Cobholm church was on Sunday 8 July 1990, which was the week preceding Christchurch's opening. When Christchurch opened the following week, the Cobholm society transferred their membership and the Cobholm chapel was closed. The church building at Cobholm was put up for sale and sold in November 1992 for £25,000 to the Upper Room Christian Fellowship Trust. Memories of the Cobholm society still survive in the Memorial Chapel at Christchurch which houses furniture from the Cobholm society, as shown in figure 13.2.

13.3.5 Beccles Road

The former Primitive Methodist church at Beccles Road in Gorleston closed in 1996 as a result of nail rot being found in the roof and expensive repairs needed. Although funds could probably have been found for the repairs, the membership decided that it would be better to close the church and the majority of members transferred to Magdalen Way Methodist church. The final service in the chapel was held on 27 October 1996 and was conducted by Rev Michael Wildgust. The building was sold and converted into four flats. Interestingly, the repairs to the roof were never made!

13.3.6 Wickhampton

The society at Wickhampton was in serious decline for many years, and by 1987 Sunday congregations had reduced to just two or three members. The building itself wasn't in bad condition, but it was likely to need repair work in a few year's time. Based on this, the trustees of the society decided that the best course of action would be to close the chapel and sell the building. In January 1988 an offer of £16,000 was received for the chapel.

Figure 13.2: Chair and table from the Cobholm society which can now be found in the Memorial Chapel at Christchurch.

This was rejected as it was deemed to be too low – the trustees were hoping to receive at least £20,000 for the building. This turned out to be a good decision as the building was sold at auction on 5 September 1988 for £23,000 to Mr and Mrs Glaister. Following estate agent's and solicitor's fees, the Acle Methodist Circuit received £22,184 for the Wickhampton chapel. From this amount, £20,657 went into the Acle Circuit Advance Fund, £1,462 went to the Connexion Advance and Priority Fund, and £65 to refund a grant from the Property Division. Ultimately, some of this money was used towards the new Methodist chapel at Acle.

13.3.7 Upton and South Walsham

In the mid 1990s, membership at Upton Methodist chapel had fallen to only seven members – several members had recently either moved away or had passed away. Finances at Upton were good, although several areas of repair work had been identified in a recent quinquennial inspection of the property. These included some re-plastering, new gutters and electrical work. By 1999, the church council considered three options for the society – to close, to reduce the number of services or to remain as they are. The church council decided to have fortnightly services at the Upton chapel for a trial period of three months.

This was continued after the trial period ended.

Urgent electrical work was found to be necessary in the year 2000, with an estimated cost of £840. Of this amount, the Acle Circuit contributed £400 with the Upton society raising the remainder. The church council meeting in the autumn of 2001 considered Upton's position once again and determined that they had received no new members and that there were fewer people who could now run the church. In addition, the members were feeling slightly embarrassed when preachers travelled to Upton to give a service for a very small congregation. A vote was then taken on whether or not to close the chapel, and the decision was in favour of the proposal to close it. The final service at Upton was held on 16 December 2001 and this included a carol service. The chapel was sold and has now been converted into a house.

The Methodist chapel at South Walsham closed rather abruptly in September 1986. Services had been planned at South Walsham for the period up until November 1986, but in the preceding September a special church council meeting had been called. The membership at South Walsham was ten, but only five of these members were actively attending the chapel and the current society treasurer had recently died. This left the society in severe difficulty in simply running the chapel. The meeting resolved that the only practical option was to close the chapel. The last service was the Harvest Festival service which was held on 21 September 1986 and taken by Mr Rodney Wicks who was a local preacher from Sutton. Only a year before its closure, the South Walsham society was not in such dire straits. They were planning to have the chapel decorated and had arranged several events for the year, including a visit from the Hickling Male Voice Choir for November 1986. Presumably this concert never took place.

The South Walsham chapel building was sold soon after its closure on 27 July 1987 for £19,000. At the time, a sale for residential use was considered unlikely due to the lack of land around the chapel. However, the chapel was subsequently converted into a house. Many of the artefacts inside the chapel were passed on to other Methodist societies in the area. The electric organ went to the Acle Sunday school, crockery went to Halvergate Methodist chapel and the notice board went to Wickhampton. The organ from the chapel was sold for £350. In 2009 the building was for sale again, but this time with an asking price of £275,000.

13.3.8 Reedham, Limpenhoe, Beighton and Cantley

The four societies at Reedham, Limpenhoe, Beighton and Cantley suffered declining memberships much the same as many Methodist societies had across the area. This led to two problems for the societies. First, a lack of members meant that the remaining members had to agree to take on more and more responsibilities in the running of the societies. Second, the smaller congregations at the societies caused a reduction in income which also made running the chapels more difficult.

Both the Reedham and Limpenhoe societies found themselves with only a few members remaining. Having such a small congregation made it increasingly difficult to support the church financially and so both societies decided that the best course of action would be to close. Limpenhoe closed in 1993 and Reedham closed a few years later in 2001. The society at Beighton was in a similar situation with only a few members, but had the added problem of the chapel needing a lot of maintenance work. Again, the society decided that the best course of action would be to close. The last service at Beighton was in 2005. The society at Cantley was established much more recently than the other societies and had operated from Cantley Village Hall, having no purpose-built chapel. As with the other societies, membership dropped and the society decided to close with the last service held in 1996.

13.3.9 Rollesby, Repps and Ludham Johnson Street

In the 1970s membership of the Ludham Johnson Street chapel had declined to such an extent that by 1979 their membership was just ten. The organist and stewards were elderly and it was unlikely that any other volunteers would be found to take on their roles should the need arise. At this time, Ludham had two Methodist chapels. The other chapel, the High Street chapel, was only about one mile away and this had a much larger congregation of 29 members. In the early 1980s a decision was made to close the Johnson Street chapel. Figure 13.3 shows a picture which was taken outside the chapel on the day of the final service.

Figure 13.3: A picture of the congregation outside the Ludham Johnson Street chapel on the day of the final service, circa 1984.

The Rollesby and the Repps Methodist societies found themselves in a similar position to Ludham Johnson Street by the end of the 1990s. Both of these societies had an elderly and declining congregation. For both societies, once it became impossible to find members who were willing and able to undertake important duties, such as being a steward, treasurer or organist, the societies were left with no option but to close. For Rollesby, closure took place in 2001 with a Service of Thanksgiving held on 10 June of that year. The service also combined a celebration of the society worshipping in the chapel for 135 years, since its opening in 1866. At the time of closure, membership of the society had reduced to just three and they transferred to Methodist societies at Repps, Martham and Hemsby. Following its closure, the Rollesby chapel was sold in December 2004 for £87,500 and subsequently converted into a house. Interestingly, as of June 2009, the building was for sale again, but now at a price of £275,000. Repps Methodist chapel closed a few years later in 2007, with the final service held on 29 April. At the present time, the Repps chapel remains unsold, although plans are progressing to offer the building for sale in the near future.

13.3.10 Fleggburgh

The chapel used by the Fleggburgh Methodist society was the original Wesleyan chapel that dated back to 1841. As time went on, the chapel became increasingly expensive to run, incurring large repair bills that were not made any less as the building was classed as a Grade 2 Listed Building. Latterly, serious problems with the electrical wiring in the chapel were identified and these required expensive repair work to be carried out. The costs of these repairs was rising and the society felt that to maintain the chapel would be beyond the society's resources. Instead, the society made a decision to sell the chapel and move services to Fleggburgh Village Hall. This would also allow the society to make improvements in terms of the worship facilities available and to reach out to the wider community.

13.4 New Churches and Improvements

The condition of several of the churches in East Norfolk was causing concern for their trustees towards the end of the twentieth century. In some cases the only practical option was to close the chapel and replace it with a new building, as happened at Thurne. For other chapels, extensive restoration and redecoration was a cheaper and better alternative. The societies at Bradwell and Catfield both decided upon this route for improving their chapels. Meanwhile, at Acle, a completely new church was built on a new site to replace the former Primitive chapel in the village. This was necessary as the new Acle bypass was to run adjacent to the chapel.

13.4.1 New church at Acle

Since the 1930s, the only Methodist chapel in Acle was the former Primitive chapel that was situated on Reedham Road, quite close to the centre of the village. In the mid 1980s, the Department of Transport began to develop plans to improve the A47 road that passed through Acle. Most significantly this was to involve re-routing the road out of the centre of Acle, and building a dual-carriageway bypass to the south of the village. The planned bypass was to pass very close to the Acle Methodist church and manse, which would mean that it would no longer be practical to continue using these once the road was in use.

In compensation for this the Department of Transport agreed to buy the manse and pay for a new church to be built, of a similar size, somewhere else in the village. A

Figure 13.4: Acle Methodist church in 2009. The church opened on 22 July 1989 having moved from the former Primitive Methodist chapel in Acle following the building of the new Acle bypass.

suitable site for the new church was found on Bridewell Lane. This was close to the centre of the village and near to Acle's new Health Centre. There was also enough land for a new manse to be built, although this was ultimately not done. Instead, a bungalow in a nearby housing estate was purchased at a cost of £53,000, the cost of which was partly offset by the £35,000 that the Department of Transport paid for the original manse. The Bridewell Road site was bought in July 1988 and building work started a few months later in September. The church was formally opened at a service held on 22 July 1989 – figure 13.4 shows the church in 2009.

13.4.2 New church at Thurne

The Methodist chapel at Thurne had been built in 1852 and enlarged in 1887. By the 1960s the trustees decided to replace the old chapel by building a new chapel on the same site. The plan was started in the late 1960s, when the society purchased a lean-to cottage for £500 that was behind the old chapel. In May of 1971 the cottage was demolished and replaced by a schoolroom, kitchen and toilets that would be used for the new chapel. Next, the old chapel itself was demolished and the new chapel built. During this time the Thurne congregation held services in the schoolroom that had just been built.

The chapel was built by a local bricklayer from Halvergate by the name of Mr W Carter. Mr Carter was at the time employed by one of the Thurne chapel trustees – Mr R Cooke. Mr Cooke loaned Mr Carter free of charge to the society to build the new chapel. Mr Clifford Cook acted as his labourer and he also worked free of charge. The cost of the new chapel was £5,000 and this money was raised over the course of two years through various fundraising events and donations.

The building work took six months to complete and a re-opening service was held on Saturday 20 November 1971. The speakers at the service were the Rev Hubert Martin, Chairman of the East Anglia Methodist District, and Venerable Aubrey Aitken, Archdeacon of Norwich. The Venerable Aitken commented during the service that "Your church must occupy just about the most important site in the whole of Broadland, everyone who comes here cannot fail to recognise the effort you have made. What a fine Christian witness you are making." The Rector of Thurne, Rev Snell, and the Superintendent Minister of the Martham Circuit, Rev Colin Riches, also took part in the service which was attended by about 130 people.

Figure 13.5 shows the new chapel as it was in 2009. During the rebuilding work, the stone plaque from the original chapel was retained and this is now used as a step into the side door of the new chapel – as shown in figure 6.6 on page 89. Rebuilding an entire chapel and schoolroom in this way, using free labour, volunteers, fundraising and donations, continued the marvellous Methodist tradition of a society pulling together to do great things. The opening of the chapel was clearly a time of great celebration, not just for the Thurne society but also for the village and the Martham circuit.

Figure 13.5: Thurne Methodist chapel in 2009. The chapel was opened on 20 November 1971 on the site of the previous chapel.

13.4.3 Bradwell

The Methodist chapel at Bradwell was built in 1891 and remained largely unaltered until the 1980s when a modernisation plan was put in place. In 1987 the society began to update the chapel by adding a new kitchen and toilet block to replace the existing one that dated back to about 1900. Modernisation continued in the mid 1990s when the society began to consider how it could best meet the needs of the twenty-first century in Bradwell. Large fundraising activities were put in place. The original wooden church pews were replaced by moveable chairs, the pulpit was replaced by a dais, and gas-fired radiators were installed throughout. During the time of these improvements the chapel was out of action. Instead, services were held in Bradwell Parish Church hall, which had kindly been offered to them by the Rector of Bradwell. The chapel was re-dedicated on 24 March 2001. Figure 13.6 shows the inside of Bradwell Methodist church in 2000 during the modernisation work and also after the work was completed.

13.4.4 Catfield

Since about 1946, concerns had been raised about the structural condition of the Catfield chapel. The building is one of the oldest Primitive Methodist chapels in East Norfolk, having been built in 1838, but was showing its age. Two alternatives were considered – undertake extensive repairs or demolish the chapel and rebuild. Building a new chapel had two major downsides – the cost of rebuilding would be expensive and obtaining the necessary licence to do this could take up to five years. The trustees decided that the best course of action would be to carry out the repair work which included repairs to the floor, redecoration of the inside and an overhaul of the roof.

Thoughts of building a new chapel did not leave the society and even during the time of the repair work a fund was set up for rebuilding it. In 1957 a second building fund was set up and in 1966 an attempt was made to purchase land for this new chapel. In 1968 an investigation into the condition of the chapel was carried out and it was discovered that the building was actually in better condition than had been originally thought. This seems to have put on hold the plans to build a new chapel, and instead £1,500 was spent on redesigning the chapel. The fixed pews were removed and replaced by chairs and repair work was carried out both inside and outside, which included new stairs, electrical rewiring and replastering. On 12 August 1970, Catfield Methodist chapel held a re-opening service with the speaker being the celebrated Methodist hymn writer Rev F Pratt Green. Of the repair costs, £335 was still outstanding although a Connexional Chapel Committee grant of £150 had been given to the society.

A kitchen and toilets were built at the chapel in 1978 at a cost of £2,000. This had first been discussed in 1966, but was deferred due to the repair work needed on the chapel itself. The kitchen was enlarged in 1985 by an extension which also served as an extra classroom for Youth Club activities. Further work was undertaken in 1986 when a beam supporting the gallery in the chapel was found to be rotten. Instead of replacing it, that part of the gallery was removed which allowed more light to enter the church.

13.5 Christchurch

One of the largest developments to occur in Methodism in East Norfolk in recent times was the conversion of Central Hall into Christchurch. Central Hall itself could trace its routes right back to the first Methodist chapel in Great Yarmouth that was in Row 8, and from there to King Street and then to Dene Side. Converting Central Hall into Christchurch represented yet another step in the ongoing development of Methodism in the town.

Figure 13.6: The upper picture shows the inside of Bradwell Methodist chapel in 2000 during work to modernise the interior. The lower picture shows the inside once the work was completed.

13.5.1 Joining of Central Hall and Middlegate

Christchurch came about through the joining of the Central Hall Methodist society and the Middlegate United Reformed Church (URC) in Great Yarmouth in the late 1980s. Both churches were based in the town centre of Great Yarmouth and during the 1980s the two societies had begun informal discussions about merging. At that time the Middlegate church was declining somewhat, although it did receive significant income by letting part of its premises for use as the town's Magistrates' Court. However, this important source of revenue was soon to end when Great Yarmouth's new Magistrates' Court opened in 1992.

An inaugural meeting of representatives from both churches took place in October 1986 to decide the best way forward for joining the societies. One of the suggestions was to arrange for joint services between the societies at their respective churches. This Joint Planning Committee was also tasked with investigating possibilities for creating a single church building for both societies to move into. Three options were put forward for consideration – using the Central Hall, using the Middlegate church, and moving to a new site. The proposals were then reported back to the two churches for discussion and further meetings of the Joint Planning Committee were held. Progress towards forming a joint society went smoothly and at a Joint Planning Committee meeting in February 1988 the proposal was confirmed.

The two societies joined formally on Sunday 8 January 1989 at an Inauguration and Covenant Service held at Middlegate URC. The service was led by Rev Crewes, who was the superintendent Methodist minister, and communion was taken by Rev Clement, who was the URC minister. Rev Gathercole, who was Moderator of the Eastern Province of the URC, was invited to preach at the service.

13.5.2 Selling Middlegate and developing Christchurch

Once the Central Hall and Middlegate societies had joined formally, decisions needed to be made regarding where the new joint church should be located. Outline plans were prepared by architects to see how each of the two buildings could be converted into a new church. One of the aims of this new church was for it to be more than a centre for Sunday worship, but also be available to the community for multiple uses. Surveys were also carried out on both buildings and options for either developing or disposing of each building were made. The conclusion of the reports was that it would be more favourable to develop the Central Hall building as the new church and to dispose of the Middlegate site.

To fund conversion of the Central Hall to Christchurch, both the Deneside Youth Department building (owned by Central Hall) and the Middlegate church would have to be sold. The Youth Department building was sold to Orbit Housing Association for £50,000, whereupon it was converted into bedsits. Sale of the Middlegate building was not so straightforward.

During the building work to convert Central Hall into Christchurch, the congregation would need somewhere for worship. In the original scheme it was planned that the congregation would move temporarily to the Middlegate church until Christchurch was ready. The conversion work was planned to start in January 1989 and be completed by December of that year. During this time the Middlegate building would be marketed, ready to be sold once the congregation moved into Christchurch. However, finding a developer who was prepared to take on the Middlegate building proved difficult to find, which led to delay. Eventually, through the perseverance of the Property Steward at Central Hall, Mr Walter Moss, a developer was found and an agreement was made to convert the Middlegate building into offices for Great Yarmouth Borough Council. These new offices were needed earlier than had been anticipated meaning that building work had to be started immediately, overlapping with the building work going on at Christchurch. This left the congregation with no church to worship in as both the Central Hall and Middlegate church were now in the hands of builders.

The Cobholm Methodist society provided the solution by inviting the now homeless Methodist/URC congregation to worship with them. The offer was taken up and joint worship began in Cobholm on 8 October 1989. The final service at the Middlegate church was held on the previous Sunday. Prior to this the congregation had been worshipping at Middlegate, following the final service at the Central Hall which took place on 30 April 1989.

13.5.3 Opening of Christchurch

The building contract to convert the Central Hall to Christchurch was completed on 25 June 1990. The last service for the Methodist/URC society at Cobholm was on 8 July 1990. Christchurch was consecrated a week later on Sunday 15 July and the official opening of Christchurch was held on Saturday 28 July, with The Rt Hon Viscount Tonypandy invited to open the new church. Lord Tonypandy had been Speaker of the House of Commons and was a former Vice-President of the Methodist Conference.

Christchurch represented a complete transformation of Central Hall. A ceiling now divided the ground floor from a new first floor at the level of the former gallery in the Central Hall. This new upstairs area formed a large worship space. Downstairs was a large open space and coffee shop, and also a smaller chapel and offices. A lift was installed to link the two areas. To compare the worship areas before and after conversion, figure 13.7 shows two pictures – one of the inside of Central Hall and the other of the inside of Christchurch, both taken from the same position at the back of the church.

Several artefacts from the Central Hall, Middlegate and Cobholm societies were retained and used in Christchurch. These serve as good reminders of the history of the new society. The pulpit and other furniture from the worship area at Middlegate were installed at Christchurch, as shown in figure 13.8. A table and some chairs from Cobholm were also retained and can be found in the Memorial Chapel at Christchurch as shown in figure 13.2. The original pulpit from Central Hall was also kept and is now downstairs at Christchurch on the stage below the Grand Arch.

Redeveloping the Central Hall into Christchurch was an expensive, but highly worthwhile, scheme. The final cost of the conversion was a sizable £479,000. The individual costs are listed below, with the most significant being the cost of the building work.

- Building work £292,000
- Furniture and fittings £40,000
- Consultants' fees £68,000
- VAT £59,000

Figure 13.7: The inside areas of the Central Hall (upper picture) and Christchurch (lower picture), both taken from the top of the gallery at the back of the church. The new floor provides space for a large number of worshippers.

Figure 13.8: The worship area at Christchurch which contains furniture that was formerly at the Middlegate URC.

- Marketing (for the sale of Middlegate) £20,000

The cost of the conversion was met largely through the money received from the sale of the Middlegate building. A breakdown of the funds used is given below:

- Sale of Middlegate building £350,000
- Sale of Youth Department building £50,000
- Circuit Advance Fund £40,000
- Interest £15,000
- Donations £20,000
- Grants £4,000

From the outset, the design of Christchurch was guided by three objectives:

1. The building should be warm and welcoming
2. The front of the building should be as open as possible
3. The whole of the building should be multi-functional.

Even now, almost 20 years after its opening, Christchurch continues to adhere to these three defining criteria. Not only does Sunday morning worship take place at Christchurch, but a whole range of other activities, including the ever popular Coffee Shop.

13.6 Acle and Loddon circuits – 2003

In 2003 the Acle Methodist Circuit joined with the Loddon Methodist Circuit. Both circuits were small and joining together was seen as a way of securing both of their futures. The Loddon circuit had three societies – Loddon, Broome and Norton Subcourse – and together these societies had a membership of about 120. This made the Loddon circuit about the same size as the Acle circuit.

The Loddon society was part of a long-standing Local Ecumenical Partnership (LEP) with the Anglican church in Loddon and had a joint membership of over 100. Norton Subcourse was also part of an LEP with churches in the Raveningham Benefice. Worship was shared among the four churches that formed the LEP. The society at Broome was much smaller and had a membership of about five. The chapel at Broome was also structurally unsafe and shortly after joining the Acle circuit the chapel was closed and subsequently sold.

Chapter 14

Methodist Church Organs

14.1 Introduction

Music has always played an important part in Methodist worship and for most churches now, this centres around an organ. In earlier times organs were rare in Methodist churches and if a society was sufficiently wealthy they may have aspired to a harmonium or piano. As time went on societies generally became more wealthy and after a period of fundraising many were able to afford an organ. In some cases, organs were moved around from one church to another – as affluent societies updated their organs, these were bought by less well-off societies.

Given the importance of organs in Methodism, this chapter describes some of the organs that have been in the Methodist societies of East Norfolk. This includes organs from the large churches in the area, such as Lowestoft Road, the Temple and Central Hall, and also some of the organs that were in a few of the smaller societies.

14.2 Lowestoft Road

The original organ at Lowestoft Road Methodist church in Gorleston was installed just after the building had been opened at around the turn of the twentieth century. Where the organ originated from is unknown, but when the organ was dismantled in the 1960s, two tablets were found which provide some clues to its history. The first tablet read:

"Enlarged and improved by Eustace Ingram, 361 Liverpool Road, London, 1897"

and the second read:

"June 1911, rebuilt by Kirkland, London."

Eustace Ingram was part of a family of organ builders which included father and two sons. Together, they built a large number of church and theatre organs across the country.

The organ was used at Lowestoft Road for over 60 years, but by the 1950s the organ was said to be "sweet and pure in tone, but its mechanism had long been decaying." The keys of the organ were connected to the organ pipes by a series of rods and wires and had started to become rather unreliable. It is reported that the organist of the time, Mr E Harry Wagstaff MA, often had to tie parts of the mechanism together with string just to keep it working!

By the 1960s the condition of the organ was of concern and on 11 July 1961 a special meeting of the trustees of Lowestoft Road church was held to discuss "special business." At this meeting the organist, Mr Wagstaff, and a member of the Lowestoft Road church, Mr Hill, also attended. During the meeting Mr Hill offered the sum of £2,500 for the purchase of a new organ in memory of his wife. The minutes from the meeting report that "The Trustees gratefully accepted the gift." A brass plaque was fitted to the new organ to commemorate the gift and read:

"This organ was presented to the church by Arthur J Hill, a chorister and member of the church on 19th October 1962 in memory of his wife Edith Emily Hill who died on 4th April 1955."

A further sum was also donated to the church by Mr and Mrs Tilsley. This allowed another row of pipes to be added which it was reported "so enriched the quality of the organ."

Following a number of tenders given by organ manufacturers to build the new organ, the firm of Alfred E Davies and Son Ltd from Northampton was commissioned to build the new organ. Even though the company was based in Northampton, they were an international firm that had build organs around the world. In an advert by the firm, they proudly announced:

"We are privileged to have been entrusted with the reconstruction of the organ in the Methodist Church, Gorleston, and we offer it as an example of careful design, excellence of construction with many exclusive engineering features and perfect electrical mechanism."

They were right! The new organ was a significant improvement over the old organ and had the advantage of being electrically operated. The organ had 505 pipes, which was 100 pipes less than the old organ, but had more facilities for using the pipes through the use of multiple wiring to make the same rank of pipes available to several stops. This allowed the new organ to be played both louder and softer than the old organ. The organ console was also moved out into the church so that the organist could hear both the organ and the singing, which had not been easy with the old organ. Figure 14.1 shows the original and new organs at the church. On 19 October 1962 a "Festival of Praise" was held to dedicate the new organ. The organ was opened by Mr Hill and a prayer of consecration then given by Rev White who was the minister at Lowestoft Road. Following oral solos and organ solos given by both Mr Hill and Mr Wagstaff, the Trust Secretary, Mr Frank Elliott, gave thanks to all those involved in arranging for the new organ.

In 2008 the Church Council at Lowestoft Road decided to have the organ restored. The firm who serviced the organ had reported that the organ was deteriorating and that if restoration was not carried out soon, it would become uneconomic to do so in the future. Fundraising and tendering was led by one of the church's two organists, Mrs Beryl Jones, and by May of 2008 the total cost of the restoration had been raised by a combination of local fundraising and two generous grants from outside of Methodism. The work was carried out by W and A Boggis from Diss during June 2008 and cost £4,477 to complete – almost twice the original cost of the organ! To celebrate the quality of the restored organ, an organ concert was given by Mr John Farmer in July of 2009.

14.3 The Temple

The Temple was one of the most, if not the most, important of the Methodist churches in Great Yarmouth. When the Temple opened in 1876, the only instrument inside was

Figure 14.1: The two organs at Lowestoft Road Methodist church. The upper picture shows the original organ that was used until 1962. This was replaced by the more modern organ in the lower picture in 1962. The later organ had its console moved into the centre of the church which allowed the organist to better see and hear the choir.

Table 14.1: Description of the various stops of the 1881 organ at the Temple.

Stop	Pipe material	Pipe length	Number of pipes
Open diapason	Metal	8ft	56 pipes
Stop diapason	Wood	8ft	56 pipes
Viol di Gamba	Metal, wood bass	8ft	56 pipes
Principal	"	4ft	56 pipes
Twelfth	"	3ft	56 pipes
Fifteenth	"	2ft	56 pipes
Harmonic flute	"	4ft	44 pipes
Trumpet	"	8ft	56 pipes
Bourdon	Wood	16ft	24 pipes

a harmonium. The Temple was a grand building, with a capacity of about 1,200 people, which made the harmonium far too small and out of place in such a building. A new organ was commissioned soon after the Temple opened and the task of building this was given to Mr William Christmas Mack of Albion Road in Great Yarmouth. The body of the new organ was painted white and the panels edged with gilt. Pipes were reportedly coloured mauve and handsomely decorated with arabesques in blue and gold. In the souvenir programme for the opening ceremony, a detailed description of the pipes that made up the organ's nine stops was included and is described in table 14.1.

Two special services to celebrate the new organ were held on 28 April 1881 – one in the afternoon and one in the evening. The afternoon service comprised a selection of organ pieces that were played by Dr Bunnett, the celebrated organist from Norwich. At the time of the organ's installation, the Temple was still £2,900 in debt. For the society to prioritise the purchase and installation of a new organ at such a time shows how important the organ was to the Temple. Two days after the services, the *Yarmouth Independent* newspaper reported on the opening of the new organ:

"Several anxious deliberations were held as to the advisability of purchasing a more handsome and powerful instrument, but there was staring·the promoters in the face a debt of some £2,900 still remaining upon the structure. However, Methodists are apparently not frightened at the thought of a little debt upon their chapels, and when the ladies were taken into confidence in the matter, their vote was unanimous as to having a suitable organ ... They at once set to work, and with what success is well known, as the result of the bazaar testifies."

It would appear that this new organ did not remain in the Temple for long. By the early 1910s a new organ had been installed in the Temple. Figure 14.2 shows this new organ in about 1924, where it can be seen to be a very grand-looking instrument. The previous organ was transferred to the Nile Road Methodist chapel in Gorleston, which at that time had only recently opened. The transfer of organs from one society to another was common practice when an organ was being replaced or a society closed. For example, when the Regent Road Methodist church closed in the 1930s, the organ was bought for £115 by the Cobholm Methodist society.

Figure 14.2: The very grand-looking new organ at the Temple which was installed in the early 1910s.

14.4 Central Hall

During the conversion of the King Street Congregational church to the Methodist Central Hall in 1938, a new organ was installed. The organ was built by the John Compton Organ Company of London in consultation with Mr WM Chapman who was then organist at the Central Hall.

In many respects the Central Hall organ was unique. The Central Hall was envisioned as not being solely used for church services, but also for concerts. This meant that the organ should ideally be able to operate in the style of a traditional church organ, but also be able to be used as a concert organ for light music. Normally, separate organs would have been required, but with this dual requirement in mind, Compton combined both types of instrument into one organ. Possibly the organ's most remarkable feature was that it produced many of the solo stops and pedal basses by electrical means. During the 1930s the Compton Organ Company had been involved in research into electrical tone production which resulted in the "Electrone" system. The Central Hall organ was one of the first organs to use the Electrone system to produce some of the very deep bass notes that would traditionally have required very long organ pipes. Using the Electrone system allowed a smaller and less expensive organ to produce effects that would normally have only been found in large church and cathedral organs. The Electrone system was also used to create oboe and clarinet tones, chimes, carillon and vibraphone effects. In fact, the Central Hall organ was the first organ to combine wind and electric tone generation, and, at the time, was the most versatile organ of its size to be built.

The mechanism of the organ was entirely electric and connected to the organ console by electric cables. The organ itself was divided into two sections and the two cabinets containing these sections were positioned at the north end of the galleries of the church. These can be seen in the upper picture in figure 13.7 on page 187. The organ console had three manuals and controlled 70 stops, two tremulants and two sustainers. Figure 14.3 shows an advert placed by the Compton Organ Company which shows off the new organ at the Central Hall.

As had originally been planned at the outset of the Central Hall, concerts would be an important use for the church. Probably the most successful and longest running of these were the concerts given by the Central Hall Choir. These were held during the summer months, primarily aimed at holidaymakers, and ran from the 1960s through to the 1990s. Figure 14.4 shows a photograph of the choir that was taken in the early 1980s, with the Compton organ at the centre, alongside the minister, Rev George Beck, and organist, Mrs Margaret Gee.

In the early 2000s, the Church Council at Christchurch (formerly Central Hall) began to investigate the possibility of replacing the original Compton organ with a more modern instrument. After over 60 years of service, the organ had started to deteriorate and it was likely that considerable amounts of money would need to spent to keep it fully operational. After careful consideration, the Compton organ was replaced by a Viscount fully electronic organ that was capable of playing hymns automatically in the event of no organist being available. The Compton organ was sold to a private collector in Diss and shortly afterwards transferred to the Mechanical Music Museum in Stowmarket. Figure 14.5 shows the new organ which was installed in 2002 at a cost of £12,500. Such was the popularity of the organ, Christchurch held a special "Farewell to the Compton Organ" recital in October 2002 which was given by David Ivory of the Cotton Organ Museum.

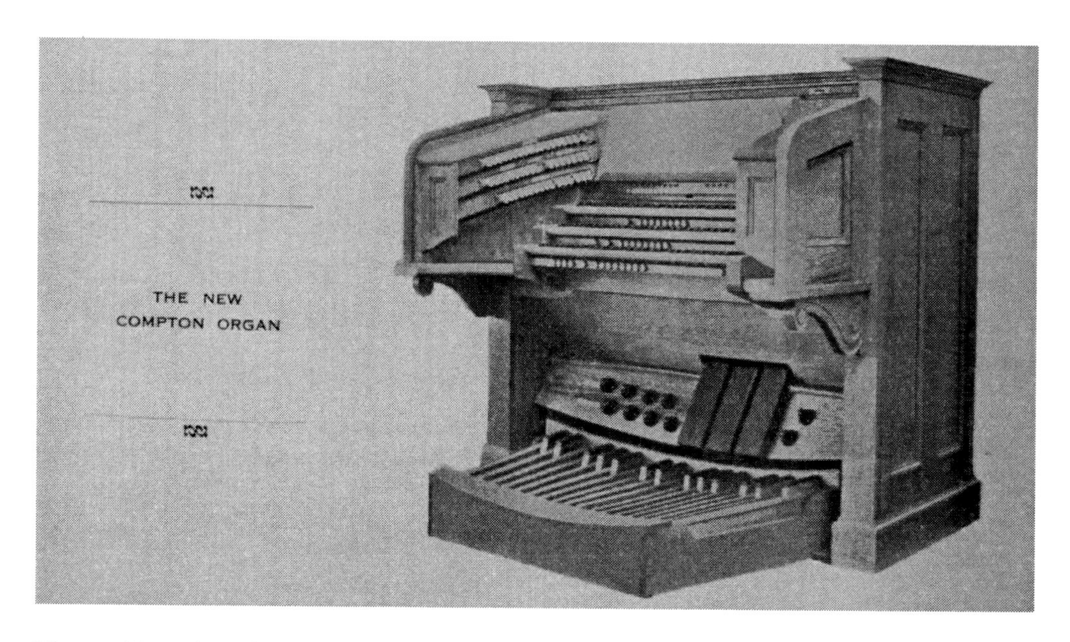

Figure 14.3: An advert by the Compton Organ Company for the new organ that was installed at the Central Hall.

Figure 14.4: The Central Hall Choir in the early 1980s. In the centre are Minister Rev George Beck and organist Margaret Gee. Choir members are – Sopranos: Olive Bignell, Peggy Irving, Jane Mackay, Jill Green, Dorothy Brown, Hilda Cuffley, Sheila Rivett, Joan Blyth and Jean Duffield; Contraltos: Jean Thompson, Jane Austin, Sylvia Milner, Alison Beck, Sheila Page and Phyllis Littlewood; Tenors: Edward Neale, Pat Page and Robert Green; Basses: Howard Bignell, Peter Green, Doug Coleman and George Austin.

Figure 14.5: The new Viscount organ at Christchurch which was installed in 2002 at a cost of £12,500. This replaced the Compton organ that had been installed in the Central Hall in 1938.

14.5 Martham and Acle

The large Methodist societies in East Norfolk were not the only ones to engage in buying and restoring their organs. Many of the smaller societies too, were equally as enthusiastic about having an organ that they could be proud of and enjoy. The organs in these smaller societies were not as big or powerful as the organs in the larger churches, but nevertheless could still produce music of high quality.

The Acle Methodist society installed an organ in their chapel on Reedham Road in 1952, having used a two-pedal harmonium for accompaniment for many years. The organ was designed specially for the Acle chapel by organ builders Bishops of Ipswich and comprised two manuals and ten stops. The organ remained there until the late 1980s at which time the chapel was closed and the society moved to a new purpose-built chapel on Bridewell Lane. The organ was considered too precious to be lost and was itself also transferred to the new chapel. The organist, Christine Brady, played the organ in both the old and new chapels and in 2007 celebrated 60 years of playing the organ at Acle, albeit in two different churches! Figure 14.6 shows the organ inside the new Acle Methodist church.

At Martham, the society set up a "Pipe Organ Fund" in 1948 to raise money for a new organ. Money came in from a wide range of sources, including:

- trustees' cheque £50.0.0

Figure 14.6: The organ at Acle Methodist church in 2009. This organ was originally installed at the old Acle (former Primitive) Methodist chapel in 1952, before being moved to the new Acle Methodist church in 1989.

- institute effort £84.6.3
- collectors book £162.2.6
- Christmas market £27.12.9
- pound stall £12.7.6
- concert £10.17.0

In total the Pipe Organ Fund raised over £400 for the new organ. In November of 1948 a new organ was bought from Spencer Shaw of London for £350 and a special concert was held to celebrate the new instrument. The excess money raised was also put to good use and enabled things such as re-lettering the Honours Board to be paid for, as well as spending 10 shillings on cakes! Figure 14.7 shows two pictures of the inside of the Martham chapel. The first was taken before the organ was installed, while the second picture was taken after the installation of the organ.

Figure 14.7: The inside of Martham Methodist chapel. The upper picture shows the inside of the chapel prior to 1948 before the organ was installed. The lower picture shows the chapel with the new organ in place. The inside of the chapel has changed little since and in 2009 looks very much the same.

Chapter 15

The East Norfolk Methodist Circuit – 2007

15.1 Introduction

This final chapter in the history of Methodism in East Norfolk describes the merger of the Great Yarmouth and Gorleston Methodist Circuit with the Acle Methodist Circuit and the Martham Methodist Circuit to become the East Norfolk Methodist Circuit in 2007. In a sense Methodism in East Norfolk has come full circle, having started with just one circuit in 1792 – the Great Yarmouth (Wesleyan) Methodist Circuit. As time went on a Primitive Circuit was formed, which later divided into the Great Yarmouth, the Acle and the Martham Primitive Methodist circuits. Similarly, Methodist New Connexion and Wesleyan Reform circuits were also established. After the mid nineteenth century, these circuits began to merge. First, the Methodist New Connexion and Wesleyan Reformers merged to form a United Methodist Circuit in 1907. Then, following Methodist Unification in 1932, the Great Yarmouth Wesleyan, Primitive and United circuits joined. Finally, in 2007, the Great Yarmouth, Acle and Martham circuits merged to leave just one Methodist circuit in East Norfolk.

These three circuits were all part of the East Anglia District of the Methodist Church, which covered the counties of Norfolk, Suffolk and Cambridgeshire. In the mid 2000s, the East Anglia District proposed a review of the areas covered by individual circuits with a view to adjusting circuit boundaries to allow smaller, less efficient, circuits to merge and thereby create a more efficient organisation. The effect of this review in the eastern part of the district was to create a new East Norfolk Methodist Circuit.

The three circuits that were merging to create the East Norfolk Methodist circuit had witnessed a great many changes over the course of their existences. This included periods of sustained growth, up to about the turn of the twentieth century, the effects of Methodist unification in 1932, the devastation of the Second World War, and finally a gradual decline in Methodism. Over this period, the Acle and Martham circuits remained relatively unchanged from their Primitive Methodist beginnings in 1883. Unification added a few non-Primitive societies to the Acle and Martham circuits and some societies closed, but essentially they encompassed broadly the same societies as they did at their formation in

1883. For the Great Yarmouth and Gorleston Methodist Circuit, the changes were more pronounced, with many more of the societies having closed, primarily due to overprovision following Methodist unification when the former Great Yarmouth Primitive circuit joined with the Wesleyan and United Methodist circuits to form the Great Yarmouth and Gorleston Methodist Circuit.

15.2 Great Yarmouth, Acle and Martham Methodist circuits

Following the proposal by the East Anglia District to review circuit boundaries, the Great Yarmouth and Gorleston, the Acle and the Martham circuits entered into discussions about a possible merger. These circuits had all witnessed significant reductions in their memberships since their peaks in the early twentieth century, and given their close proximity to each other, merging to create a single larger circuit was a logical move. At the time of these discussions, the Great Yarmouth and Gorleston circuit was the largest of the three circuits and had 302 members that were spread across seven churches and served by three ministers. In comparison, the Martham circuit was much smaller and had a membership of 146, nine churches and one minister. The Acle circuit was larger, having recently, in 2003, acquired the Loddon Methodist Circuit, which gave it 238 members, six churches and one minister. Merging the three circuits as they stood would create a big new circuit with almost 700 members, spread across 22 churches with five ministers. Tables 15.1, 15.2 and 15.3 list the churches that made up the three circuits, along with their individual membership numbers.

Table 15.1: Great Yarmouth and Gorleston Methodist Circuit churches and membership in 2007.

Church	Membership
Christchurch	103
Scratby	8
Magdalen Way	79
Lowestoft Road	26
Bradwell	22
Newtown	29
Caister	35
Total	302

By June of 2006, the three circuits had formulated and agreed on a plan to merge. This would take place on 1 September 2007 with the name of the new circuit agreed as being the East Norfolk Methodist Circuit. It was decided that the churches in the Acle circuit that joined from the Loddon circuit in 2003, namely Loddon and Norton Subcourse, would join the Lowestoft and East Suffolk Circuit. As an addition to the new East Norfolk circuit, the Methodist society at Sutton was also to join. Sutton had previously been part of the North Walsham and Aylsham Circuit and brought with it a membership of 18. Preparations for the new circuit had already begun at a high level with Rev Chris Shreeve agreeing to become the new superintendent minister – he had previously

Table 15.2: Acle Methodist Circuit churches and membership in 2007. Note – the Loddon Methodist society is part of a Local Ecumenical Partnership with the Anglicans and the membership is joint, hence its relatively high figure.

Church	Membership
Acle	57
Freethorpe	37
Halvergate	10
Lingwood	15
Loddon	112
Norton Subcourse	7
Total	238

Table 15.3: Martham Methodist Circuit churches and membership in 2007.

Church	Membership
Martham	32
Hemsby	9
Thurne	31
Catfield	17
Winterton	7
Horsey	8
Potter Heigham	17
Ludham	19
Fleggburgh	6
Total	146

been superintendent minister of the Martham Circuit. A preliminary circuit meeting for the new East Norfolk Methodist Circuit was held on 20 June 2007 at Potter Heigham Methodist church, at which arrangements began to be put in place for the forthcoming merger.

For the Great Yarmouth and Gorleston circuit, this also marked the end of Rev John Fenn's superintendency of the circuit. A combined farewell service for the Great Yarmouth circuit and Rev Fenn was held at Magdalen Way Methodist church on Sunday 29 July 2007, starting with a tea and followed by the service. The Martham circuit also celebrated their final service of their circuit with a special "First Sunday" service which included a display of memorabilia that had been collected during the course of the circuit's life.

15.3 The East Norfolk Methodist Circuit

The East Norfolk Methodist Circuit was established on 1 September 2007 with a welcome service that was held at Magdalen Way Methodist church in Gorleston. This was led by Rev Graham Thompson, who was the Chairman of the East Anglia District of the Methodist Church. At the same service, a new minister for the circuit, Rev Betty Trinder, was also welcomed. The new circuit had a membership of 585, 21 churches and five full-time ministers. Figure 15.1 shows a map of east Norfolk as of 2007, with the locations of the 21 churches illustrated.

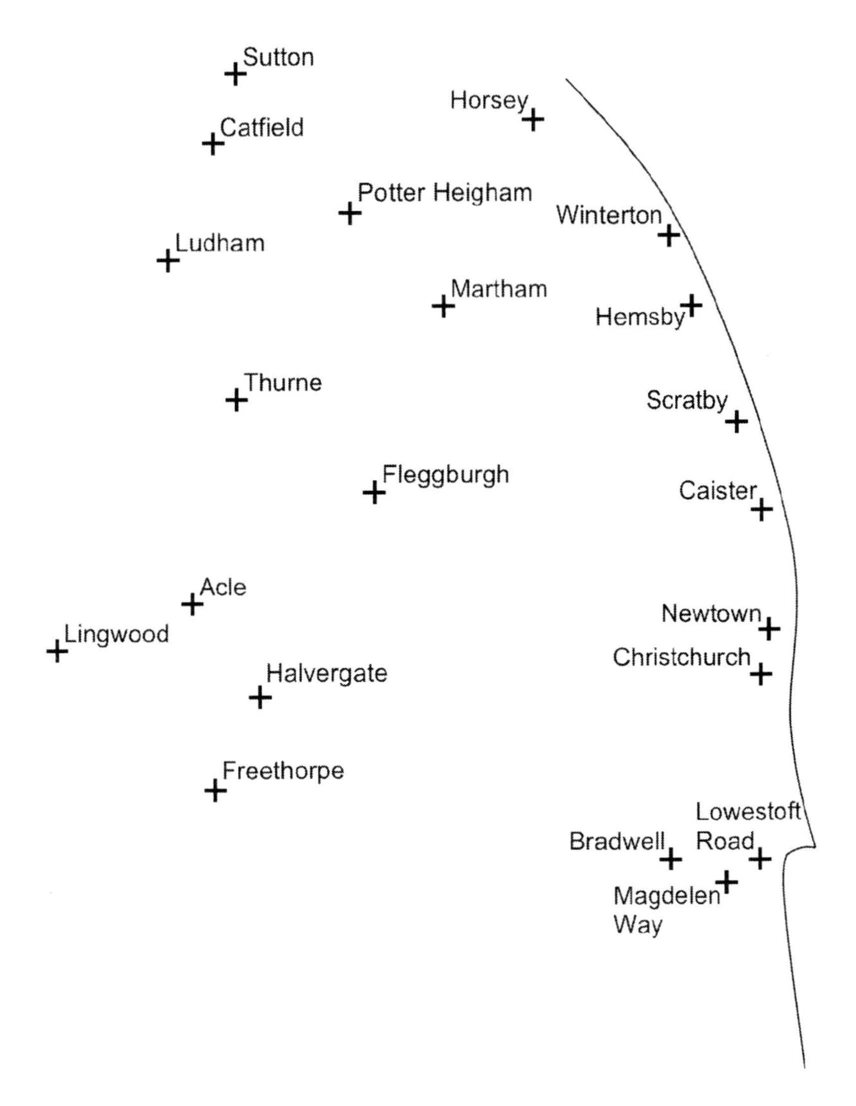

Figure 15.1: Map showing the 21 churches that made up the East Norfolk Methodist Circuit in 2007.

The merger of the Great Yarmouth, Acle and Martham circuits into the single East Norfolk Methodist Circuit was a significant event for Methodism in the area as these circuits had operated independently for the last 124 years. With the formation of the East Norfolk Methodist Circuit, the organisation of Methodism in east Norfolk was returning to how it had been prior to 1883, when many of these societies were part of the Great Yarmouth Primitive Methodist Circuit. Out of the 21 societies in the East Norfolk Methodist Circuit, 12 of them could trace their origins back to the Great Yarmouth Primitive

Table 15.4: List of societies in the East Norfolk Methodist Circuit in 2007, showing the opening date of the present building and the origin of the society (Wesleyan, Primitive, United or post-1932).

Church	Opening date	Origin	Former circuit
Christchurch	1990	Wesleyan	Great Yarmouth and Gorleston
Scratby	1894	Primitive	Great Yarmouth and Gorleston
Magdalen Way	1957	Post-1932	Great Yarmouth and Gorleston
Lowestoft Road	1899	Wesleyan	Great Yarmouth and Gorleston
Bradwell	1891	Primitive	Great Yarmouth and Gorleston
Newtown	1907	United	Great Yarmouth and Gorleston
Caister	1886	Wesleyan	Great Yarmouth and Gorleston
Acle	1989	Primitive	Acle
Freethorpe	1896	Primitive	Acle
Halvergate	1878	Primitive	Acle
Lingwood	1867	Primitive	Acle
Martham	1882	Primitive	Martham
Hemsby	1879	Primitive	Martham
Thurne	1971	Primitive	Martham
Catfield	1838	Primitive	Martham
Winterton	1877	Primitive	Martham
Horsey	1958	Primitive	Martham
Potter Heigham	1956	Primitive	Martham
Ludham	1866	Wesleyan	Martham
Fleggburgh	–	Wesleyan	Martham
Sutton	1899	Primitive	North Walsham and Aylsham

Methodist circuit – Scratby, Bradwell, Acle, Freethorpe, Halvergate, Martham, Hemsby, Thurne, Catfield, Winterton, Horsey and Potter Heigham. A further two were also former Primitive societies – Sutton and Lingwood – but these were not originally part of the former Great Yarmouth Primitive Methodist Circuit. Five of the societies were former Wesleyan – Lowestoft Road, Caister, Ludham, Fleggburgh and Christchurch (considering Christchurch's evolution from the Central Hall and before that, Dene Side). One of the societies was formerly United Methodist – Newtown – and another was formed after Methodist unification in 1932 – Magdalen Way. Table 15.4 lists the societies making up the East Norfolk circuit and gives details of their origin (Wesleyan, Primitive, United or post 1932) and the date that the current building was opened. The table shows that the more rural circuits of Acle and Martham comprised mostly ex-Primitive societies, whereas the ex-Wesleyan and ex-United societies were mainly around Great Yarmouth. This is with the exception of Ludham and Fleggburgh which are both ex-Wesleyan, although both of these villages did at one time have Primitive societies as well.

15.4 Conclusion

At the formation of the East Norfolk Methodist Circuit in 2007, Methodism had been in East Norfolk for just over 250 years, having started when Thomas Olivers first attempted to bring Methodism to Great Yarmouth in 1754. Over the course of these 250 years, Methodism in East Norfolk has witnessed many changes. The number of societies peaked at around the turn of the twentieth century, with 48 societies in existence, spread across five circuits. By the time of Methodist unification in East Norfolk in 1938, the number of societies was almost unchanged at 44, but these were now spread across just three circuits. By 2007, these three circuits had merged and now comprise 21 societies.

However, Methodism in East Norfolk continues to flourish. One of the most recent events in the circuit was a Faith Tea that was held at Acle Methodist church on 8 March 2009. This was followed by community hymn singing and a service led by the superintendent minister, Rev Chris Shreeve. The sermon was given by Mr David Walton, who was the vice-President of the Methodist conference in 2009, and additional singing was provided by both the Martham Singers and the Acle Singers. So, the tradition of Methodist gatherings, faith teas, community hymn singing and fellowship continues in East Norfolk as it has done for the last 250 years. Long may it continue!

Appendix A

Organisation and Structure of the Methodist Church

Several names and terms used in this book are specific to the Methodist Church and its organisation. This appendix gives a brief description of these with respect to the Methodist Church.

Local Church
The church is the main contact that members have with the wider Methodist Church. Churches were often referred to as *societies*. In the early days of Methodism these societies would meet in someone's home, in a rented room, or even outside on a village green or farmer's field. As the societies grew they progressed to more permanent buildings and eventually to building or buying their own chapel or church. Within the churches, smaller groups of worshippers often met in *classes* for Bible study, prayer and fellowship. The local churches are organised through a group of lay volunteers that are now called *stewards*, but were originally known as *trustees*.

Circuit
A circuit comprises a group of churches that are led by a team of *ministers*. Each minister will usually look after the pastoral needs of several churches in the circuit, along with the help of *local preachers*. A circuit is led by the *Circuit Superintendent*, although most decisions are made at *Circuit Meetings* which typically take place every three to six months. These circuit meetings were formally known as *Quarterly Meetings*.

District
A district is made up from a number of circuits and is led by the *Chairman of the District*. The district normally holds two meetings each year which are known as *District Synods*.

Conference
The Methodist Conference meets annually and is made up from representatives from each of the districts. The first Methodist Conference took place in 1744 under Rev John Wesley and continues in a similar format today. Representatives from each district attend the Conference which is led by a *President* and *Vice-president*. John Wesley was the first President of the Methodist Conference.

Appendix B

Circuit Ministers

This appendix provides lists of ministers who have worked in some of the circuits that have existed in East Norfolk. It has not been possible to create a full set of circuit lists, nor to identify all ministers within a particular circuit, and so gaps do appear. The circuits for which lists of circuit ministers have been created are shown below; the lists are in the following pages:

- East Norfolk Methodist Circuit: 2007–
- Great Yarmouth and Gorleston Circuit: 1963–2007
- Central Hall Circuit: 1938–1963
- Acle Methodist Circuit (Primitive from 1883–1932): 1883–2007
- Martham Methodist Circuit (Primitive from 1883–1932): 1883–2009

Table B.1: Ministers of the East Norfolk Methodist Circuit: 2007–.

Rev Betty Trinder	2007–
Rev Tibbs Naidoo	2007–
Rev Ian Worsfold	2007–2008
Rev Heather Sorrell	2007–
Rev Chris Shreeve	2007–

Table B.2: Ministers of the Great Yarmouth and Gorleston Methodist Circuit: 1963–2007. Note – the list is incomplete.

Rev Tibbs Naidoo	2006–2007
Rev Ian Worsfold	2003–2007
Rev David Clarke	2000–2003
Rev John Fenn	1999–2007
Rev Michael Wildgust	1994–2006
Rev Derek Lund	1998–2000
Mrs Kath Lund	1998–2000
Rev Alan Burgess	2000–2000
Rev Al Loades	1993–1999
Rev Edmee Hurst	1995–1998
Deacon Alan Middup	1993–1996
Rev J Brian Kirkby	1993–1995
Rev Mary Bailey	1993–1994
Rev Ronald Crewes	–
Rev George Beck	–
Rev Ronald Hoare	–
Rev Hammond	–
Rev Povey	–
Rev Eric Bilton	–

Table B.3: Ministers of the Central Hall Circuit: 1938–1963.

Rev Eric Bilton	1957–1963
Rev John E Trevithick	1951–1957
Rev Percy C Oliff	1948–1951
Rev Dr James R Course	1941–1948
Rev A Stanley Parker	1938–1941

Table B.4: Ministers of the Acle Primitive Methodist Circuit (1883–1932) and Acle Methodist Circuit (1932–2007)

Rev Heather Sorrell	2004–2007
Rev N Roy Coppack	1996–2003
Rev D Jones	1992–1996
Rev Stephen Robinson	1984–1992
Rev Robert A Austin	1977–1984
Rev A Leslie Jones	1972–1977
Rev George R Nunnerley	1967–1972
Rev Percival E Cooper	1962–1967
Rev Cecil G Deeks	1956–1962
Rev Charles T Staden	1953–1956
Rev William Howard	1948–1953
Rev George Jackson	1936–1948
Rev Ernest S France	1931–1936
Rev Abraham Hill	1924–1931
Rev Ernest S France	1918–1924
Rev H W Matthews	1914–1918
Rev Abraham Hill	1908–1914
Rev Samuel Smith	1907–1908
Rev William L Spooner	1904–1907
Rev Nathaniel Brown	1899–1904
Rev Samuel Willetts	1895–1899
Rev George Griffin	1893–1895
Rev Robert Betts	1890–1893
Rev James B Knapp	1886–1890
Rev Arthur Temple Wardle	1883–1886

Table B.5: Ministers of the Martham Primitive Methodist Circuit (1883–1932) and Martham Methodist Circuit (1932–2007)

Rev Christopher Shreeve	2001–2007
Rev Ralph Webb	1993–2001
Rev Stephen Yelland	1985–1993
Rev N Roy Coppack	1976–1985
Rev Colin Riches	1967–1976
Rev George Nunnerley	1961–1967
Rev W Nicholas	1955–1961
Rev L G Jones	1952–1955
Rev Alan Roughley	1951–1952
Rev E Wagstaffe	1950–1951
Rev J E Ogden	1946–1950
Rev H W Pope	1942–1946
Rev H Hart	1938–1942
Rev A B Gowers	1935–1938
Rev Abraham Hill	1930–1935
Rev F S France	1924–1930
Rev E Hudson	1920–1924
Rev J Morton	1918–1920
Rev H Didcock	1916–1918
Rev H Lawson	1912–1916
Rev F C France	1902–1912
Rev M S Flushing	1899–1902
Rev James Cooper	1895–1899
Rev William Moore	1891–1895
Rev George Rudrum	1886–1891
Rev Normandale	1883–1886

Appendix C

Bibliography

- RE Davies, *Methodism*, Penguin Books, 1963
- J Ede, N Virgoe and T Williamson, *Halls of Zion : Chapels and meeting houses in Norfolk*, University of East Anglia, 1994
- CJ Palmer, *The Perlustration of Great Yarmouth with Gorleston and Southtown*, 1872
- AW Patterson, *From Hayloft to Temple*, 1903
- B Taylor, *A Brief History of Methodism in Gorleston to 1866*, Great Yarmouth and District Archaeological Society, 1992
- C Tooke, *Methodism in Caister*, Great Yarmouth and District Archaeological Society, 1996
- A Watmough, *A History of Methodism in the Town and Neighbourhood of Great Yarmouth*, J. Kershaw Publisher, 1826
- *Cook's Directory of Great Yarmouth, Gorleston and Southtown*, 1896
- *Kelly's Directory of Great Yarmouth, Gorleston and Southtown*, 1957
- Articles from Norfolk Record Office

Index